THE
ULTIMATE
QUESTION 2.0

THE ULTIMATE QUESTION 2.0

How **NET PROMOTER** Companies
Thrive in a Customer-Driven World

FRED REICHHELD

WITH ROB MARKEY

BAIN & COMPANY

Harvard Business Review Press

Boston, Massachusetts

Library of Congress Cataloging-in-Publication Data

Reichheld, Frederick F.
The ultimate question 2.0 : how net promoter companies thrive in a customer-
driven world / Fred Reichheld with Rob Markey. -- Rev. and expanded ed.
       p. cm.
   Previously published under title: Ultimate question.
   Includes bibliographical references and index.
   ISBN 978-1-4221-7335-0 (hardback)
  1. Customer relations.   2. Consumer satisfaction.   3. Customer loyalty.
4. Employee motivation.   5. Employee loyalty.   6. Leadership.
7. Success in business.   I. Markey, Rob.   II. Reichheld, Frederick F.
Ultimate question.   III. Title.
   HF5415.5.R439 2011
   658.8'72--dc22

                                                          2011013248

Much has changed in this revised and expanded edition—but not its dedication, which remains steadfast: to my wife Karen, with love and loyalty.

Contents

Preface

This book shows how companies can put themselves on the path to true growth—growth that occurs because their customers and employees love doing business with them and sing their praises to neighbors, friends, and colleagues. This is the only kind of growth that can be sustained over the long term. Acquisitions, aggressive pricing strategies, product line extensions, cross-sell strategies, new marketing campaigns, and all the other implements in a CEO's toolkit may give a company a short-term boost. But if these gambits don't ultimately result in delighted customers, the growth won't last. So it is with market share. A dominant position in the marketplace often gives a company economic advantage. But again: if that potential isn't utilized to make customers smile, neither the advantage nor the dominant share will last.

This lesson has taken on new importance as a quiet revolution sweeps across the business world. The revolution, like many others shaking up the current world order, has been stoked and accelerated by the development of social media tools. Customers and employees blog, tweet, and text about their experiences in real time, overwhelming the carefully crafted messages proffered by advertising and public relations departments. Power is shifting from the corporation to those who buy from it and those who work for it.

To come out on top in this revolution, business leaders must find ways to enable frontline teams to delight customers. Most leaders *want* customers to be happy; the challenge is how to *know* what customers are feeling and how to establish *accountability* for the customer experience. Traditional satisfaction surveys just aren't up to this job. They ask too many questions and inspire analysis instead of action. Financial reports aren't up to it, either. As we'll see, conventional accounting can't even distinguish a dollar of good profits—the kind that lead to growth—from a dollar of bad profits, which undermine it.

What the book offers instead is a wholly new approach. Companies begin this approach by asking one question—the Ultimate Question—in a regular, systematic, and timely fashion. Based on the answers, a company can identify the customers who love it, those who hate it, and those who don't care much one way or the other. It can compile a simple, easily understandable score—its Net Promoter® score—that shows how it is faring on the customer-relations front. It can track that score week in and week out, in much the same way every business already tracks its financial performance.

Then the company can begin the real work: closing the loop with customers, listening to what they have to say, fixing the problems that lead to unhappiness or anger, and creating experiences that lead to more and more delight. It can engage every employee in the quest to build a true customer focus into their daily operations. Just as managers now use financial reports to make sure they and their team members are meeting profit goals, they can use the Net Promoter score to make sure they are meeting customer-relationship goals. This system is helping companies win the quiet revolution by illuminating the path toward greatness.

The companies that have pioneered the use of the system—you will read about them in the chapters that follow—have already learned this lesson and are *way* out ahead of their competitors. They range from small neighborhood businesses to Silicon Valley superstars and global giants such as General Electric. ("This is the best customer-relationship metric I've seen—I can't understand why any of you wouldn't want to try it!" exclaimed General Electric CEO Jeff Immelt to a meeting of his senior leaders in 2005.) Different as they are in other respects, these companies have one big thing in common, which is that they take seriously the principle of the Golden Rule: treat others as you would want to be treated. These businesses want customers who are so pleased with how they are treated that they willingly come back for more and bring their friends and colleagues with them. Incidentally, though most of the book's examples are drawn from the business world, organizations of any kind—schools, hospitals, charities, even government agencies—can put these ideas to practical use as well. Nonbusiness organizations also have customers or constituents; they, too, need to delight the people they serve; and they, too, can benefit greatly from a management system based on timely, regular feedback from customers.

Once you have read the book, please visit the Web site www.netpromotersystem.com. Our hope is that together we can create a community of people who believe that the purpose of companies and other organizations is to enrich the lives they touch and to create relationships worthy of loyalty—and who think that an organization's best chance for long life, prosperity, and greatness requires measuring performance on this dimension just as carefully as it measures profits.

A word of advice to those who read the first edition of *The Ultimate Question*. Every chapter of this new edition includes important additions and clarifications, and many of the chapters are completely new. If you are already deeply familiar with the original, be sure to read the introduction (wholly new), skim chapters 1 through 4, and study chapter 5 as if you were reading it for the first time, since some of the most costly implementation errors resulted from incomplete understanding of the principles explained in this chapter. Part II of the book (chapters 6 through 10) is nearly all brand-new material. These chapters describe and analyze the accomplishments of Net Promoter practitioners since publication of the original book.

Introduction

From Score to System

It always seemed to me that success in business and in life should result from your impact on the people you touch—whether you have enriched their lives or diminished them. Financial accounting, for all its sophistication and influence, completely ignores this fundamental idea. So several years ago, I created a new way of measuring how well an organization treats the people whose lives it affects—how well it generates relationships worthy of loyalty. I called the metric Net Promoter score, or NPS.[1] Thousands of innovative companies, including Apple, Allianz, American Express, Zappos.com, Intuit, Philips, GE, eBay, Rackspace, Facebook, LEGO, Southwest Airlines, and JetBlue Airways, adopted NPS. Most used it at first to track the loyalty, engagement, and enthusiasm of their customers. They liked the fact that NPS was easy to understand. And they liked it because it focused everyone on one inspirational goal—treating customers so well that those customers become loyal promoters—and led to action in pursuit of that goal. They also appreciated the fact that it was an open-source method, which they could adapt for their own needs.

Over time, these companies developed and expanded the metric. They used it to help build employee engagement and commitment. They discovered new methods to extend its impact, not just to measure loyalty but to transform their organizations. They shared ideas with one another, and they built upon one another's applications. In a remarkable explosion of creative intelligence, NPS soon morphed into something much more than a metric. Though the science is still young, it became a management system, an entire way of doing business. The initials themselves, NPS, came to mean Net Promoter *system* rather than just Net Promoter score.

And what a difference this system seems to have made. Listen to what some of these companies' leaders have to say about it:

> NPS has galvanized our thinking and enabled the entire organization to focus on the customer. During the 1970s and '80s, total quality management revolutionized the cost of quality in manufacturing. NPS is having a comparable impact in the current age.
> —*Gerard Kleisterlee, CEO, Philips*

> NPS was a natural fit for Apple. It has become part of the DNA of our retail stores.
> —*Ron Johnson, SVP and founding executive, Apple Retail*

> NPS completely changed our world. It has become an integral part of our process and culture. Now, you couldn't take it away if you tried.
> —*Junien Labrousse, executive vice president and chief product and technology strategist, Logitech*

> NPS provides the litmus test for how well we are living up to our core values—it is the first screen I look at when I boot up my computer each morning.
> —*Walt Bettinger, CEO, Charles Schwab*

> NPS is the most powerful tool we have ever deployed. The reason is that it is so actionable.
> —*Dan Henson, then chief marketing officer, General Electric*

We use NPS every day to make sure we're WOWing our customers and our employees.

   —*Tony Hsieh, CEO of Zappos.com, author of* Delivering
     Happiness

In chapter 6 you'll read nearly a dozen stories about how companies such as these have put the Net Promoter system to work and about the results they have achieved. NPS was a key part of Charles Schwab's turnaround, a period in which the company's stock tripled. It has been a central element of Apple's famous retail stores, which are believed to have the highest sales per square foot of any retailer anywhere. It has enabled Ascension Health to give its patients better care, Progressive Insurance to gain market share and retain more of its policyholders, American Express to provide better service to cardholders while lowering its costs—and on and on. The Net Promoter system has proved to be a powerful engine of growth and profitability.

But I don't want to stop with *system*, because there is another *S* that permeates the companies that have achieved the most impressive results with Net Promoter. These companies embody a Net Promoter *spirit* of leadership, a distinctive philosophy that energizes the system. Leaders who exhibit this spirit believe that the mission of any great organization is to enrich the lives it touches— to build relationships worthy of loyalty. A great organization must have a positive impact on its shareholders, of course, but also on its employees, its business partners, and especially its customers. Unless it earns the loyalty of all these stakeholders, its returns to shareholders will soon evaporate. Moreover, these leaders themselves recognize that their personal reputation, their legacy, will be defined by how well they achieve that mission.

Phrases such as *personal reputation*, *Net Promoter spirit*, and *enriching lives* might lead you to infer that NPS is soft and nebulous. On the contrary, Net Promoter is where mission meets mathematics. A mission without a measurement, without an accurate gauge of success or failure, is just so much hot air. Only by systematically measuring its effect on people and their relationships can an organization gauge whether it is really achieving its mission and enriching lives. That's NPS's reason for being. It provides a practical measurement process that can accurately assess a company's progress. It provides a management system that can help a company capture the spirit and drive toward greatness.

This book tells the story of NPS, where it began, how it evolved, and where it is headed. It shows you how you can use the system to improve your business—and your life.

In the Beginning

NPS first saw the light of day in *Harvard Business Review*, in late 2003. That article—"The One Number You Need to Grow"—eventually led to a book titled *The Ultimate Question*, which appeared in 2006. Both article and book described a simple, practical way to categorize customers based on their answer to a single question, typically phrased something like this:

> *On a zero-to-ten scale, how likely is it that you would recommend us (or this product/service/brand) to a friend or colleague?*

I also instructed companies to ask at least one follow-up question:

> *What is the primary reason for your score?*

The simplicity of the zero-to-ten scale allows companies to take a quick measurement of customers' feelings and attitudes. The open-ended follow-up question enables them to hear the reasons for these attitudes in the customers' own words. It avoids the distortions imposed by the preconceived response categories of traditional customer-satisfaction questionnaires.

When my colleagues and I studied the use of these questions, we found that customers typically fall into three well-defined groups. Each group of customers exhibits a distinct pattern of behavior as well as a distinct set of attitudes. And each calls for a different set of actions from the company.

- *Promoters.* People who respond with a nine or a ten are signaling that their lives have been enriched by their relationship with the company. They behave like loyal customers, typically making repeat purchases and giving the company a larger share of their spending. They talk up the company to their friends and colleagues, just as their answer to the question implies. They take the time to respond to surveys, and they offer constructive feedback and suggestions. We called this group *promoters*, because in their energy and enthusiasm that's exactly how they act. Any company should want to maintain the promoters' enthusiasm, to learn economical ways to create even more customers who feel and act that way, and to provide recognition and rewards to the teams or individual employees who do so.

- *Passives.* People who give the company a seven or an eight got what they paid for, nothing more. They are passively satisfied customers, not loyal ones, and they exhibit a markedly different set of attitudes and behaviors. They make few referrals— and when they do make one, it's likely to be qualified and unenthusiastic. If a competitor's discount or glitzy ad catches their eye, they are likely to defect. We called this group *passives*, because they bring little energy to the company and cannot be counted on as long-term assets. A company's goal for this category is to improve its services, products, or processes, where possible, to the point where it can delight these customers and turn some of them into promoters.

• *Detractors.* And then there are the people who give a rating of six or below. Their score indicates that their lives have been diminished by their dealings with the company. They are not a happy crew. They are dissatisfied, disaffected, even dismayed by how they are treated. They bad-mouth the company to their friends and colleagues. If they can't easily switch providers—for instance, if they have long-term contracts or if there aren't any competitors with similar offerings—they make nuisances of themselves, registering complaint after complaint and driving up costs. Their surly behavior destroys employee motivation and pride. Companies confronted with detractors have to probe for the root cause of their disappointment, then apologize and determine ways to solve the problem. If there is no economically rational solution to the detractors' discontent, then the company must learn not to acquire this type of customer in the first place.

If one central goal of a company is to enrich the lives of its customers, these three categories are a measure of how well it's doing. Promoters represent successes. Customers don't give a nine or ten score unless the company delivers something very special—unless it truly has a positive effect on their lives. Passives are just satisfied. They can't be considered successes unless the company's goal is to achieve mediocre results. Detractors, of course, represent serious failures. Something has gone badly wrong, and an interaction that should have had a positive effect instead has had a negative one.

But categorization was just the first step. We then wanted one simple number that could be tracked week in and week out to gauge a company's progress and focus its improvement efforts. We

EXHIBIT I-1

Net Promoter score: tracking lives enriched minus lives diminished

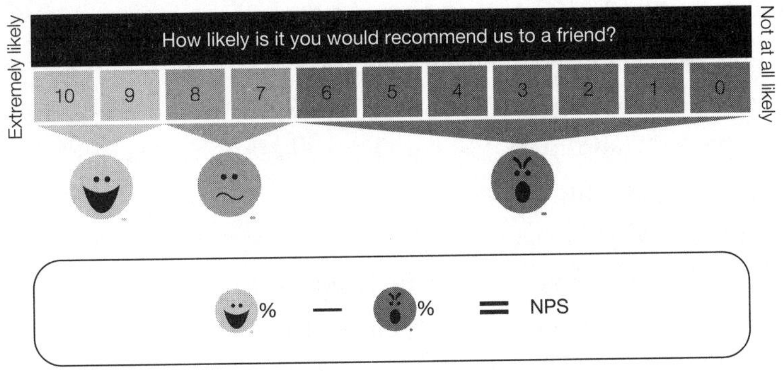

wanted a metric that was simple, powerful, and easy to understand, a bottom-line number akin to net profit or net worth. So we decided to take the percentage of customers who are promoters and subtract the percentage who are detractors. The result is Net Promoter score (exhibit I-1).

The Evolution of NPS

When *The Ultimate Question* was originally published, we very much wanted to put *Net Promoter* in the title. But that was a nonstarter: back then, hardly anyone had ever heard of NPS. The whole idea was in its infancy, just moving from theory to practice. The theory was backed up by some compelling research, and it had given rise to promising experiments by early adopters such as Intuit and General Electric. But it was a theory, nonetheless. The book highlighted companies that we had found to have high NPS relative to their competitors. (We had learned to measure NPS across an industry with what we now call the top-down market benchmark approach, which assesses companies' overall relationships with their customers rather than rating individual transactions.) But the exemplary firms did not themselves utilize the NPS framework and tools to achieve their success for the very good reason that, in 2006, these tools and processes did not yet exist. NPS had just been invented.

The situation has changed dramatically as this edition goes to press. Thousands of companies have adopted NPS. Many have achieved extraordinary results. Firms like Apple, Intuit, Philips, Rackspace, and the others mentioned earlier have put NPS at the center of their management processes. They have fleshed out the microeconomics that support the theory—for example, they can put a dollar value on the conversion of a passive to a promoter. They have developed metrics, tools, and processes that now underpin the standard Net Promoter system of management. This system has helped them discover better methods to hire, train, and reward their people. It has led them to reexamine policies, redesign products, and improve business processes. In short, they have discovered that the Net Promoter system holds the power to transform a company. They have also seen that, though the concept is simple, the journey toward building an army of promoters is both more challenging and more rewarding than they initially expected.

My colleagues and I have had the privilege of working with many of these companies as they pursued their NPS journey. We created forums, conferences, Web sites, and online communities to accelerate the learning and encourage the sharing of best practices. The centerpiece of this burgeoning business movement is the NPS Loyalty Forum, a membership organization sponsored by Bain & Company, the global consulting firm that has been my professional home for the past thirty-two years. Forum companies meet several times a year, usually at the headquarters of a member (see the box "NPS Loyalty Forum" for a partial list of attendees). The meetings allow the group to interact with a broad range of the host organization's team, from CEOs and finance chiefs to operations managers, marketing execs, and frontline customer-service reps. This cross-fertilization turns out to be particularly valuable because NPS has significant implications for every function and level of an organization.

We were also supported by Satmetrix, another early collaborator in the development of NPS metrics and tools, in creating public conferences. The conferences have taken place twice a year, one in the United States and one in Europe, and in the first few years attracted more than 3,200 managers. In addition, we developed a three-day certification course, which at this writing has already been taught around the world and has graduated more than 1,000 executives. The course is now available online.

Participating in these forums, conferences, and training programs helped me understand the evolution of NPS from score to system and beyond. Indeed, one of the fundamental lessons that these practitioners have learned is that the power of NPS extends far beyond the theme implied by the original book title. The score provided a starting point, but it is the system that has helped leaders create cultures that inspire employees to become more customer focused.

The ultimate question of the book's title was the "how likely is it that you would recommend" question mentioned earlier. That phrasing was a shorthand wording of a more basic question, which is, *Have we treated you right, in a manner that is worthy of your loyalty?* The shorthand form seemed to work best for most businesses—that is, it produced a score that correlated reliably with customer behaviors—though some companies found that slightly different wordings worked even better. But the question itself wasn't really the heart of things. After all, no company can expect to increase its growth or profitability merely by conducting surveys, however the question or questions might be phrased.

Rather, the question has led to the development of a management system with three central components. One is *categorizing*

NPS Loyalty Forum

The following is a partial list of companies that have participated in at least one meeting of the NPS Loyalty Forum:

24 Hour Fitness

Advance Auto Parts

Aggreko

Allianz

American Express

Archstone

Ascension Health

Asurion

Atlas Copco

Avid Technology

BBVA Bancomer

Belron

Cancer Treatment
    Centers of
    America

Charles Schwab

Chick-fil-A

Cintas

Cisco

Deutsche Post (DHL)

Deutsche Telekom

eBay

E.ON

Ermenegildo Zegna

Experian Consumer
    Division

Facebook

FranklinCovey

GE Healthcare

General Electric
    Company

Gilbane Building
    Company

Grocery Outlet

Honeywell Aerospace

Humana

ING Group

Intuit

JetBlue Airways

Joie de Vivre
    Hospitality

LEGO

LexisNexis

Lloyds Banking Group

Logitech

Macy's

Medtronic

Nike

Nokia

Paul Davis Restoration

Philips

Pricewaterhouse-
    Coopers

Progressive Insurance

Qantas

Rackspace

RSC Equipment
    Rental

Safelite

Schneider Electric

Sodexo

Stora Enso

SunTrust

Swiss Reinsurance
    Company

Symantec
    Corporation

TD Bank

TD Canada Trust

Teach For America

Tech Data

Teleperformance

Thermo Fisher
    Scientific

T-Mobile

TPG

Vanguard

Verizon

Volaris

Westpac Group

Zappos

customers into promoters, passives, and detractors through a simple survey. Another is *creating an easy-to-understand score based on that categorization.* Those are the elements that produce the Net Promoter score. But then comes a third essential component: *framing progress and success in these terms, thereby motivating everyone in the organization to take the actions required to produce more promoters and fewer detractors*—in other words, systematically and regularly learning to use scores and related feedback to drive improvements. That's how a company can better its results and strive toward greatness. That's what turns NPS from a score into a system.

Because so many noteworthy companies have adopted the Net Promoter system, awareness of the term has grown to the point where this revised and expanded version can finally include the words *Net Promoter* in the title. The core ideas in the original book remain valid, but with five years of experience, we can now position and characterize them more accurately. Since this edition also contains so much second-generation material and insights, we decided to call it *The Ultimate Question 2.0: How Net Promoter Companies Thrive in a Customer-Driven World.*

What You'll Find in This Book

What will you find in this revised and expanded version of *The Ultimate Question?*

Part I of the book describes the fundamental idea. It begins with the depressing proliferation of customer-unfriendly practices and the "bad profits" they generate. It relates the origin of NPS and describes in detail what our research showed. It also explains and quantifies the logical connection between NPS and a company's growth. This connection is becoming even more relevant and immediate as Web-based communication tools proliferate. Customers get real-time access to information about company practices and performance and so have moved ever more firmly into the driver's seat. Part I also looks at some of the practicalities of measuring customer attitudes. It tells the inspiring story of Enterprise Rent-A-Car, developer of the system I used as the initial model for NPS, and it outlines the rules for timely, accurate, and reliable measurement of something as slippery as how customers feel.

Part II—nearly all of it new in this edition—focuses on how leaders have achieved remarkable successes with the Net Promoter system. It recounts some of the best practices of leading companies and summarizes the key lessons. It highlights the fundamental changes these leaders had to make in order to drive the cultural shift toward building an army of promoters. Just as a movie trailer hits the highlights of a film, I will preview some of those lessons here.

NPS is a flexible, adaptable, open-source system. There's as little orthodoxy as possible in the system. Most companies have found that the zero-to-ten scale works best, but it's not the only one possible. (Enterprise uses a one-to-five scale.) Most companies prefer the "how likely" question the way I phrased it here, but some find a different question works better. Plenty of companies have unique names for their system. Schwab calls it Client Promoter Score. Thermo Fisher Scientific calls it Customer Loyalty Score. Chick-fil-A uses the phrase Raving Fan Index.

But there are three fundamental elements that you can't do without. Flexible it may be, but without the following three elements, NPS just won't work:

- *Companies must systematically categorize promoters and detractors* in a timely, transparent fashion. The categories and resulting feedback must make intuitive sense to frontline employees, not just to statisticians, and this information must be systematically compiled and communicated throughout the organization so people can take action and track their results. Otherwise, what's the point?

- *Companies must create closed-loop learning and improvement processes and build them into their daily operations.* NPS doesn't accomplish anything unless companies actually act on what they learn—unless, that is, they "close the loop" between learning and action. The closed-loop processes can't be an add-on; they have to be part and parcel of everyday management.

- *CEOs and other leaders must treat creating more promoters and fewer detractors as mission critical.* NPS isn't something that can be relegated to the market-research department. Earning the loyalty of customers and employees is either central to a company's philosophy and strategic priorities or it isn't—and if it isn't, adopting an improved customer feedback process won't make much difference.

NPS, in short, isn't something to be entered into lightly. Which brings us to perhaps the most important lesson of all:

NPS ultimately is a business philosophy, a system of operational practices, and a leadership commitment, not just another way to measure customer satisfaction.

This requires a word of explanation.

For starters, ask yourself: Why would a company even care what its customers and other stakeholders think? Many companies don't, and most of them seem to get by without going broke. (See all the examples of bad profits in chapter 1.) To be sure, I believe that NPS can make a business more successful. But I also believe that caring about your customers is the right thing to do. It makes for a better company, a better society, and a better life.

Think for a moment about the Golden Rule, the principle that you should treat others the way you would want to be treated if you were in their shoes, in a manner that brings honor and dignity to both parties. In one form or another, the Golden Rule is a pillar of most of the world's great religions. But it's hardly foreign to business. Companies such as Southwest Airlines, Four Seasons, and Chick-fil-A make the Golden Rule a centerpiece of their missions. If people can live up to the Golden Rule, they can reasonably assume they are living a worthwhile life; they are having a positive effect on those whose lives they touch. The "how likely" question is merely a practical shorthand for the question of whether you are observing the Golden Rule. It brings the whole thing back to earth, and to business. The purpose of a survey, after all, is not to begin a philosophical discussion or to launch a lifelong relationship. It is to create workable categories and a score that can facilitate action. It is a way of making business relationships better.

But the underlying philosophy is important to examine, because it reflects the values that inform and guide an organization. If you truly care about your company's effect on its customers' lives, you won't even be tempted to stop with a score. You will use the score as a prod, an incentive, a reminder that you can get better as an organization. You will begin to hire people, as Ron Johnson of Apple's retail division puts it, who "care about a customer's heart, not just her pocketbook." You will redirect your strategic investments and redesign your processes to create more promoters and fewer detractors, not just to increase your profits (though it will) but because it's the right thing to do. You will also begin to extend NPS, so that it measures the attitudes and behaviors of other stakeholders in the business—employees, major investors, suppliers, and other business partners—and unlocks insights into how to earn their loyalty. Organizations touch many lives, and you need to know what your company's impact is wherever and however it affects people.

Every leader of a business leaves a legacy when he or she departs, and it is that legacy by which a leader is judged. If you want to leave a legacy that extends beyond profits, a legacy of caring about customers and employees and about the kind of company you have built or contributed to, a legacy of enriching the lives you touched, NPS is an indispensable tool.

The Challenge of Making NPS Work

The ideas behind NPS seem so simple and intuitive that executives may be lulled into thinking that implementation will also be simple. It isn't. The companies that have adopted NPS have learned that it takes time and hard work to establish reliable, trustworthy measurements, to understand what the scores are telling you, and to create closed-loop processes that actually bring about change. NPS touches every part of the organization, including finance, operations, marketing, product design, human resources, and information technology. It reaches from the CEO and board all the way to the frontline employees who serve customers. It challenges established practices, priorities, and decision processes. Simple it may be, but it requires serious commitment on the part of senior leaders. Without that commitment, companies are likely to experience loss of momentum, confusion, resistance to new ways of doing things, and other pitfalls. Support and perseverance from the top of the organization are essential.

You may also find that merely broaching the idea of NPS runs into a wall of opposition from a group of critics that practitioners have dubbed *Net Pro-moaners* (discussed further in chapter 10). No surprise here: there's already a well-developed industry that purports to measure customer and employee satisfaction through long and largely ineffective research surveys, and an open-source solution such as NPS threatens the economic models on which most of the research firms depend. The firms' closed-source, black-box models are designed so that their algorithms remain closely guarded secrets. If the algorithms weren't secret, no one would pay these companies to use their models or seek advice on how to boost scores.

With NPS, by contrast, every company is welcome to adopt the process for free, and its transparency makes it easy to understand and improve. Little surprise that market-research traditionalists have scurried to write white papers and academic articles claiming that NPS doesn't work. Similarly, Encyclopedia Britannica does not hold Wikipedia in high regard, and proprietary software makers have little nice to say about open-source technologies. It's worth remembering the famous Upton Sinclair dictum: it is difficult to get a man to understand something when his salary depends upon his not understanding it.

When you shake up the existing order, you can expect opposition and obstacles. So what? This is a destination that is worth the trip, a journey that is worth the trouble. The knowledge you can gain from implementing the Net Promoter system is in fact priceless. It will help you run a better business, do more satisfying work, and build relationships that yield a more fulfilling life.

Before I close this introduction, I want to take the opportunity to welcome my colleague Rob Markey to a more public role on my writing team. Rob and I have worked together at Bain for almost twenty years now. He was an important reader and adviser on the first edition of this book, and he has played such a substantial role in the creation of this edition's new material that he deserves to be recognized as coauthor. Rob leads the NPS Loyalty Forum and is the head of Bain's Global Customer Strategy and Marketing practice. His depth of experience working with clients on NPS-related issues is unparalleled. This book is the stronger for his contributions.

In years to come, we intend to write more books about the Net Promoter system. But this book provides the starting point, the foundation. It will help you understand what the movement is all about, where it came from, and what it hopes to accomplish. And it will give you a taste of the remarkable success stories of companies that practice—and continue to learn from—the system. Perhaps someday we will be writing about your company as well. I hope so.

—Fred Reichheld
   Wellesley, Massachusetts
   April 2011

Part One

The Fundamentals of the Net Promoter System

1

Bad Profits, Good Profits, and the Ultimate Question

Most companies these days are striving to focus more closely on their customers—to become more customer-centric. Little surprise here: we live and work in a Web-savvy world in which customers have near-perfect information. Only companies that put the customer at the very center of their operations can successfully compete in such a world.

Many companies also want to make themselves more *mission* driven than *profit* driven. Again, no surprise. Their leaders understand that they can't win and keep customers without first winning and keeping the best possible employees. And most talented employees want to pursue a mission, a purpose that transcends profits for shareholders.

But despite all the effort companies have put into these twin tasks, focusing on customers and inspiring employees, the vast majority of firms haven't made much progress. Their cultures remain staunchly profit-centric, ruled by financial budgets and accounting metrics. Managers must make their numbers; business-unit heads, their sales and profit goals. Chief financial officers must report quarterly earnings to Wall Street. Leaders *know* the catechism of customer centricity, and most can recite it by heart. Question: *why do we want loyal customers?* Answer: *because loyal customers come back more often, buy additional products and services, refer their friends, provide valuable feedback, cost less to serve, and are less price sensitive.* But what leaders track, discuss, and manage each day are the financial indicators.

This is a major disconnect. Our accounting systems—both financial and management accounting—don't have anything to say about feelings of loyalty, enthusiasm, repeat purchases, referrals, and all the other emotions and behaviors that determine the economics of individual customers. Executives and employees know how to meet their immediate financial goals, and they know they will be held accountable for doing so. But customer loyalty and the company's mission, as objectives, are soft, slippery, seemingly impossible to quantify. In the rush of daily decisions and priorities, of budget pressures and sales quotas and cost accounting, the gravitational pull toward short-term profits is powerful. And so companies, despite the best of intentions, drift into a vortex. They begin making decisions that alienate customers and employees. They spend too much time focusing on the wrong things. They allow themselves to be seduced by the easy lure of what can only be called *bad profits*.

Consider some examples.

Bad Profits

The year was 1992. Computer users were growing more numerous by the day, and the online services business was booming. A brash young company known as America Online, or AOL, seemed poised for takeoff. Thanks to an initial public offering of stock, AOL had more than $60 million in its coffers.

AOL wanted to spend that money on growth—and the path to growth, its executives decided, was to invest in customer acquisition.

So over the next several years, the company carpet-bombed the United States with free software diskettes that allowed computer users to try out the service. It tucked the diskettes into the pages of magazines. It packaged them with the snacks served to airline passengers. It inserted them in cereal boxes and displayed them at the checkout stands of grocery stores. Most of the diskettes wound up in trash containers and then in landfills, and AOL's marketing campaign became a kind of national joke. Still, enough people signed up that the company could declare its strategy a success. Membership grew from 350,000 in early 1993 to about 4 million by the end of 1995.

Unfortunately, AOL's management team at the time wasn't spending commensurate amounts on improving the company's service capacity. Soon the flood of new users was straining the company's operating network. AOL earned a new nickname, "America On Hold." A full-day blackout in the summer of 1996— the longest in a series of service interruptions around this time, as it turned out—made headlines across the country and frustrated millions of members. AOL's monthly customer churn rate rose to 6 percent, an annual rate of 72 percent. Searching for a way to boost current earnings, AOL began to inundate customers with irritating pop-up ads and sales pitches. Though the company's membership continued to grow, more and more customers grew frustrated and disillusioned with what AOL was offering.

In January 2000, AOL merged with Time Warner, in a stunning deal that initially valued AOL at more than $190 billion. But it wasn't long before AOL began to stumble. Broadband was spreading rapidly, and AOL lost many customers to broadband service providers. It even lost some to dial-up competitors MSN and Earthlink. AOL shifted its strategy to become a free content provider, more like Yahoo! and Google, with much of its support provided by advertisers. But it continued to annoy its customers.

People who wanted to complain or terminate their contracts, for instance, struggled to find the carefully hidden 800 number. If they did succeed in finding it and actually reached an operator, they got a sales pitch to extend their contract instead of the service they were seeking. "Long ago," wrote Randall Stross in the *New York Times* in late 2005, "the company's culture became accustomed to concentrating energy on trapping customers who wished to leave."[1] In 2006, a disgruntled customer recorded a call with AOL in which he attempted to quit the service and was stonewalled at every turn. The recording went viral on the Internet, and once again AOL was a national joke.

In late 2009, Time Warner finally gave up on the AOL brand, spinning it off to shareholders at a valuation of $3.2 billion—a destruction of roughly $187 billion in shareholder value in just nine years.

Too many companies these days are like AOL back then. They want to make the most of their innovations. They want to build a great brand with world-class loyalty. But they can't tell the difference between good profits and bad. As a result, they let themselves get hooked on bad profits.

The consequences are disastrous. Bad profits choke off a company's best opportunities for true growth, the kind of growth that is both profitable and sustainable. They blacken its reputation. The pursuit of bad profits alienates customers and demoralizes employees.

Bad profits also make a business vulnerable to competitors. Companies that are not addicted—yes, there are many—can and do zoom right past the bad-profits junkies. If you ever wondered how Enterprise Rent-A-Car was able to overcome big, well-entrenched companies to become number one in its industry, how Southwest Airlines and JetBlue Airways so easily steal market share from the old-line carriers, or how Vanguard soared to the top of the mutual fund industry, that's your answer. These companies manage to balance the need for profits with the overarching vision of providing great results for customers and an inspiring mission for employees. They have figured out how to avoid bad profits, and their revenues and reputations have flourished.

The cost of bad profits extends well beyond a company's boundaries. Bad profits provide a distorted picture of business performance. The distortion misleads investors, yielding poor resource decisions that hurt our economy. Bad profits also tarnish the position of business in society. That tarnished reputation undermines consumer trust and provokes calls for stricter rules and tighter regulations. So long as companies pursue bad profits, all the noisy calls for better business ethics are pretty much meaningless.

By now you're probably wondering how in heaven's name *profit*, that holy grail of the business enterprise, can ever be bad. Short of outright fraud, isn't one dollar of earnings as good as another? Certainly, accountants can't tell the difference between good and bad profits. All those dollars look the same on an income statement.

While bad profits don't show up on the books, they are easy to recognize. They're profits earned at the expense of customer relationships.

Whenever a customer feels misled, mistreated, ignored, or coerced, profits from that customer are bad. Bad profits come from unfair or misleading pricing. Bad profits arise when companies shortchange customers the way AOL did, by delivering a lousy experience. Bad profits are about extracting value from customers, not creating value. When sales reps push overpriced or inappropriate products onto trusting customers, the reps are generating bad profits. When complex pricing schemes dupe customers into paying more than necessary to meet their needs, those pricing schemes are contributing to bad profits.

You don't have to look far for examples. Financial services firms, for instance, like to throw around terms like *fiduciary* and *trust* in their advertising campaigns, but how many firms deserve these monikers? Mutual funds bury their often exorbitant administrative fees in the fine print, so that customers won't know what they're paying. Brokerage firms slant their research to support investment-banking clients, thus bilking their stock-buying clients. Retail banks charge astonishing fees for late payments or bounced checks. The resentment toward financial institutions after the 2008 economic meltdown was so pronounced that it spawned legislation to protect consumers from predatory practices.

Or take health care. No wonder the market doesn't work and governments have had to step in. Most U.S. hospitals won't reveal the deals they have cut with insurance companies, so consumers can't know the real price of any particular procedure. If the regulations established by the 2010 reform law should be postponed or overturned—their fate is uncertain at this writing—most insurers will continue to do their best to exclude people who might actually need coverage; and whatever the outcome, if you do have coverage, they're sure to drown both you and your doctor in a deluge of complicated paperwork. Many pharmaceutical companies pay doctors to push their drugs, while carefully quashing studies suggesting that a potentially lucrative new drug may be ineffective or dangerous. And many health maintenance organizations promise to provide cradle-to-grave coverage, yet balk at paying for many procedures their own physicians recommend.

Travelers face their own set of inhospitable tactics. They must pay most airlines $100 to change a ticket and as much as $100 for an extra piece of checked baggage. If they are so foolish as to use a hotel phone, they may find they have run up charges larger than the room rate. If they return most rental cars with less than a full tank, they will be charged more than triple the market price for the fill-up. Of course, they also have the option of buying a full tank at the beginning of the rental and then trying to manage their mileage so precisely that only fumes remain—they get no credit for unused gas.

At times, customers must conclude that businesspeople lie awake nights thinking up new ways to hustle them. Most airlines change their prices frequently—often by hundreds of dollars—so nobody can know what the "real" fare is. Banks develop algorithms that process the largest checks first each day, so that depositors will be hit with more insufficient-funds penalties. Many mobile-phone operators have created pricing plans that cleverly trap customers into wasting prepaid minutes or incurring outrageous overages. In 2010, one Boston-area family hit the headlines because it had received a monthly bill for *$18,000* from its wireless provider—all because the family's college-age son had unwittingly downloaded a stream of data to his phone after the introductory rate had expired. If only the father had been encouraged to sign up for the $150 unlimited data plan, he could have avoided three years of haggling over that bill.

Ironically, the best customers often get the worst deals. If you are a patient, loyal user of your telephone or cable company, your mobile-phone provider, and your Internet service company, chances are good that you are paying more than disloyal switchers who signed up more recently. In fact, you're probably paying more than you need to, regardless of when you signed up, just because you didn't know about some special package the company offers. Customers who discover an extra charge of $20, say, for using text messaging might find that unlimited text messaging is available for $5 per month—if only they had asked for it in advance.

How Bad Profits Undermine Growth

Bad profits work much of their damage through the *detractors* they create. Detractors are customers who feel badly treated by a company—so badly that they cut back on their purchases, switch to the competition if they can, and warn others to stay away from the company they feel has done them wrong.

Detractors don't show up on any organization's balance sheet, but they cost a company far more than most of the liabilities that traditional accounting methods so carefully tally. Customers who feel ignored or mistreated find ways to get even. They drive up service costs by reporting numerous problems. They demoralize frontline employees with their complaints and demands. They gripe to friends, relatives, colleagues, acquaintances—anyone who will listen, sometimes including journalists, regulators, and legislators. Detractors tarnish a firm's reputation and diminish its ability to recruit the best employees and customers. Today, negative word of mouth goes out over a global PA system. In the past, the accepted maxim was that every unhappy customer told ten friends. Now an unhappy customer can tell ten thousand "friends" through the Internet.

Detractors strangle a company's growth. If many of your customers are bad-mouthing you, how are you going to get more? If many of your customers feel mistreated, how can you persuade them to buy more from you? In 2002, surveys showed that a whopping 42 percent of AOL customers were detractors. No wonder the company was on a downward spiral. Right now, churn rates in many industries—cellular phones, credit cards, auto insurance, and cable TV—have deteriorated to the point where a company may lose half of its new customers in less than three years. People have to fly whichever airline takes them where they want to go, but many airlines have created so much ill will that customers are itching for alternatives. For a while, US Airways dominated many routes into and out of Baltimore-Washington International Airport (BWI). By 1993, its market share at BWI had reached 41 percent. With this market power, the airline was able to charge high fares while delivering mediocre service. Customer resentment grew, but there were few options: if you wanted a nonstop flight, you often had to take what US Airways offered. Then Southwest Airlines entered the market with lower fares, superior service, and none of those irritating bad-profit tactics. Travelers flocked to the new carrier, and even when US Airways dropped prices to match Southwest, the customer exodus continued. By 2010, Southwest had corralled a 53 percent share of the market at BWI, while US Airways' share had diminished to only 6 percent.

True growth is hard to find these days. How hard? A recent study by Bain & Company found that only 9 percent of the world's major firms achieved real, sustainable profit and revenue growth of even 5.5 percent a year over the ten-year period from 1999 to 2009.[2] It seems like no coincidence that so many companies are having trouble growing and so many companies are addicted to bad profits. To change metaphors, business leaders have become master mechanics in siphoning out current earnings, but they fumble for the right wrench when it comes to gearing up for growth.

Granted, companies can always buy growth, just as AOL did. They can encourage the hard sell and pay fat commissions to the salespeople who master it. They can discount heavily, offering temporary rebates, sales, or "free" financing. They can launch heavy advertising and promotional campaigns. And of course, they can make acquisitions. All such techniques may boost revenues, but only for a while. It's also true that many factors usually contribute to a troubled company's downfall: AOL was hurt, for instance, by the increasing popularity of broadband as well as by its seeming disregard of the customer experience. But technologies and strategies are always changing, and companies that listen to their accountants more closely than to their customers are likely to find it hard to make a transition to a new business model.

Consider the experience of Blockbuster. Once a thriving, successful company, it had a leading market share in the video rental business. As video rentals gave way to online rentals and video on demand, it might have morphed into an equally successful company in an adjacent market—as a competitor to Netflix, for instance, or even as an owner of movie theaters. But Blockbuster was addicted to bad profits and thus had more than its share of detractors. Rent a movie for a long weekend for only $5.99! But if you return it even an hour late, the fee is doubled. And if you forget to return it for a week, you might owe more than $40. In our town, the Blockbuster store had no serious competition, so customers had to put up with this nasty practice. But they often took out their frustration on the store's clerks, which made it harder to attract good employees. Soon the store was understaffed and the checkout lines long. The aisles were cluttered with DVDs that were never properly sorted. More and more customers were accused of failing to return videos. More and more accounts were turned over to collection agencies.

If Blockbuster had built a loyal customer base, it would have had a strong set of strategic options. But it chose to fund its growth with bad profits. What may have seemed like smart pricing tactics ended up alienating customers and employees and set the stage for the company's rapid decline: Blockbuster's share of the movie rental business dropped quickly, its losses mounted, and its market value plummeted. Despite management changes, it was never able to recover, and in 2010 it had to file for bankruptcy.

Shifting technology and resulting new business models don't have to sound the death knell for companies, as Netflix illustrates. Netflix went out of its way to avoid bad profits. It developed innovative ways to make its Web site more customer friendly. It eschewed late fees and "gotcha" pricing tactics, and it invested heavily in creating great customer service. If customers lost a DVD, they faced no threats from collection agencies; they simply had to explain the circumstances. Netflix trusted them unless and until an unreasonable number of recurrences demonstrated that it couldn't. As technology shifted to enable online streaming of videos, Netflix wasn't a victim. The enormous customer loyalty it had built helped the company lead the transition to the new technology.

Buying growth through discounts, sales promotions, and advertising is expensive. It tends to create a profit squeeze, which in turn usually deepens a company's addiction to bad profits. Retail banks, for example, now depend on nuisance fees for as much as one-third of reported earnings. One mobile-phone operator calculates that proactively putting customers in the plan that was best for them would cut profits by 40 percent. This addiction to bad profits demotivates employees, diminishes the chances for true growth, and accelerates a destructive spiral. Customers resent bad profits—but investors should, too, because bad profits undermine a company's prospects. Like the addicts they are, enterprises dependent on bad profits have no future until they can break their habit.

The Alternative: Good Profits

But it doesn't have to be this way. Some companies grow because they have learned to tell the difference between bad profits and good profits—and to focus their efforts on the good kind.

Good profits are dramatically different. If bad profits are earned at the expense of customers, good profits are earned with customers' enthusiastic cooperation. A company earns good profits when it so delights its customers that they willingly come back for more—and not only that, they tell their friends and colleagues to do business with the company. Satisfied customers become, in effect, part of the company's marketing department, not only increasing their own purchases but also providing enthusiastic referrals. They become *promoters*. The right goal for a company that wants to break the addiction to bad profits is to build relationships of such high quality that those relationships create promoters, generate good profits, and fuel growth.

The Vanguard Group of mutual funds offers a compelling illustration of the difference between bad profits and good. Not long ago, Vanguard *reduced* prices by as much as one-third for customers who had recently made large investments or who had maintained healthy balances for an extended period. Vanguard's management recognized that the economies of scale generated by those large-balance and long-tenured investors could be shared with them. The company had the opportunity to deliver more value to its best customers, widening the pricing gap they would experience compared to competitors' offerings. It would have been more profitable to continue to charge these customers the same prices paid by newer and smaller-balance customers. To Vanguard, however, this didn't make good business sense. Why not share the benefits of scale with the very customers who created them? When the company did this, its core customers were so delighted that they increased their holdings and boosted referrals. That helped turbocharge Vanguard's growth, and pushed the company toward leadership in the mutual funds industry.

Nor is Vanguard alone in its pursuit of good profits. For example:

> Amazon.com could easily afford to advertise more than it does; instead, it channels its investments into free shipping, lower prices, and service enhancements. Founder and CEO Jeff Bezos has said, "If you do build a great experience, customers tell each other about that."[3]

Zappos.com, the online shoe and apparel retailer, followed a similar path. By avoiding investments in sales and marketing, Zappos was able to channel its resources into delivering a great customer experience. CEO Tony Hsieh's strategy was to grow through repeat purchase and customer referral, which helped the company reach sales of more than $1 billion in just ten years. Amazon was so impressed with Zappos that it acquired the firm for $1.2 billion in 2009.

Southwest Airlines doesn't charge for flight changes or for checked baggage; the carrier has also replaced the industry's elaborately segmented pricing structure with a transparent pricing policy. Southwest now flies more domestic passengers than any other U.S. airline and boasts a market capitalization that tops the rest of the industry.

Costco, the leader in customer loyalty among warehouse retailers, rocketed from start-up to the *Fortune* 50 in less than twenty years while spending next to nothing on advertising and marketing. Its customers are so loyal that the company can rely on positive word of mouth for its growth.

Among Internet companies, the impressive early growth of eBay offered a remarkable contrast to the stalled growth of AOL. The eBay Web site says this:

eBay is a community that encourages open and honest communication among all its members. Our community is guided by five fundamental values:

- *We believe people are basically good.*
- *We believe everyone has something to contribute.*
- *We believe that an honest, open environment can bring out the best in people.*

- *We recognize and respect everyone as a unique individual.*
- *We encourage you to treat others the way you want to be treated.*

eBay is firmly committed to these principles. And we believe that community members should also honor them—whether buying, selling, or chatting with eBay friends.

Of course, anyone can list high-minded principles on a Web site or a recruiting brochure. But eBay has found ways to translate these principles into daily priorities and decisions. The result: by 2010, eBay managed to turn more than 70 percent of its customers into promoters. (Only Amazon had a higher percentage of promoters—76 percent—in the online shopping sector that year, though by 2011, Zappos was large enough to show up on the surveys, and its Net Promoter score was in a statistical dead heat with eBay's.) Referrals generate many of eBay's new customers, creating multiple economic advantages across the business. The company has found that referred customers cost less to serve because they've already been coached by a promoter on how the site works and they usually have friends who help solve their problems instead of relying on eBay employees. EBay has also learned to tap the creativity of an entire online community, not just its own employees. The company encourages members to point out areas in which they believe eBay isn't living up to its principles, and to identify new opportunities to better serve members. Community members are invited to rate sellers after each transaction, and the ratings are then shared with everybody. This process enables each member to establish a reputation based not on public relations or advertising spin but on the cumulative experience of members with whom they've done business. EBay's virtual world is just like a small town: a good name is essential for success.

Conventional wisdom encourages companies to consolidate market power and then extract maximum value from customers.

Yet eBay has done just the opposite. Although it has come to dominate the online auction market, the company tries to consider the needs of community members as well as the long-term interests of its shareholders when it makes decisions. Running a company like a community enables eBay to look beyond the next quarter's stock price and to continually find ways to enrich the lives of community members. For example, the company created a group health insurance plan for its so-called PowerSellers—typically small merchants—who don't have access to the scale economies of corporate health plans. Although eBay facilitates the program, it doesn't take a profit margin. The company's acquisition of PayPal, in addition to being an astute business move, helps create trusted communities of buyers and sellers with additional protection from fraud built into the system. EBay's consistent values platform made it a credible home for PayPal—one more example of a loyal customer base enabling a move to an adjacent business that strengthened the core and provided enormous growth of its own.

Moves like this demonstrate a way of thinking that is radically different from the thinking of bad-profits companies. Airlines that dominate particular routes have repeatedly used their market power to raise prices, sometimes to levels that can only be described as price gouging. AOL alienated customers not just with those service failures and pop-up ads, but also by continuing to charge for minutes used and resisting a move to flat monthly fees. EBay could easily increase profits by boosting ad revenue—but management recognizes that lots of expensive ads would make the site less valuable to community members and possibly put small merchants at a disadvantage relative to large players.

This way of thinking also demonstrates a deep respect for the power of word of mouth in today's economy. Just as detractors have a bullhorn for spreading their negative word of mouth, promoters have one for spreading their positive word of mouth. Promoters bring in new people. They talk up a company and burnish its reputation. They extend the company's sales force at no cost. They make it possible for a company to earn good profits and thereby to create growth that is both profitable and sustainable.

This approach to customers boils down to a simple precept: treat them the way you would like to be treated. What's surprising is that so many company leaders articulate it in exactly these homespun terms. EBay founder Pierre Omidyar literally says, "My mother always taught me to treat other people the way I want to be treated and to have respect for other people."[4] Other leaders invoke the Golden Rule as well:

> Colleen Barrett, retired president of Southwest Airlines: "Practicing the Golden Rule is integral to everything we do."

> Isadore Sharp, founder and chairman of the Four Seasons hotel group: "Our success all boils down to following the Golden Rule."

> Andy Taylor, CEO of Enterprise: "The only way to grow is to treat customers so well they come back for more, and tell their friends about us. That's how we'd all like to be treated as customers." Taylor concluded, "Golden Rule behavior is the basis for loyalty. And loyalty is the key to profitable growth."

A truly customer-centric company is one that lives up to the Golden Rule. Employees treat customers the way they would want to be treated if they were customers. That means avoiding bad profits entirely.

Bad and Good Profits: How Can Companies Tell the Difference?

"Loyalty is the key to profitable growth," said Andy Taylor of Enterprise. That makes sense as far as it goes. But it raises as many questions as it answers. Most companies can't even define loyalty, let alone measure and manage it. Are customers sticking around out of loyalty, or just out of ignorance and inertia? Are they trapped in long-term contracts they would love to get out of? Anyway, how can managers really know how many of their customers love the company and how many hate it? What practical gauge can distinguish good profits from bad?

Without a systematic feedback mechanism, after all, the Golden Rule is self-referential and simplistic, unreliable for decision making. I might think I'm treating you the way I would like to be treated, but you may strongly disagree. Where companies are concerned, satisfaction surveys often delude executives into thinking that their performance merits an A, while their customers are thinking C– or F. Business leaders need a hard, no-nonsense metric—an honest grading system—that tells them how they are *really* doing.

The search for that metric—the missing link between the Golden Rule, loyalty, and sustainable growth—turned out to be a long and arduous quest.

At Bain & Company, we began investigating the connection between loyalty and growth almost thirty years ago. We first compiled data demonstrating that a 5 percent increase in customer retention could yield anywhere from a 25 percent to a 100 percent improvement in profits. Later, we showed that companies with the highest customer loyalty (we labeled them *loyalty leaders*) typically grew revenues at more than twice the rate of their competitors.

Of course, not everybody was eager to learn about the mysterious *loyalty effect*, which explained how building relationships worthy of loyalty translated into superior profits and growth. The corporate generals at places like Enron and WorldCom couldn't have cared less about treating customers right. Some Wall Street firms in recent years seem to have been ignoring customers in favor of racking up big profits through proprietary trading. But the vast majority of senior executives generally buy into the concept. After all, it doesn't take a rocket scientist to see that a company can't grow if it is churning customers out the back door faster than the sales force can drag them in the front.

Still, there's a puzzle lurking here. Survey after survey demonstrates that customer loyalty *is* among most CEOs' top priorities—yet the colonels, captains, and corporals in their organizations continue to treat customers in ways that ensure these customers won't be coming back anytime soon. If the CEOs are as powerful as they are said to be, why can't they make their employees care about customer relationships?

The reason, of course, is just what we alluded to earlier in this chapter: employees are held accountable for increasing profits. Financial results are what companies measure. Financial results determine how managers fare in their performance reviews. Trouble is, accounting procedures can't distinguish a dollar of good profits from a dollar of bad. Did that $10 million in incremental profit come from new hidden surcharges, or did it come from loyal customers' repeat purchases? Did that $5 million in cost reduction come from shaving service levels, or from cutting customer defection rates? Who knows the answer to any such question? And if nobody knows, who cares? Managers trying to run a department or division can't be faulted for paying attention to the metrics by which they will be judged.

Whatever the CEO might think, in short, companies that measure success primarily through the lens of financial accounting tend to conclude that loyalty is dead, relationships are irrelevant, and the treatment of customers should be governed by what seems profitable rather than by what seems right. With only financial metrics to gauge success, managers focus on profits regardless of whether those profits represent the rewards from building relationships or the spoils from abusing them. Ironically, customer loyalty provides companies with a powerful financial advantage—a battalion of credible sales and marketing and PR troops who require no salary or commissions. Yet the importance of these customer promoters is overlooked because they don't show up on anybody's income statement or balance sheet.

Finally, at a European conference on loyalty, a Bain colleague provided a crucial insight into this conundrum. Watching the executives file out of the room after a presentation, seemingly pumped up about loyalty as never before, he shook his head. "You know, it's sad," he said. "Right now, they all understand that their businesses can't prosper without improving customer loyalty. But they'll get back to their offices and soon recognize that there is no one in their organization to whom they can delegate the task. There is no system to help them measure loyalty in a way that makes individuals accountable for results."

Bingo. *Accountability* is one of those magic words in business. Any experienced manager will tell you that where there is individual accountability, things get done. *Measure* is another magic word: what gets measured *creates* accountability. With no standard, reliable metric for customer relationships, employees can't be held accountable for them and so overlook their importance. In contrast, the precise, rigorous, daily measures of profit and its components ensure that those same employees—at least the ones who wish to stay employed—feel personally accountable for costs, revenues, or both. So the pursuit of profit dominates corporate and individual agendas, while accountability for treating people right, for enriching lives, for building good relationships, all gets lost in the shadows.

Several years ago, we thought we had solved this measurement challenge. We had helped companies develop a whole set of key measures, such as retention rate, repurchase rate, and "share of wallet." But then we had to face reality. Most organizations found it difficult to collect accurate and timely data on these loyalty metrics. The companies were simply unable to rebalance their priorities and establish accountability for building good relationships with customers. Though the science of measuring profits had progressed steadily since the advent of double-entry bookkeeping in the fifteenth century, measuring the quality of relationships remained stuck in the dark ages. Companies lacked a practical, reliable operational system for gauging the percentage of their customer relationships that were growing stronger and the percentage that were growing weaker—and for getting the right employees to take appropriate actions based on this data.

So we went back to the drawing board. What we needed was a foolproof test—a practical metric for relationship loyalty that would illuminate the difference between good profits and bad. We had to find a metric that would permit individual accountability. We knew that the fleeting attitudes expressed in satisfaction surveys couldn't define loyalty; only actual behaviors can gauge loyalty and can fuel growth. So we concluded that behaviors must be the real building blocks. We needed a metric based on what customers would actually do.

After considerable research and experimentation, some of which you'll read about in the following chapters, we found one such metric. We discovered the one question you can ask your customers that usually links so closely to their behaviors that it is a practical surrogate for what they will do. By asking that question thoughtfully and systematically, and by linking results to employee rewards, you can tell the difference between good profits and bad. You can manage for customer loyalty and the growth it produces just as rigorously as you now manage for profits.

Customer responses to this question yield a simple, straightforward measurement. This easy-to-collect metric can make your employees accountable for treating customers right. It's one number that lets you determine how much progress you are making in your quest to become customer-centric. We called this question the ultimate question because it helps you see whether you have succeeded in your mission to enrich the lives you touch. Upon reflection, though, perhaps we should have called it the penultimate question since it always needs to be followed up by one additional question: why?

Asking the Ultimate Question

What is the question that can tell good profits from bad? Simplicity itself: *how likely is it that you would recommend this company, or this product or service, to a friend or colleague?* The metric that it produces is the *Net Promoter score.*

Net Promoter score (NPS) is based on the fundamental observation that every company's customers cluster into three groups, each with its own distinct patterns of behavior. *Promoters,* as we have seen, are loyal enthusiasts who keep buying from a company and urge their friends to do the same. *Passives* are satisfied but unenthusiastic customers who can be easily wooed by the competition. And *detractors* are unhappy customers trapped in a bad relationship. Customers can be categorized according to their answer to the question. Those who answer nine or ten on a zero-to-ten scale, for instance, are promoters, and so on down the line.

A "growth engine" running at perfect efficiency would convert 100 percent of a company's customers into promoters. The worst possible engine would convert 100 percent into detractors. The best way to gauge the efficiency of the growth engine is to take the percentage of customers who are promoters and subtract the percentage who are detractors. That's what NPS is—promoters minus detractors.

In concept, it's just that simple. All the complexity arises from learning how to ask the question in a manner that provides reliable, timely, and actionable data—and, of course, from learning why the customer feels this way and then learning how to take actions that create more promoters, produce fewer detractors, and thus improve your score.

How do companies stack up on this measurement? The range of scores varies by industry, as shown in exhibit 1-1. But the leaders in each industry demonstrate some very impressive levels of growth-engine efficiency. For example, Net Promoter stars such as Apple, Amazon.com, Costco, and USAA operate at NPS efficiency ratings from 60 to more than 80 percent. So even they have some room for improvement. But the average firm sputters along at an NPS efficiency of only 10 to 20 percent. In other words, promoters barely outnumber detractors. Many firms—and some entire industries—have *negative* Net Promoter scores, which means that they are creating more detractors than promoters day in and day out. These abysmal scores help explain why so many companies can't deliver profitable, sustainable growth, no matter how aggressively they spend to acquire new business.

Our research over a ten-year period confirms that, in most industries, companies with the highest ratio of promoters to detractors in their sector typically enjoy both strong profits and healthy growth. This might seem counterintuitive. After all, the high-loyalty firms tend to spend much less on marketing and new-customer acquisition than do their competitors. They also focus intensely on serving existing customers and are highly selective in pursuing new customers, which you might suspect would limit these firms' growth. But the data doesn't lie: NPS leaders tend to grow at more than twice the rate of their competitors. And do you remember the 9 percent of companies that had registered sustained, profitable growth over a ten-year period? The Net Promoter scores of those companies, on average, were 2.3 times the scores of the other firms in their respective industries.[5]

EXHIBIT 1-1

Net Promoter score ranges and leaders by industry (U.S.)

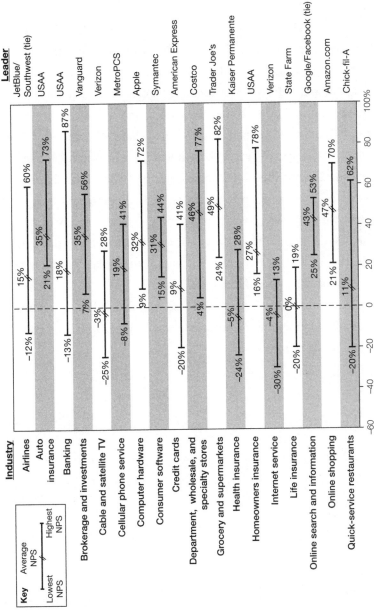

Key

Average NPS

Lowest NPS ⊢────⊬────┤ Highest NPS

Industry	Leader
Airlines	JetBlue/Southwest (tie)
Auto insurance	USAA
Banking	USAA
Brokerage and investments	Vanguard
Cable and satellite TV	Verizon
Cellular phone service	MetroPCS
Computer hardware	Apple
Consumer software	Symantec
Credit cards	American Express
Department, wholesale, and specialty stores	Costco
Grocery and supermarkets	Trader Joe's
Health insurance	Kaiser Permanente
Homeowners insurance	USAA
Internet service	Verizon
Life insurance	State Farm
Online search and information	Google/Facebook (tie)
Online shopping	Amazon.com
Quick-service restaurants	Chick-fil-A

Source: Satmetrix 2011 Net Promoter Benchmark Study of U.S. Consumers; Bain analysis.

Most business leaders desperately need to become more customer-centric in order to grow. They need it to boost their stock price. They need it to attract and motivate talent. Whatever language they may use, they probably know that creating more customer promoters is vital. But without a simple, practical way to assign accountability and measure progress, they can't align their organizations around this goal. Indeed, most don't realize how deeply addicted to bad profits they have become. Inflated customer-satisfaction scores have lulled them into complacency—yet our research shows that for the average firm, more than two-thirds of customers are passives (bored) or detractors (angry). Given this sad fact, most attempts to buy growth simply burn up shareholder funds. The efforts amount to throwing money into advertising and sales only to dissipate the impact through the poisonous emissions of unhappy customers.

Bad profits have undermined true growth and have given business a bad name. But it's not too late to change. Some companies have already begun.

2

The Measure of Success

Scott Cook was worried. His financial-software company, Intuit, was on a slippery slope, and he wasn't sure what to do about it.

Granted, his problems might not have looked overwhelming to an outsider. Intuit had grown like gangbusters ever since its birth in 1983. Its three major products—Quicken, QuickBooks, and TurboTax—dominated their markets. The company had gone public in 1993, and by the end of the decade was racking up sizable profits. Intuit had also been lauded by the business press as an icon of customer service, and Cook—a mild-mannered, bespectacled Harvard MBA who had done a stint at Procter & Gamble before cofounding the company—had a gut-level grasp of the importance of customer promoters. "We have hundreds of thousands of salespeople," he told *Inc.* magazine as early as 1991. "They're our customers." Intuit's mission? "To make the customer feel so good about the product they'll go and tell five friends to buy it."

But now—was that really happening? Cook wasn't sure. When the company was in its start-up phase, operating out of cozy offices in Silicon Valley, he had known every employee personally, and he could coach them all on the importance of making products and delivering services that customers truly loved. They could all hear him working the service phones himself, talking to customers. They could see him taking part in Intuit's famous "follow-me-home" program, where employees asked customers if they could watch them set up the software in order to note any problems. But now the company had thousands of people in multiple locations. Like many rapidly growing businesses, it had hired a lot of professional managers, who had been trained to run things by the numbers.

And what were those numbers? There were two requirements for growth, Cook liked to say: *profitable* customers and *happy* customers. Everyone knew how to measure profits, but the only measurements of customers' happiness were vague statistics of "satisfaction"—statistics derived from surveys that nobody trusted and nobody was accountable for.

So managers naturally focused on profits, with predictable consequences. The executive who cut staffing levels in the phone-support queue to reduce costs wasn't held accountable for the increased hold times or the resulting customer frustration. The phone rep who so angered a longtime customer that he switched to another tax-software product could still receive a quarterly bonus, because she handled so many calls per hour. Her batting average on productivity was easy to measure, but her batting average on customer goodwill was invisible. The marketing manager who kept approving glitzy new features to attract more customers was rewarded for boosting revenues and profits, when in fact the added complexity created a bewildering maze that turned off new users. Now, Cook was hearing more complaints than in the past. Some market-share numbers were slipping. For lack of a good system of measurement—and for lack of the accountability that accurate measurement creates—the company seemed to be losing sight of exactly what had made it great: its relationships with its customers.

The Challenge: Measuring Customer Happiness

In a way, Cook's experience recapitulated business history. Back in the days when every business was a small business, a proprietor could *know* what his customers were thinking and feeling by the looks on their faces. He knew them personally. He could see with his own eyes what made them happy and what made them mad. Customer feedback was immediate and direct—and if he wanted to stay in business, he paid attention to it.

But soon companies were growing too big for their owners or managers to know every customer. Individual customers came and went; the tide of customers ebbed and flowed. Without the ability to gauge what people were thinking and feeling, corporate managers naturally focused on how much those customers were spending, a number that was easily measurable. If our revenue is growing and we're making money, so the thinking ran, we must be doing something right.

Later, of course—and particularly after the arrival of powerful computers—companies tried to assess customers' attitudes more directly. They hired market-research firms to conduct satisfaction surveys. They tried to track customer-retention rates. These endeavors were so fraught with difficulties that managers outside marketing departments generally, and wisely, ignored the efforts. Retention rates, for example, track customer defections—how fast the customer bucket is emptying—but say nothing on the equally important question of how fast the bucket is filling up. They are a particularly poor indication of attitudes whenever customers are held hostage by high switching costs or other barriers. (Think of those US Airways Baltimore-Washington travelers before Southwest Airlines arrived on the scene.)

Conventional customer-satisfaction measures are even less reliable. There is only a tenuous connection between satisfaction rates and actual customer behavior, and between satisfaction rates and a company's growth. That's why investors typically ignore reports on customer satisfaction. In some cases, indeed, the relationship between satisfaction and performance is exactly backward. In the spring of 2005, for example, General Motors was taking out full-page newspaper ads trumpeting its numerous awards from J.D. Power and Associates, the biggest name in satisfaction studies. Meanwhile, the headlines in the business section were announcing that GM's market share was sinking and its bonds were being downgraded to junk status. A few years later GM would find itself in bankruptcy proceedings.

So as we continued our study of loyalty, we searched for a better measure—a simple and practical indicator of what customers were thinking and feeling about the companies they did business with. We wanted a number that reliably linked these attitudes to what customers actually did, and to the growth of the company in question.

What a chore it turned out to be! We started with the roughly twenty questions on the Loyalty Acid Test, a survey Bain designed several years ago to assess the state of relations between a company and its customers. (Sample questions: How likely are you to purchase Company X's products or services again? What was your overall satisfaction with the products and services provided by Company X?) Then we sought the assistance of Satmetrix Systems Inc., a company that develops software to gather and analyze real-time customer feedback. (Full disclosure:

Fred serves on Satmetrix's board of advisers and worked with the company to develop its NPS certification course.)

The process began with the recruitment (from public lists) of thousands of customers in six industries: financial services, cable and telecommunications, personal computers, e-commerce, auto insurance, and Internet service providers. We then obtained a purchase history for every person surveyed. We also asked these people to name specific instances when they had referred someone else to the company in question. When this information wasn't immediately available, we waited six to twelve months and then gathered information on subsequent purchases and referrals by those individuals. Eventually we had detailed information from more than four thousand customers, and we were able to build fourteen case studies—that is, cases for which we had sufficient sample sizes to measure the link between individual customers' survey responses and those same individuals' purchase or referral behavior.

Discovering the Right Question

All this number crunching had one goal: to determine which survey questions showed the strongest statistical correlation with repeat purchases or referrals. We hoped to find for each industry at least one question that effectively predicted what customers would do, and hence helped predict a company's growth. We took bets on what the question would be. Our own favorite—probably reflecting our years of research on loyalty—was, "How strongly do you agree that Company X deserves your loyalty?"

But what we found was different, and it surprised us all. It turned out that the same question—the ultimate question— worked best for *most* industries. And that question was, "How likely is it that you would recommend Company X to a friend or colleague?" In eleven of the fourteen cases, this question ranked first or second. In two of the three others, it was so close to the top that it could serve as a proxy for those that did rank number one or number two.

Reflecting on our findings, we realized they made perfect sense. Loyalty, after all, is a strong and value-laden concept, usually applied to family, friends, and country. People may *be* loyal to a company that they buy from, but they may not describe what they feel in those terms. If they really love doing business with a particular provider of goods or services, however, what's the most natural thing for them to do? Of course: recommend that company to someone they care about.

We also realized that two conditions must be satisfied before customers make a personal referral. They must believe that the company offers superior value in terms that an economist would understand: price, features, quality, functionality, ease of use, and other such factors. But they also must *feel* good about their relationship with the company. They must believe the company knows and understands them, values them, listens to them, and shares their principles. On the first dimension, a company is engaging the customer's head. On the second, it is engaging the heart. Only when both sides of the equation are fulfilled will a customer enthusiastically recommend a company to a friend. The customer must believe that the friend will get good value—but he or she also must believe that the company will treat the friend right. That's why the "would recommend" question provides such an effective measure of relationship quality. It tests for both the rational and the emotional dimensions.

We don't want to overstate the case. Though the "would recommend" question is far and away the best single-question predictor of customer behavior across a range of industries—and not just referrals but repeat and expanded purchases, along with willingness to provide constructive feedback—it's not the best for every industry. In certain business-to-business settings, a question such as "How likely is it that you will continue to purchase products or services from Company X?" or "How likely is it that you would recommend that we do more of our business with Company X?" may work better. So companies need to do their homework. They need to validate the empirical link between survey answers and subsequent customer behavior for their own business. But once that link is established, as we will see in chapter 3, the effect is powerful: it provides the means for gauging performance, establishing accountability, and making investments. It shows the connection between this measure of customer centricity and profitable growth.

Scoring the Answers

Of course, finding the right question to ask was only the beginning. We now had to establish a good way of scoring the responses.

To be useful, the scoring of responses must be as simple and unambiguous as the question itself. The scale must make sense to customers who are answering the question. The categorization of answers must make sense to the managers and employees responsible for interpreting the results and taking action. The right categorization will effectively divide customers into groups that deserve different attention and different responses from the company based on their behavior, their value to the company, and their differing needs. Ideally, the scale and categorization would be so easy to understand that even outsiders—investors, regulators, journalists—could grasp the basic messages without the need for a handbook and a course in statistics.

For all these reasons we settled on a simple zero-to-ten scale, where ten means extremely likely to recommend and zero means not at all likely. When we mapped customers' behaviors on this scale, we found—and have continued to find in our subsequent work with clients—three clusters corresponding to different patterns of behavior:

- One segment was the customers who gave a company a nine or ten rating. We called them *promoters*, because they behaved like promoters. They reported the highest repurchase rates by far, and they accounted for more than 80 percent of referrals.

- A second segment was the "passively satisfied" or *passives*; they rated the company seven or eight. This group's repurchase and referral rates were a lot lower than those of promoters, often by 50 percent or more. Motivated more by inertia than by loyalty or enthusiasm, these customers typically stay on only until somebody offers them a better deal.

- Finally, we called the group who gave ratings from zero to six *detractors*. This group accounts for more than 80 percent of negative word-of-mouth comments. Some of these customers may appear profitable from an accounting standpoint, but their criticisms and attitudes diminish a company's reputation, discourage new customers, and demotivate employees. They suck the life out of a firm.

Grouping customers into these three categories—promoters, passives, and detractors—provides a simple, intuitive scheme that accurately predicts customer behavior. Most important, it's a scheme that drives action. Frontline managers can grasp the idea of increasing the number of promoters and reducing the number of detractors a lot more readily than the idea of raising the customer-satisfaction index by one standard deviation. The ultimate test for any customer-relationship metric is whether it helps the organization act in a customer-centric manner, thereby tuning the growth engine to operate at peak efficiency. Does it help employees clarify and simplify the job of delighting customers? Does it allow employees to compare their performance from week to week and month to month? The notion of promoters, passives, and detractors does all this.

We also found that what we began to call Net Promoter score, or NPS—the percentage of promoters minus the percentage of detractors—provided the easiest-to-understand, most effective summary of how a company was performing in this context.

We didn't come to this language or this precise metric lightly. For example, we considered referring to the group scoring a company nine or ten as "delighted," in keeping with the aspiration of so many companies to delight their customers. But the business goal here isn't merely to delight customers; it's to turn them into promoters—customers who buy more and who actively refer friends and colleagues. That's the behavior that contributes to growth. We also wrestled with the idea of keeping it even simpler— measuring only the percentage of customers who are promoters. But as we'll see in later chapters, a company seeking growth must increase the percentage of promoters *and* decrease the percentage of detractors. These are two distinct processes that are best managed separately. Companies that must serve a wide variety of customers in addition to their targeted core—retailers, banks, airlines, and so on—need to minimize detractors among noncore customers, since these customers' negative word of mouth is just as destructive as anybody's. But investing to delight customers other than those in the core may yield little economic return. Net Promoter scores provide the requisite information for fine-tuning customer management in this way.

Individual customers, of course, can't have an NPS; they can only be promoters, passives, or detractors. But companies can calculate their Net Promoter scores for particular segments of customers, for divisions or geographic regions, and for individual branches or stores. NPS is to customer relationships what a company's net profit or net worth is to financial performance. It provides a bottom line that can drive learning and accountability. That is not to say this or any other bottom line is the only number you need to manage a business. Just as you need to know the details of revenues and costs to analyze that most famous of bottom lines, net profit, so too do you need detailed data on promoters, passives, and detractors to peel the onion of your Net Promoter score. But the clarity and focus that come from tracking a single number for loyalty—Net Promoter score—simplifies communication and calls attention to the instances that require deeper analysis.

Solving Intuit's Problem

Intuit—worried as it was about slipping customer relationships—jumped at the idea of measuring its NPS and began an implementation program in the spring of 2003. ("Just one number—it makes so much sense!" exclaimed Scott Cook when he learned of the idea.) The company's experience shows some of what's involved in measuring promoters and detractors. It also shows how this measurement can transform a company's day-to-day priorities.

Intuit's first step was to determine the existing mix of promoters, passives, and detractors in each major business line. Cook suggested that this initial phone-survey process focus on only two questions. The team settled on these: first, What is the likelihood you would recommend (TurboTax, for example) to a friend or colleague? Second, What is the most important reason for the score you gave?

Customer responses revealed initial Net Promoter scores for Intuit's business lines ranging from 27 to 52 percent. That wasn't bad, given that the average U.S. company has an NPS of 10 to 20 percent, but Intuit has never been interested in being average. In later years, the company's leadership team came to understand that the most relevant NPS comparisons were with competitive alternatives in each market. At the time, though, the team was looking at absolute numbers—and the scores simply weren't consistent with the company's self-image as a firm that values doing right by its customers. There was, they believed, plenty of room for improvement.

The initial research revealed something else as well: the telephone-survey process used by the company's market-research vendor was woefully inadequate. First, there was no way to close the loop with customers who identified themselves as detractors—no way to apologize or probe for the root cause of the problem, no way to develop a solution for whatever was troubling them. Second, the open-ended responses the vendor reported were intriguing, but managers had a tendency to read into them whatever they already believed. Third, the responses were often confusing and contradictory. For example, promoters frequently praised a product's simplicity, while detractors of that same product griped about its complexity. The teams obviously needed a way of drilling deeper if they were to understand the root causes of promotion and detraction.

In addition to these customer-relationship scores, some of the business units began to add the "would recommend" question to the brief transaction surveys they were already using to manage the quality of their various interactions with customers. These responses provided a steady flow of NPS insights that illuminated hot spots and trouble spots relating to customers' experience with the company. For example, Intuit had decided to charge all QuickBooks customers for tech-support phone calls—even new customers who were having trouble getting the program up and running. Net Promoter scores for customers who called tech support were drastically below the QuickBooks average, and it was immediately apparent that the policy was at fault. The business team tested several alternatives to see what effect they would have on scores; eventually the team found that the most economical solution was to offer free tech support for the first thirty days of ownership. Net Promoter scores from customers who called tech support increased by more than 30 points as a result.

The Consumer Tax Group, home of the industry-leading TurboTax product line, faced a particularly tough challenge. TurboTax's market share in the increasingly important Web-based segment had plummeted by more than 30 points from 2001 to 2003. Managers in the division knew that they had to get a better handle on customer issues. One successful initiative was the creation of a six-thousand-member "Inner Circle" of customers whose feedback would directly influence management decisions. Customers who registered to join this e-mail community were asked some basic demographics and were also asked the "would recommend" question so that the company could determine whether they were promoters, passives, or detractors. Then they were asked to suggest their highest-priority improvements for TurboTax and to vote on suggestions made by other Inner Circle members. Software sifted the suggestions and tracked the rankings, so that over time the most valuable ideas rose to the top of the list.

The results were eye-opening. For detractors, the top priority was improved quality of technical support. To address that issue, the management team reversed a decision made two years earlier and returned all phone tech-support functions from India to the United States and Canada. The team also boosted tech-support staffing levels. The second-biggest priority for detractors was to improve the installation process. That became a top priority for TurboTax's software engineers, who in the 2004 edition of the program achieved a reduction of nearly 50 percent in installation-related tech-support contacts.

Promoters had a different set of priorities. Topping the list was the rebate process: some complained that it took longer to fill out all the rebate forms than to install TurboTax and prepare their taxes! After getting this feedback, the division general manager assigned one person to own the rebate process and held that individual accountable for results. Soon the proof of purchase was simplified, the forms were redesigned, the whole process was streamlined—and turnaround time was reduced by several weeks. Over time, it became clear that even these improvements were not sufficient, and the division finally realized that the right solution for the customer would be to eliminate rebates entirely. It made this bold move as part of a complete repricing strategy.

The Consumer Tax Group continued to study Net Promoter scores, examining various customer segments. New customers, the group found, had the lowest scores of any cluster. Executives called a sample of these customers to find out why, and what they discovered was startling and unsettling. All the features that had been added year after year to appeal to diverse customer groups with complex tax needs had yielded a product that no longer simplified the lives of standard filers. In fact, more than 30 percent of new customers never used the product a second time. In response, the management team issued new priorities for the design engineers: make the program simpler. Soon the interview screens were revised according to new design principles. Confusing tax jargon was eliminated—a new editor hired from *People* magazine got the job of making the language clear and easy to understand. In tax year 2004, for the first time, the NPS of first-time users was even higher than that of longtime users.

Intuit's Results: Happy Customers and Shareholders

Over the two-year period from the spring of 2003 to the spring of 2005, Net Promoter scores for TurboTax jumped. The desktop version, for instance, rose from 46 to 61 percent. New users' scores climbed from 48 to 58 percent. Most important, retail market share, which had been flat for years, surged from 70 to 79 percent—no easy feat in a maturing market. Scores improved at most of Intuit's major lines of business. Thanks to this success, Net Promoter scores became part of the company's everyday operations. "Net Promoter gave us a tool to really focus organizational energy around building a better customer experience," said Steve Bennett, who was CEO at the time. "It provided actionable insights. Every business line [now] addresses this as part of their strategic plan; it's a component of every operating budget; it's part of every executive's bonus. We talk about progress on Net Promoter at every monthly operating review."

At the firm's 2004 Investor Day, when executives update securities analysts and major investors on the company's progress, challenges, and outlook for the future, Cook and Bennett unveiled their renewed commitment to building customer loyalty. They described how Net Promoter scores had enabled the team to convert the historically soft goal of building better customer relationships into a hard, quantifiable process. Just as Six Sigma had helped Intuit improve its business processes to lower costs and enhance quality, Net Promoter scores were helping it set priorities and measure progress toward the fundamental goal of stronger customer loyalty.

Yes, there was still a long way to go. But Cook and Bennett pointed out that the new initiative was simply a return to the original roots of Intuit's success. As the company grew larger, the need increased for a common metric that could help everyone balance today's profits against the improved customer relationships that feed future growth. "We have every customer metric under the sun," said Cook, "and yet we couldn't make those numbers focus the organization on our core value of doing right by the customer. The more metrics you track, the less relevant each one becomes. Each manager will choose to focus on the number that makes his decision look good. The concept of one single metric has produced a huge benefit for us—customers, employees, and investors alike."

By showcasing Net Promoter scores as the central metric for revitalizing growth in the core businesses, Cook and Bennett were signaling to their own organization that this was not some here-today, gone-tomorrow corporate initiative. On the contrary: it was a business-critical priority so important to Intuit's future that it deserved to be understood by shareholders. Intuit's leaders were also signaling to shareholders that at the next Investor Day, these investors would be entitled to learn more about the company's progress on Net Promoter scores. Maybe the event even foreshadowed the day when all investors will insist on seeing reliable performance measures for customer-relationship quality—because only then can investors understand the economic prospects for sustainable, profitable growth.

Meanwhile, Intuit keeps on finding ways to delight customers and convert more of them into promoters. Most recently, the company introduced an innovative personal tax product that makes it easy to prepare and file some returns via smart phones. Customers with fairly simple tax returns take a photo of their W-2 with their smartphone device, and the information automatically imports and populates the appropriate parts of the returns. After answering a few simple questions, customers can view, print, and file their tax return without ever leaving the smartphone, all for a remarkably low price. This new product, SnapTax, was released nationwide in tax year 2010 and generated an NPS of 72, the highest score for a new product in the company's history.

3

How NPS Drives Profitable Growth

erard Kleisterlee, CEO of Royal Philips Electronics, faced a daunting challenge. The company had become one of the largest electronics companies in the world on the basis of its strong engineering and product-oriented culture. Kleisterlee had a deep appreciation of that strength—he himself had been trained as an engineer and had worked at Philips for his entire career, as had his father before him. But now he felt the company's culture had to change. The marketplace was far more competitive than before. Customers expected more than they had in the past. Unless Philips could become more customer focused, Kleisterlee believed, its growth would stagnate.

So Kleisterlee charged his chief marketing officer at the time, Geert van Kuyck, with investigating and evaluating approaches to culture change, and with finding the best approach for Philips. The ideal approach would have to fit with the company's strategic philosophy of "sense and simplicity." It would need to provide a level of rigor and discipline that could earn the respect of Philips's engineers. It would also have to be scalable to a global level. With 2010 revenues of more than €25 ($33) billion and about 125,000 employees in more than sixty countries, Philips was a vast, sprawling enterprise. Its businesses were spread across three sectors: health care (including imaging systems such as CT scanners, MRI

machines, and X-ray machines plus patient monitoring, infor-
matics, and home health-care monitoring), consumer lifestyle
(shavers, coffeemakers, mother and child-care products, kitchen
and domestic appliances, TVs, DVD and Blu-ray players, and electric toothbrushes), and lighting (professional, household, and
automotive). Kleisterlee knew that changing a culture in so large
and complex a company represented a substantial challenge, so he
made it clear to his board that this must become a mission-critical
priority for the entire leadership team.

Van Kuyck understood what it was like to work in customer-
centric organizations, having been part of both Procter & Gamble
and Starbucks prior to joining Philips, and he realized what a massive change would be involved. So he examined the full range of
options that could help Philips achieve this shift to customer
focus. After evaluating all of the approaches taken by major firms
throughout the world, Van Kuyck settled on NPS with the following explanation:

> We liked NPS because it represented a single standard on
> which all the businesses could agree. Every sector had devel-
> oped its own unique approach to customer satisfaction met-
> rics and they all wanted to continue with their existing system,
> but few of them were getting results, and none of the existing
> systems linked to financial performance. That's why we had to
> look outside for the right solution. That's one of the biggest
> advantages of NPS—it ties directly to revenue growth, and it
> drives action.

"It ties directly to revenue growth . . ." When they investigated
NPS, van Kuyck and the executive team found a strong relationship between Philips's score, compared to that of its strongest
competitor, and its rate of growth relative to competitors in the
market. The analysis is summarized in exhibits 3-1 and 3-2. In

EXHIBIT 3-1

Best basis for comparison is against direct competitors using a top-down approach

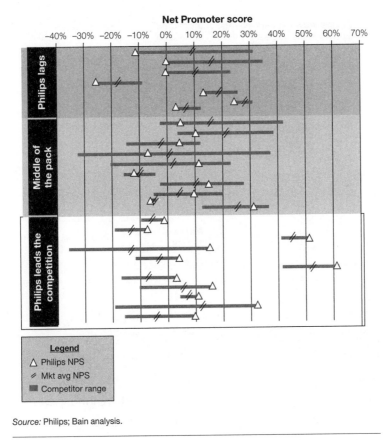

Source: Philips; Bain analysis.

exhibit 3-1, the range of competitive NPS for a given business is represented by the bar; the average is shown by a hash mark; and the NPS of the Philips business is marked by the triangle. Like other companies, Philips has learned that leading the competition on NPS matters more than achieving a specific score level. For each carefully defined business—for example, shavers in China—the median growth rate of businesses in outright leadership positions

EXHIBIT 3-2

Philips divisions that lead their competitors grow faster and gain share

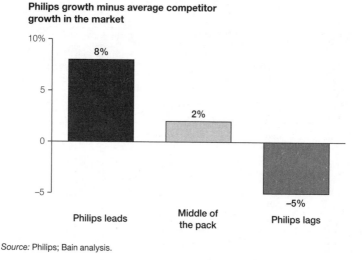

Philips growth minus average competitor growth in the market

Source: Philips; Bain analysis.

was eight percentage points greater than the growth rate of competitors in that market. Where Philips trailed all its direct competitors, growth was slower than the competition by five percentage points (exhibit 3-2). When local Philips teams turned up the microscope to a higher magnification and gathered more detailed data on NPS and local growth and market-share changes, they found even stronger relationships. For example, in Philips's U.S. health-care business, the team found that relative NPS explained 90 percent of the changes in market share between Philips and its key competitors.

A number of corporations around the world have performed similar analyses, and the results are much the same. The giant Allianz insurance group, for instance, examined its relative NPS and growth in the same fashion as Philips and found similar results. Both firms have set strategic targets based on this framework and have shared them with investors and stock market analysts. Philips's 2009 annual report updated the relative-NPS analysis and announced that 60 percent of the company's revenue now came from businesses in NPS leadership or coleadership positions. The long-term goal that Kleisterlee and his team have built into executive bonuses for all Philips managers is now based on outright leadership alone (coleadership is no longer enough). The goal is 50 percent in NPS leadership positions by 2015.

". . . And it drives action." While the score was helpful for setting goals and measuring progress, van Kuyck and the leaders of Philips's business units particularly liked how NPS helped drive action. The feedback was specific, tangible, and immediate. Team members up and down the organization could relate to what the score meant and what response would be appropriate. For example, leaders in the business-to-business (B2B) health-care sector quickly identified opportunities to improve service on MRI, CT scan, ultrasound, and other products based on specific feedback received directly from customers in imaging labs and hospital administration departments. They could also incorporate this feedback in setting priorities for product and service redesigns and upgrades. In subsequent chapters, we'll share more examples from Philips and other firms illustrating how NPS not only links to growth but also inspires the actions that drive growth.

The Economic Power of High-Quality Relationships

To understand the connection between customer relationships and profitable growth, begin with a simple fact: in business, every decision ultimately involves economic trade-offs. Every company would want better relationships with customers if these relationships were free. Every CEO would rather meet earnings goals with good profits than with bad if there were no cost involved. Indeed, the abuse of customers would end tomorrow if ending it had no effect on companies' financial performance. But of course, building high-quality relationships does cost something—often a considerable amount. It requires investment. It requires reducing a company's reliance on bad profits. There is no way to deceive or exploit customers and build better relationships with them at the same time, at least not in the long run. Often, building high-quality relationships may require investing more than competitors in product value, services, staffing, training, or technology. Many great companies—fast-growing, profitable enterprises such as Apple Retail, Costco, Vanguard, TD Bank, and Chick-fil-A—have maintained such high investments in relationships and yet have achieved excellent financial outcomes. To some investment analysts, the success of a Costco or a TD Bank is almost mysterious. Some expenses seem high, while some revenue lines seem low according to their accounting-based analyses. Yet the companies continue to earn healthy profits and grow faster than their competitors.

The real question, therefore, is not just how much it may cost to build great relationships—the costs are usually easy to see on the P&L or on management accounting reports—but the magnitude of benefit that results, and of course how that benefit stacks up against the costs. To answer the question, companies need to understand the economic value of better customer relationships. They must be able to answer questions such as these: What would it be worth to turn a detractor into a passive or a promoter? What would it be worth to raise our relative NPS by 10 points? Where and when would this improvement show up in our financials? At the moment, few managers can answer these questions. This chapter will begin to clarify the economics in terms that numbers-oriented executives will understand. The analysis may seem complex at first, but it is worth pursuing, because this is where the Net Promoter rubber meets the economic road.

Let's start by examining individual customer economics. The value of a promoter or a detractor can be quantified. Indeed, given the vital role that promoters play in building a business, the value of improvements in NPS must be quantified and put into financial terms. You may not have all the data you need at your fingertips, but most companies can produce it. Remember, of course, that this quantification is still an emerging science—even after years of experience, most practitioners are still developing a more complete picture of the economic benefits and better ways to calculate them. So don't let the perfect be the enemy of the good. If exact figures aren't available, use reasonable estimates—and keep innovating.

The first step is to calculate the lifetime value of your average customer. This process is described in chapter 2 of Fred's first book on loyalty economics, *The Loyalty Effect*.[1] (For your convenience, we are also providing a set of resources for calculating lifetime value on our Web site www.netpromotersystem.com). The fundamental approach is to tally up all the cash flows that occur over the life of a typical customer relationship and put them into today's dollars. You don't need a graduate degree in finance to understand that a dollar today does not have the same value as a dollar tomorrow, so you will need to convert future cash flows into today's dollars using a reasonable discount rate. Then, using the lifetime value of an average customer as a baseline, tally up the differences in lifetime value for promoters, passives, and detractors. They often exhibit dramatically different behaviors and produce significantly different economic results. The following list describes several factors that distinguish the categories and offers some tips for estimating their economic effects on your business.

- *Retention rate.* Detractors generally defect at higher rates than promoters, which means that they have shorter and less profitable relationships with a company. By tagging customers as promoters or detractors based on their response to the "would recommend" question, you can determine actual retention patterns over time and quantify their impact. You can estimate the average tenure of your current population of detractors and promoters even before gathering the time-series data. Just ask them on the same survey with the "would recommend" question how long they've been customers, and then use this average tenure to infer likely retention patterns. (Note that this can be a little bit tricky—chapter 2 of *The Loyalty Effect* and the www.netpromotersystem.com Web site explain how to get it right.)

- *Pricing.* Promoters are usually less price sensitive than other customers. Typically, they did not initially choose to do business with you primarily on the basis of price, and they appreciate the overall quality and value they receive from your company. They want your business to prosper. The opposite is true for detractors: they're often more price sensitive to begin with, and they have no interest in helping keep your business healthy. You'll need to examine the market basket of goods or services purchased by promoters and detractors over a six- to twelve-month period and then calculate the margin on each basket, keeping track of discounts and price concessions.

- *Annual spend.* Promoters increase their purchases more rapidly than detractors. The reason is that they tend to consolidate more of their category purchases with their favorite supplier. Your share of wallet increases as promoters upgrade to higher-priced products or services and respond with enthusiasm to new product or service offerings. Promoters' interest in new offerings and brand extensions far exceeds that of detractors or passives.

- *Cost efficiencies.* Detractors complain more frequently, thereby consuming customer-service resources. Some companies also find that credit losses are higher for detractors. (Perhaps that is how some detractors exact revenge.) Similarly, in some businesses, most of the legal expenses should be attributed to detractors, since lawsuits by promoters are rare. Sales, marketing, advertising, and other customer-acquisition costs are also lower for promoters, due to the longer duration of their relationships and their higher propensity to respond to offers or seek out additional products and services. Average order size is often larger for promoters; their purchase patterns can be more predictable (and can sometimes be adjusted to help smooth your production process), resulting in lower administrative and inventory costs. Finally, perhaps the biggest productivity boosters that should be allocated to promoters— albeit the ones most difficult to quantify—are the positive energy and morale boost in the frontline employees who receive their positive feedback. That produces another round of productivity improvement and cost savings from lower employee turnover.

- *Word of mouth.* This component of NPS merits a somewhat more detailed consideration because it is so important and because it seems to be the one that stumps most analysts. Begin by quantifying (by survey if necessary) the proportion of new customers who selected your firm because of reputation or referral. For those customers who cite more than one reason for selecting your company, estimate the importance of the referral or reference in their decision. The lifetime value of these new customers, including any savings in sales or marketing expense, should be allocated to promoters. (Between 80 and 90 percent of positive referrals come from promoters.) Keep in mind that referred customers usually have superior economics themselves; they also have a higher propensity to become promoters, which accelerates the positive spiral of referrals.

Detractors, meanwhile, are responsible for 80 to 90 percent of the negative word of mouth, and the cost of this drag on growth should be allocated to them. Perhaps the easiest way to estimate the cost is to determine how many positive comments are neutralized by one negative comment and how many potential referrals have therefore been lost. This number can be accurately determined only through customer interviews, but for an initial estimate (based on the experience of Bain clients and reports by other researchers) it's safe to assume that each negative comment neutralizes from three to ten positives. For example, consider the process you might go through in searching for a dentist when you move to a new town. If you hear one negative comment about a particular dentist from a trusted friend or colleague, how many positive comments will you need to hear before you select that dentist?

Bain teams around the world regularly apply this framework to quantify lifetime customer economics utilizing clients' internal customer data. Of course, those results must remain confidential, but we can demonstrate how to apply the model from the outside in, utilizing public information and some market research—as you might want to do in evaluating an acquisition candidate or competitor. Let's begin with an example where a Bain team used the approach to estimate the customer-level NPS economics for retail banks in North America in 2008. First the team conducted a survey of 4,300 banking customers in North America. The survey responses allowed us to sort customers for each bank into promoters, passives, and detractors. We also included questions about which banking products and services they had purchased, their account balances, how long they had been customers, how they had become customers of their bank, whether they intended to remain with their current bank, and to what extent they made personal referrals to the bank.

The team found significant differences in these profit-driving behaviors among promoters, passives, and detractors. These differences were well in line with what we had found in our work with retail bank clients over the years. Promoters give their primary bank almost 45 percent more of their household deposit balances than detractors do. They buy, on average, 25 percent more products from the bank than detractors, and their mix of products skews toward more profitable checking and savings accounts. Attrition rates among promoters average only one-third those for detractors. Promoters make nearly seven times as many positive referrals as detractors.

To estimate the financial impact of these behaviors, we used industry-average net interest margins on deposits and loans and industry-average overhead and other costs to create an average retail bank P&L. We could then convert this to an average customer-level P&L by simple division. We plugged promoter, passive, and detractor behavior into a simple model to estimate the financial impact of their different behaviors, converting them to lifetime value by discounting the future cash flows. Based on this analysis, a promoter is worth roughly $9,500 more to a bank than a detractor (exhibit 3-3). In fact, detractors have a *negative* lifetime value: they actually destroy value for shareholders and employees.

This analysis still leaves some elements of value unaccounted for. For example, our work shows that the new customers referred by promoters are significantly more likely to become promoters themselves, and therefore more valuable than the average new customer. Had we

EXHIBIT 3-3

Among affluent customers, promoters are worth $9.5K more than detractors

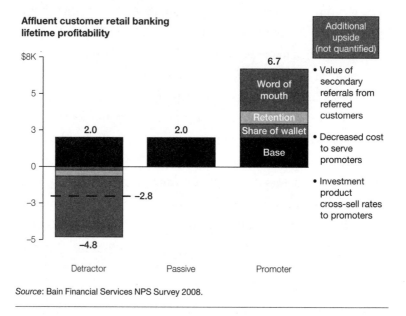

Source: Bain Financial Services NPS Survey 2008.

been less conservative, we would have attributed this incremental customer value to the promoters. Similarly, Bain clients have found that
detractors cost significantly more to serve than promoters. They put
more demands on call centers, raise more problems that need to be
resolved, and are less likely to use self-service tools like online banking. Allocating these additional cost differences would have further
improved the precision of the estimated value differences.

Word-of-Mouth Economics at Dell

In the banking example, the Bain team had to estimate the value of
customer referrals, both positive and negative. As you can see from
exhibit 3-3, much of the difference in value between promoters

and detractors can be attributed to this word-of-mouth impact. We have seen similar patterns in many businesses in our work with clients. Yet management teams are often reluctant even to attempt to calculate the value of referrals because there is little in existing financial or management literature on the topic. It is important, however. A good reputation can generate significant new business, while a bad reputation can sink your efforts to grow.

Another Bain team used a similar approach to quantify the value of promoters and detractors in the personal computer business. The team focused on Dell, which at the time was experiencing serious customer-relationship problems. We calculated the value of detractors and promoters for Dell's consumer business utilizing an economic model that took into account the variables we have mentioned. Securities analysts at the time estimated that the average consumer was worth $210 to Dell. Disaggregating this average, the team's analysis revealed that a detractor cost the company $57, while a promoter generated $328. Let's review the process the team followed, focusing especially on the economics of word of mouth.

Working with Satmetrix, which screened public lists for Dell customers, the team first developed a brief e-mail survey. Researchers then asked those customers a series of questions, including why they had selected Dell over its competitors. The results showed that a little more than 25 percent of Dell's new customers came to the company through referral from friends or colleagues. The survey also asked the "would recommend" question to determine the customer's status as promoter, passive, or detractor, along with how many positive or negative comments they had made to friends or colleagues. The responses revealed that 60 percent of Dell's customers at that time were promoters, 25 percent were passives, and 15 percent were detractors. Based on the number of positive and negative comments reported by these promoters, passives, and detractors, the team then estimated that the 8 million consumers who were Dell customers at the beginning of the research period made about 40 million positive and 5 million negative comments.

Now, here's a step-by-step calculation of the value of this positive word of mouth:

• In our survey, 25 percent of new customers said the primary reason they chose Dell was referral. So 1 million of the 4 million new customers Dell acquired that year came from positive word of mouth.

• Since each new customer was worth an average of $210 each, those 1 million new customers were worth $210 million to the company.

• If 40 million positive comments generated $210 million in value, each positive comment was worth $5.25.

• Given that the average promoter reported making positive comments to about eight people a year, the promoter's positive word of mouth is worth $42 ($8 \times \$5.25$).

The survey also asked customers about their average annual spending, their tenure, and the number of times they called Dell's customer support, all of which enabled the team to estimate the other economic advantages of promoters. Overall, the researchers found that promoters were worth $118 more than an average customer, or $328. If this analysis were done with Dell's internal data, the number would probably be higher, since it would be possible to quantify the superior value of referred customers over time. It would also be possible to track more accurately the repeat-purchase behaviors of promoters.

When estimating the cost of detractors, the researchers first found that detractors accounted for most of Dell's negative word of mouth. To estimate the cost of these negative comments, the survey asked customers how many positive comments from friends or colleagues were required to neutralize each negative comment. On average, customers reported that it required at least five positive comments to neutralize one negative. Since survey data indicated that each detractor made negative comments to about four people a year, each detractor was neutralizing twenty positive comments that would have been worth $5.25 each. So on this count alone, each detractor was costing the company $105 a year.

The survey also revealed that detractors called customer-service reps almost three times more frequently than average customers, spent less per year, and were less likely to repurchase from Dell. Over the life of their relationship with Dell, detractors generated a total of $267 less than average customers, meaning that each detractor actually was destroying $57 in value for Dell and its shareholders.

As in the retail bank analysis, this calculation surely underestimates the full cost of detractors. Our analysis ignored the effect of negative word of mouth on existing customers; it ignored the negative spillover that unhappy consumers might be having on Dell's corporate business; and it ignored any negative impact of dealing with unhappy customers on the motivation and commitment of Dell employees. We also ignored several potentially important economic effects that would require inside information to estimate, such as bad debts, legal expense, and employee motivation. Nevertheless, the analysis provides a reasonable estimate for evaluating investments targeted to building better relationships.

The Bain team's approach reveals the powerful economics of customer promoters. At that time, as noted, Dell had about 8 million individual customers. The 15 percent who were detractors cost the company about $68 million (1.2 million detractors at $57 loss per detractor). Converting just half of those detractors into average customers—probably not an unrealistic target, given that other companies in Dell's industry with high Net Promoter scores typically generate only 3 to 8 percent detractors—would have added more than $160 million annually to the bottom line (600,000 detractors at $267 improvement per conversion). This simple math could help Dell managers place the right level of priority on reducing detractors and increasing promoters. Dell or any other company can evaluate major investments aimed at improving the customer experience, because these proposals can now be subjected to the same rigorous economic analysis already applied to other investments.

In short, by moving beyond traditional customer-satisfaction surveys and by rigorously tracking NPS economics, you can finally create a link between customer feedback and cash flow. You can begin to squeeze bad profits out of your income statement and tune up your growth engine for consistently superior performance.

The Link Between NPS and Growth: Relative or Competitive NPS

This micro view of customer economics provides the foundation for cost-benefit analyses to support investment decisions aimed at building stronger customer relationships. Leaders need a macro view as well, however. They must be able to determine how valuable, overall, it would be to improve NPS so they can set goals for improvement and hold executives accountable for achieving that improvement.

While it is tempting to set absolute goals for year-to-year improvement or to compare NPS across industries or geographies, advanced NPS practitioners such as Philips and Allianz have found it is better to focus on improving faster than their competitors in each well-defined business (that is, the competitors in a geographic region from which local customers can realistically buy). The reason is that averaging NPS across different lines of business or across disparate geographic units can be misleading. Some business lines and some regions have inherently lower NPS than others; for example, almost all the auto insurers in Australia have negative NPS. But, just as in a basketball game, it doesn't matter how high your own score is; it matters whether you score more points than your competitor. That's why experienced practitioners have learned to rely on *relative* NPS or "competitive benchmark NPS" as the basis for setting corporate priorities and goals. (Note that in exhibit 3-1 for Philips, the variations in relative growth were not based on average NPS; rather, they were based on NPS for each business in each distinct geographic area.)

To manage their business portfolios, these companies allocate resources toward growth opportunities in business units that enjoy NPS leadership, and then to unit managers who develop compelling business cases that should enable them to drive NPS past the current leaders. This is wise from a strategic point of view, because only the most efficient players will survive as businesses mature. Margins inevitably decline, and the companies that rely on expensive and inefficient customer-acquisition engines—those with low NPS—will no longer be able to compete with companies that are generating growth through customer loyalty (those with the highest NPS in the industry).

Given this vital role in competitive strategy, it's essential to determine the NPS for your businesses relative to the NPS of key competitors. You can start by developing a representative sample of customers not only of your company but also of your competitors.

The most rigorous approach requires what market researchers often call a *double-blind research design*, where the customers remain anonymous and the researchers don't reveal who is sponsoring the survey. This minimizes bias both in the sample itself and in the way customers respond to the survey. It creates a level playing field for comparison. After you have calculated each competitor's Net Promoter score, you can determine your company's relative NPS by subtracting your best competitor's score from your own.

The Bain team that examined North American retail bank customer-level economics also examined the relationship between NPS and organic growth by these same banks. It found that differences in relative Net Promoter scores within a region explained most of the differences in relative growth rates of retail deposits. But to understand the relationship between relative NPS and relative organic growth rates, it's essential to define the relevant competitive set carefully. For example, Bank of America competes against TD Bank in the northeastern United States but not in the western part of the country, where TD Bank has no branches. So a customer's basis for evaluating Bank of America depends, in part, on which other banks he or she believes are practical alternatives. Moreover, the strength of the retail operations of Bank of America or Wells Fargo might differ significantly from one region to another, since these banks are composed to a significant extent of acquisitions made in recent years. In fact, the pace of mergers and acquisitions among banks made the analysis even more difficult. Growth rates reported by competitors were affected quite dramatically by branch or bank acquisitions. We controlled this effect by removing the artificial gain resulting from mergers and acquisitions from the bank's overall growth. Finally, because bank

EXHIBIT 3-4

NPS correlates with organic deposit growth in the Midwest region

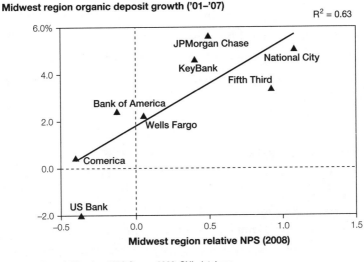

Midwest region organic deposit growth ('01–'07)

$R^2 = 0.63$

Source: Bain Financial Services NPS Survey 2008, SNL database.

revenue is so dependent on interest rates, and because interest rates fluctuate so dramatically, we needed a measure of growth that reflected customer behavior more than it reflected macroeconomic trends. For retail banks, retail deposit balances (which are reported publicly) turned out to be a good indicator of organic growth.

The results of the Bain team's analysis can be seen in exhibit 3-4, which plots relative NPS versus growth among banks in the Midwest region of the United States. (A second chart, illustrating an approach to recombining the data on a national basis, weights the regional results based on relative total deposits to create a weighted-average NPS and organic growth rate at a national level.

This chart appears on our Web site.) The bank example, of course, is only one industry. But as we have worked with Bain clients, members of the NPS Loyalty Forum, and others over the past several years, we have learned that the relationship between NPS and organic growth within a closely defined competitive set is quite strong for most businesses. We have built a robust fact base that includes multiple industries across many countries; examples of the analysis and data are available at www.netpromoter system.com.

Other Considerations

Let's be clear: NPS does not explain relative growth in every industry situation. Factors other than customer loyalty can play an important role. Companies with deep pockets can open loads of new stores or flood the market with promotions or steep price discounts. Mergers and acquisitions can distort the underlying relationships, as in the retail banking example. Companies with monopolies and companies that dominate distribution channels sometimes grow despite weak Net Promoter scores. (Think of your local cable company.) And technological breakthroughs can create growth surges. But even in situations like these, it makes sense for companies to segment customers into promoters, passives, and detractors. Doing so will help managers generate faster and more efficient growth. No company can sustain its growth over a longer time frame and over multiple product-design and technology cycles without building good relationships. Moreover, the negative effect of low NPS on employee morale eventually takes its toll. This explains why even mighty Microsoft has decided to link executive compensation to customer-feedback scores. While loyalty isn't the only factor determining growth, profitable organic growth cannot long be maintained without it.

Another important caveat: a high NPS in and of itself is not the real objective, because a high NPS by itself does not guarantee success. NPS merely measures the quality of a company's relationships with its current customers, and high-quality relationships are a necessary but not a sufficient condition for profitable growth. For example, HomeBanc Mortgage Corporation, which was featured in the first edition of this book, had the highest NPS among mortgage banks at the time. But it still fell victim to the mortgage meltdown of 2007, which swept HomeBanc and many of its competitors into bankruptcy. A company must build an army of promoters, as HomeBanc did, but it will squander the potential they create if it can't then make effective decisions about risk, pricing, innovation, cost management, and everything else necessary for sustainable, profitable growth.

Relative NPS and Market Share

The goal of most corporate strategies is to build competitive advantage and to gain the highest market share possible. Growing the number of promoters and reducing the number of detractors should, over time, help a company grow faster and more profitably. As noted, many of the early leaders in adopting the Net Promoter system have learned how improving NPS relative to the competition can help them outgrow their competitors and gain market share.

The irony is this: as firms gain share, the more dominant they become—and the more likely they will stumble into the trap of bad profits. Even if CEOs have no desire to book bad profits, because they recognize the deleterious effects bad profits have on growth, they and their executive team are always under pressure to grow earnings. That alone makes executives susceptible to the temptation to milk customer relationships.

At the extreme, some companies enjoy monopolies or near monopolies. If you want to fly from one second-tier city to another, you will probably find that one airline dominates the nonstop flight schedules. If you want to sign up for cable service in many cities, you have only one choice. You may find that only one mobile-phone provider offers you good reception at your home, at your office, and during your commute. If that provider insists on a two-year contract in return for a reasonable pricing plan, it has essentially trapped you in a temporary monopoly. All such strategies generate substantial profits, but the customers who pay for them are more vulnerable than ever to abusive, manipulative, and coercive treatment. The cell-phone provider with the best network coverage, for example, is more likely to offer lackadaisical service, complicated billing, onerous overage and roaming fees, and unhelpful customer-service reps.

Does it make sense for such companies, which have earned or bought their way to dominance in particular markets, to invest in building good relationships? Or are they better off simply maximizing near-term profits? Consider the cable TV companies that negotiated exclusive contracts with municipal governments. In cable, there is little historical correlation between relative growth and relative Net Promoter scores because growth is driven more by increases in population and income in a given market than by the cable company's service levels. Indeed, Net Promoter scores in the cable and satellite TV industry are embarrassingly low, averaging negative 3 percent. Customers are rarely enthusiastic when they have limited choice—and anyway, many local cable companies have ratcheted up prices while providing mediocre service.

But no monopoly lasts forever. New technologies emerge. Regulations change. Building good customer relationships prepares a company for the possibility of increased competition. What's more, superior NPS boosts a company's growth potential by enabling it to expand into adjacent service areas. For example, one of the most profitable expansion opportunities for cable companies has been to move into the telecommunications business—and it turns out that NPS works well to explain companies' relative success in this market. Bain teams analyzed a series of local telephone markets in the United States and Canada, examining the rate at which the local cable firm was able to cross-sell telecom services to existing customers. The best single explanation of relative success was the difference between the NPS the cable company received from its core cable customers and the NPS given the local phone company by its core phone customers. Where the difference was positive—with the cable NPS higher than the phone company's NPS—the cable company's telecom penetration was rapid. The bigger the difference, the faster the penetration.

NPS leaders recognize the value of market-share leadership. Intuit enjoys 80 percent retail market share or more in its top three businesses; Southwest Airlines has an 80 percent share of takeoffs and landings at its top twenty-five airports; Enterprise has overwhelming leadership in the home-market sector of car rentals. But what keeps these firms growing is not their worship of market share; it is their ability to keep their people focused on earning good profits. Good customer relationships not only expand the core business, they also open the door for successful extensions into adjacent businesses. For example, Enterprise was able to profitably expand into airport rentals and used-car sales because of its great service record in the home-market rental business. The iPhone's dazzling new technology allowed it to dominate the smart-phone business, with long lines of customers queuing up for each new model. But leaders at Apple stores worked diligently to ensure that frontline employees remained kind and helpful rather than arrogant or complacent. As a result, customers welcomed the iPad with equal enthusiasm, and they increased their purchase of Macs as well. Superior market share is an excellent goal. To achieve it, and to sustain it, you must find a way to track NPS and build better relationships—not only because it is the right thing to do, but because it makes economic sense.

4

The Enterprise Story—Measuring What Matters

urnberry Isle Resort, Florida, 1996. The mood at the Enterprise Rent-A-Car senior management retreat should have been festive. It was Enterprise's most successful year so far. The company was growing fast and had just overtaken Hertz as the number one rental-car agency in the United States. But the opening presentation at the meeting hit a sobering note. Customer-satisfaction scores were flatlining. In a satisfaction study of insurance adjusters (a prime source of customer referrals), some adjusters had ranked Enterprise below one of its competitors.

When that slide hit the screen, CEO Andy Taylor remembers, "there was an audible gasp in the room." All eyes turned toward founder and chairman Jack Taylor, Andy's father, who had devoted his life to building a company that would serve customers better than any other. Jack was upset. After the morning presentations, Jack met privately with Andy, and his message was short. "Andrew," he said, ever the paterfamilias, "we've got a *big* problem."[1]

Andy Taylor, who hadn't been called Andrew by his father (or anyone else) since childhood, remembers this as a defining moment. He had been named president and chief operating officer of the closely held company in 1980, CEO in 1991. Now, he knew, it was up to him to change things. He vowed to ensure that Enterprise set new standards of excellence in service and customer relationships. The only question was how to go about it.

The company had been experimenting with customer-satisfaction surveys ever since 1989, when it first began marketing car rentals to consumers. But back then, many managers doubted that the surveys really meant much. Sure, the numbers indicated a few problems. But wasn't the company growing? Wasn't it making money? Any difficulties, some of the managers said, weren't systemic; they could be addressed locally. That was more in keeping with Enterprise's decentralized tradition.

But by the early 1990s, Andy Taylor was worried, partly because he himself had been hearing more complaints than usual from customers. So he assigned a team of senior managers to work on the surveys. That team designed a new instrument—and like a lot of such instruments, it suffered from "question creep." The initial version, one page long, included nine questions and asked for seventeen separate responses, including an open-ended "How could we have served you better?" At the top, however, was the question that would turn out to be central to the whole endeavor: "Overall, how satisfied were you with your recent car rental from Enterprise?" The five boxes a customer could check ran from "completely satisfied" to "completely dissatisfied." Taylor and his team decided that the company would calculate the percentages in each category for this question. They would call the scores the Enterprise Service Quality index, or ESQi.

Thus did Enterprise launch the measurement process, as Taylor later told *Fortune Small Business*, that "enabled us to go from being a nearly $2 billion business in 1994 to a $7 billion-plus business" in 2004.[2] By 2009, Enterprise Holdings had grown to over $12 billion, including the purchase of Alamo and National. That summer, Andy

Taylor explained to a conference of insurance executives, "The first thing we did when the deal was final was to implement our ESQi process at National and Alamo—so we had NSQi and ASQi. The reason was that it communicated how vital this framework was to the Enterprise family—and it provided a baseline to ensure that subsequent changes through the merger process would not weaken customer relationships."

But in 1994, there was still a long way to go. Making ESQi into a useful, credible tool turned out to be a long, involved, and contentious process.

Learning to Measure

Enterprise's first questionnaires went out in July 1994, and the company reported its first three months' worth of results to senior managers in October. Overall, the ratings were only fair. Eight-six percent of respondents reported themselves at least moderately satisfied. But only 60 percent checked the "top box," as the company called it, to indicate they were completely satisfied. That score, Taylor felt, was far lower than it should be.

Worse, there were huge disparities between the various regions, with some registering top-box scores in the 80 percents and others in the low 50s. One of the company's biggest and most profitable regions came in at a dismal 54 percent. "We were pretty much at or near the bottom of the whole company," acknowledged the region's senior vice president for rental. "To competitive people like us, that was a real difficult pill to swallow, especially in front of our peers."

Maybe not surprisingly, the first reaction among some managers was to shoot the messenger. Low scorers, Taylor remembers, "ripped the measurement, the survey questionnaire, and the sampling technique behind it." The process didn't allow for differences in branch size, the managers argued. It didn't take into account that different regions of the country might have different expectations about customer service. Besides, they added, what did it all prove? ESQi might be a valid measurement of satisfaction, but did it have anything to do with growing the company? Was there really a connection between customer satisfaction and financial results?

So Taylor and his team continued to examine and refine their methods. They found that branch size and geographical region didn't matter much—top performers and poorer ones could be found in any category. The team challenged the notion that senior managers already knew where the problems lay. When asked to rank their various operations above or below the company's service average without looking at the latest ESQi scores, for example, the managers couldn't peg more than half, the same as guessing.

The team also made three changes to the scoring process that would prove definitively important:

- *Reliable and granular.* Since the customer experience was primarily controlled by the local branch, team members reasoned, the company needed to score not just its regions but each of its numerous branches. (Enterprise Rent-A-Car at the time had more than eighteen hundred branches; today Enterprise Holdings has more than seventy-six hundred branches, including National and Alamo.) Only with this degree of granularity could regional managers reliably hold the branches accountable for building good customer relationships. Each branch, moreover, would need feedback from at least twenty-five customers a month, so the sample size had to increase. A three-month moving average of this feedback would produce a reliable ranking.

- *Timely.* Listening to the company's field managers, the team also decided that the information had to be more timely.

Customer-satisfaction scores that were gathered once a quarter and disseminated long after the quarter's end didn't really tell you much. Who could remember what had happened during that quarter to move the scores one way or the other? In fact, Taylor and his team wanted data in as close to real time as possible, so that frontline staffers could remember events that had influenced the feedback. Timely feedback would also allow branches to test new ideas and then to evaluate them when the survey scores arrived. To speed things up, the researchers switched from mail to telephone surveys and began reporting ESQi monthly, just like the monthly reporting of profits and other performance measures.

• *Linked to behaviors.* Finally, since executives wanted proof that investments to increase ESQi scores would actually pay off, the team analyzed how well various questions on the surveys linked to customer behaviors such as repurchases and referrals—behaviors that drove growth. Researchers called back hundreds of customers who had taken the survey months earlier, asking how many positive and negative referrals those customers had made. They asked the customers how many cars they had rented since taking the survey and what Enterprise's share of those rentals had been. These questions struck pay dirt: the one question at the top of the page, "Were you completely satisfied?" accounted for a startling 86 percent of the variation in customer referrals and repurchases. Those who gave the company a perfect 5 on a 5-point scale—the equivalent of promoters—were three times more likely to return to Enterprise than a customer giving a lower score. And nearly 90 percent of positive referrals were made by top-box customers. The bottom line: high top-box scores translated directly into growth and profit.

All these findings quieted the skeptical executives. The measurements meant something. But nothing actually seemed to be *improving* the company's scores, as the 1996 meeting showed. So Andy Taylor's next challenge was to get his executives and his branches to do something about the measurements. It was, he wrote, a "time for leadership, time to put some teeth into our efforts."

Taking ESQi Seriously

Taylor's first step was to link ESQi scores to corporate recognition. At Enterprise, the granddaddy of recognition programs is the prestigious President's Award, a coveted prize given to people who make truly exceptional contributions to the company. After 1996, you weren't eligible unless your branch or region was at or above the corporate average for ESQi. Southern California's Group 32, which had won a disproportionate number of these awards in the past, came up empty-handed for the following two years. The point hit home. "People said, 'You know what? This company is serious about ESQi,'" remembered Tim Walsh, a former officer of Group 32.

Step two delivered an even stronger message. The company redesigned its monthly operating reports to highlight ESQi, listing every branch's score right alongside the net profit numbers. The reports ranked every branch, region, and group manager in the company, so everyone immediately knew how he or she stacked up against everyone else. Moreover, the company announced that no one with a below-average ESQi score was eligible for promotion— and backed up its announcement by passing over a well-regarded California executive who Taylor says "would have been a shoo-in under the old system."

Step three: communication and more communication. "ESQi became a key topic of *every* speech I gave internally," says Taylor.

"Customer satisfaction went on the agenda of *every* management and operations review meeting at all levels. When I was present, I would go right to the bottom of the ESQi rankings and pointedly ask the managers responsible to explain what was going on and what they were doing about it. Those were apt to be the first questions in a sustained grilling."

Before long, ESQi was an inextricable part of Enterprise's corporate culture. The promotion requirement of above-average ESQi came to be known as "jacks or better," as in the traditional poker-table requirement of a pair of jacks or better to open the betting. The branches or groups that were below average and thus ineligible for promotions were said to be in "ESQi jail." And gradually, ESQi scores began to improve. In 1994 the average had been around 67. By 1998 it had risen to 72, and by 2002 it hit 77. The gap between top performers and those at the bottom narrowed, shrinking from 28 points in 1994 to only 12 in 2001. Even Southern California brought its number up to above average, and again was winning some President's Awards.

Why ESQi Works

Enterprise's ESQi system is designed to help frontline managers pursue two objectives: get more top-box ratings and fewer scores of neutral or worse. In the language of this book, the goals are to increase the number of customer promoters and reduce the number of detractors. The most effective example we had yet seen of a relationship-measurement process, ESQi has several distinctive features.

Tight focus. Unlike much market research, ESQi is not designed by headquarters staff to address every question or pet project someone in the company might have. Quite the opposite. Over time, the company dropped all those questions on the initial questionnaire in favor of just one: *how satisfied were you with your most recent rental experience?* If the customer is dissatisfied, the surveyor expresses regret and says, we would like to have someone give you a call about this whenever it would be convenient. That's it. If marketing or any other department wants to learn about other issues, Enterprise commissions separate customized research. In effect, the customer survey was transformed from a market-research instrument to a practical process—an operating system.

Operational accountability. The organizational process for managing the research was similarly transformed. Since it was line managers who would be relying on the tool, the company moved ESQi out of the market-research department entirely. Dan Gass, the manager responsible for running the system, reports directly to Greg Stubblefield, one of the corporate executives responsible for Enterprise's rental business. While the phone surveys themselves are handled by an outside vendor, Gass stays closely involved. He regularly visits the vendor's facility to talk with the phone staff. He monitors calls at least fifteen hours a month. This alerts him to any major issues that require executive attention, and it helps him discover ways to improve the overall process.

Timeliness and high participation rates. Enterprise computers regularly upload a random sample of recently closed rental tickets to the survey vendor to ensure that customers are surveyed within a few days of renting a car. Because the survey is so short, the rate of customer cooperation among those who answer the phone exceeds 95 percent. The high response rate eliminates sample bias and enhances the reliability of scores.

The closed loop. One decision that was critical to ESQi's success was not to ask the survey vendor to diagnose the root causes of a customer's score. Much to the vendor's dismay, Taylor and his team insisted that attempting to generate both the score and the diagnosis with the same survey would lead to failure on both counts.

The reasoning was compelling. Anyone who has done root-cause analysis knows that it takes at least four or five follow-up questions to determine the problem that needs attention. And probing for the root cause of an individual customer's concerns often requires knowing something about both the customer and the transaction. For example, it may be essential to know whether the branch was temporarily understaffed, whether the transaction was a first-time rental, or what the customer's historic rental pattern has been. No outside phone interviewer can possibly have all that knowledge and understanding.

So whenever a customer communicates any dissatisfaction on the ESQi survey, the phone rep asks the "would you accept a call from the branch manager" question. More than 90 percent of these customers agree to be called—at which point an e-mail alert, including the customer's phone number and the survey score, is automatically forwarded to the branch involved. Branch managers have been trained to call right away, to apologize, to probe for the root cause of the customer's disappointment, and then to develop an appropriate solution. In some cases, the apology itself is all it takes to fix the problem. In others, a free rental is more appropriate. The primary diagnosis is always performed at the front line so that the branch can learn what needs to be fixed and fix it.

A link to the economics of the business. Thanks to the closed loop, Enterprise has been highly successful in reducing detractors: the proportion of customers who rate their experience neutral or worse has declined from 12 percent to 5 percent since 1994. This drop by itself has improved the firm's economics—there is less negative word of mouth. The increase in the percentage of promoters also improves the economics, both by driving growth and by reducing costs. For instance, Enterprise can spend less on advertising than Hertz and still grow faster due to Enterprise's word-of-mouth advantage. Measuring and managing the number of customer promoters created at each branch allows the company to turn word of mouth from a soft benefit into a quantifiable competitive weapon.

Continuous evolution. Of course, the system is constantly evolving and is much more effective today than it was when it started. The survey vendor's call efficiency has grown from twelve completed calls per hour in 1996 to almost twenty today, which means that the cost per branch to run the system is less than $550 per year. Enterprise has also continued its drive to deliver more timely data. A while ago, the corporate average seemed stuck at 77 percent. As Dan Gass searched for explanations for this stall, he noticed a seasonal effect: most branches' scores dropped off during the summer. Summer was a time when a lot of new hires were coming on board and attention was drifting away from ESQi. To maintain the focus on customer service, Gass pushed Enterprise to report ESQi at the regional level on a weekly basis. In 2004, with this new data available, there was no decline in summer scores. Simply generating the numbers more frequently to keep the organization focused did the trick. By November, the company was averaging nearly 80 percent top-box results.

How ESQi Drives Improvement

ESQi itself, of course, is only a measurement; the real challenge is to keep on improving the scores. Enterprise's improvement efforts fall into several categories:

- *Training.* Gass developed a comprehensive training program around the concept of the service cycle. Enterprise employees interact with customers at a whole series of points during a rental, from the initial call on through pickup, arrival at the branch, signing the contract, and so on. The training program sets standards for each point in the cycle and includes tips on how employees can ensure a pleasant experience for the customer at every step.

- *On-the-spot fixes.* Managers discourage the use of customer-survey language in their branches. Branch employees are strongly discouraged from asking a customer if he or she was completely satisfied; instead, they'll probe for what they can do to make the rental experience better, and then take immediate action. The goal is to make sure that customers come back repeatedly and tell their friends. But management also watches costs, because there is little benefit to any Enterprise manager who runs a branch that gets a high ESQi score but isn't also growing profitably.

- *Experimentation.* Individuals and teams try new approaches, new tactics, and new strategies, then watch to see whether these changes improve outcomes. In effect, Enterprise's more than seventy-six hundred branches and twelve monthly feedback scores allow more than ninety-one thousand experiments to drive learning every year. Experimentation is particularly important when it comes to generating more promoters. Detractors presumably want their problems solved, but what do promoters want? As it turns out, generating promoters requires initiatives such as offering a free bottle of chilled water on the shuttle bus. This idea was pioneered by a driver who experimented with putting a small cooler in his bus; his branch's growing ESQi score alerted others to the success of the innovation. In fact, most of Enterprise's enhanced services, including picking you up at your home, office, or repair shop, bubbled up from individual branch successes.

• *Closing the loop even faster.* If you rent from Enterprise, you'll experience an interesting phenomenon: when you drop off your car at the end of the rental, you will probably be asked two or three questions by the crew member who processes your return. How was our service? What could we have done to make your experience better? If there was a problem, how can we make it up to you? The crew member will make every effort to correct any complaints on the spot. In most branches, this kind of direct feedback is tabulated at the end of each day; it provides the agenda for the next morning's preopening team huddle.

• *Learning from the best.* Enterprise has found that the best ideas rarely come down from headquarters executives; they are developed, field-tested, and revised out in the branches. The trick for the company is to create forums in which the really good ideas can be identified and shared. This is why Enterprise spends so much time on ESQi at area, regional, and national manager meetings—and why the results are widely published. At national gatherings, some session leaders ask branch managers to display their ESQi scores on their name tags. Branch managers at these meetings thus know at a glance who has something to teach them. The ranking system ensures that when managers are looking for good ideas, they seek advice from the branches with the best scores rather than from those who are best at spinning impressive stories.

Since Enterprise links customer-feedback scores to promotions, it's surprising that you don't hear employees pleading with customers for top-box ratings. But unlike car dealers, Enterprise branches don't post sample surveys on the wall with the top boxes suggestively filled in. Instead, Enterprise teaches its employees that manipulating scores is not only unethical—as unethical as stealing from the cash register or fudging profits—but also contrary to the real goal of their company, which is to provide a superior customer experience.

Of course, some employees have been tempted to bend the rules and game their results. Enterprise calls this *speeding* and regards it as grounds for dismissal. Shortly after the branch-specific process was implemented, for example, it was rumored that a few branches were changing phone numbers on the records of unhappy customers. A number altered by only one digit meant that a phone surveyor would never connect and the branch would avoid a bad score. At Enterprise, though, it's difficult to hide this kind of malfeasance for long, since employees are frequently transferred across branches and anyone caught doctoring phone numbers can be fired. The company now keeps track of how many phone numbers fail to connect to the customer of record, identifies outlier branches, and scrutinizes their process.

As another safeguard against gaming, area managers occasionally ask to have the customer-exception reports forwarded to them for follow-up, and then talk directly to detractors. The executives also call a few customers randomly to ask about their experience. "ESQi, like any system, is effective only if the input is pure and honest," says Andy Taylor. Indeed, any question about the appropriateness of gaming ESQi would appear to be covered by the company's value statement: "Personal honesty and integrity are the foundation of the company's success." To deter any attempt at loose interpretation, Taylor expects his top managers to continually reinforce the importance of the integrity of ESQi. Stories about attempts to game the system—and the career-ending consequences—become tribal knowledge at regional gatherings of branch managers. The stories are repeated so often that everyone understands the consequences of cheating on ESQi.

Vote for Growth

One of the most significant breakthroughs in building effective teamwork at Enterprise branches is a process known as "The Vote."

Neil Leyland, a manager responsible for several branches in London, noticed a conundrum: his branch employees always seemed to think their ESQi scores should be higher than they were, but their scores never seemed to move much. Leyland decided that the employees weren't working together as effectively as they could be in each branch. Nor were they holding each other accountable for results.

So he came up with a plan. Every Monday morning, before his branches opened, each of the team members was asked to rank-order all the others, from best to worst, based on the quality of their customer service over the past week. The votes were tallied and posted for all to see. Leyland asked employees to keep their comments positive, to explain the rationale for their rankings, and to provide specific examples of good and bad behaviors. Typical comments included: "I rated you last because I noticed that you didn't answer the phone before the third ring several times, and I had to leave my customer to cover for you." Or "You seem to have a hard time looking the customer in the eye when you shake his hand." The group worked hard to ensure that their comments were constructive, and everyone had to offer suggestions to the team-mates whom they ranked below average. On subsequent Mondays, Leyland presented awards to the top-rated employee and to the employee whose rankings were most improved that week.

At first, other managers found this mutual feedback extreme. Some feared that the program would lead to contentious, uncon-structive behavior or would wreck team spirit. But soon Leyland's laggard branches rocketed from the bottom to the top of the ESQi rankings, and their annual growth rate accelerated to more than

50 percent. When Dan Gass saw those numbers, he became a believer—and so did many branch managers throughout the system. Some managers implemented The Vote but chose to gather the rankings confidentially and share only the final tallies. Most found that an open ballot was the most effective at making each team member feel personally accountable for creating change.

Within two years, more than half of Enterprise's worldwide branches had adopted The Vote as a core tool for improving customer service. Senior managers who feared that the process would be too extreme began inviting top-ranked employees out to lunch. That provides both a reward for the employees and a source of new ideas for the managers. For example, one winner routinely noted personal details on the customer's rental contract (like "visiting son in hospital") as a reminder to ask how the visit went when the car was returned.

Meanwhile, back in Leyland's home territory, the United Kingdom, Enterprise continued its upward trajectory. With The Vote driving performance, Enterprise handily outstripped its competitors, achieving NPS leadership of more than 25 points in an independent assessment. Growing at an average of 20 percent per year while the competition was shrinking, Enterprise thus consistently gained market share. Many companies have been unable to repeat their success in one country when they set up shop in another. Enterprise seems to have found the secret, and has built a rigorous process to ensure that its customer-centric strategy works well all around the globe.

A Unique System

Enterprise's homegrown system of assessing customer relationships differs a little from the system we describe in this book. Enterprise doesn't use the terms *promoters* and *detractors*. It relies on a 5-point scale rather than the zero-to-ten scale used by NPS practitioners. ESQi is based only on top-box results—the percentage of promoters—rather than *net* promoters, or promoters minus detractors. We believe that the extra step of calculating a Net Promoter score is worth the trouble, because it ensures that a company will pay attention to both groups and because NPS correlates with growth rates more closely than does the number of promoters alone.

But no one can argue with success. Indeed, the more closely one studies Enterprise's ESQi measurement process, the more impressive it becomes. The company's closed-loop system ensures that measurements tie into action. Improvements keep bubbling up from the branches. The percentage of customers who are promoters continues to expand. And even though Enterprise doesn't include its detractors in the ESQi score, it pays close attention to them and works to cut their number by reducing operational mistakes.

Andy Taylor credits ESQi as the single biggest reason that Enterprise has been able to maintain superior growth in its core business despite its enormous scale. ESQi has enabled his branches to focus their creativity on delivering a better customer experience, not on artificially boosting accounting profits. The resulting customer loyalty has allowed the firm to expand into adjacent markets, such as airport rentals and used-car sales, with the wind at its back. By jettisoning traditional satisfaction-survey methods and replacing them with one reliable number, Enterprise continues to grow, to prosper, and to set the industry standard for generating more promoters and fewer detractors.

5

The Rules of Measurement

Traditional methods of measuring customer satisfaction have so many shortcomings that we devoted an entire chapter to them in the original version of this book. Today, these shortcomings have become widely recognized, and we will only mention some of the most common:

- Most surveys are too long. They create unnecessary complexity and waste customers' time.

- They are designed to generate research reports, not to drive daily frontline learning and behaviors.

- They are often anonymous, which eliminates the possibility of closing the loop with individual customers.

- They are structured in the language of the researcher, not the customer.

- Response rates are typically low, so the results are unreliable.

- Often, the wrong customers respond—especially in business-to-business settings, where the senior executives responsible for purchase decisions rarely take the time to fill out surveys.

- The results are easily gamed and manipulated (think of the last time you dealt with a car dealer who pleaded for a top-box score).

If you want to read the entire critique of customer-satisfaction surveys from the original edition, please visit the Web site www. netpromotersystem.com. But for the moment, let's go on to more pressing matters.

The goal of this chapter is to show how you can measure and manage customer feedback as rigorously as you now measure and manage profits. This means developing a measurement process as effective as Enterprise's or Apple's while avoiding the pitfalls of traditional satisfaction surveys. It isn't easy! The Net Promoter system may be simple in concept, but building a reliable scoring process is hard work. You'll probably need to put at least as much effort and resources into it as you are currently spending (or squandering) on satisfaction surveys. If true customer centricity is your top priority, you may even need to match the resources you now allocate to generating reliable financials.

When it comes to the *how*, of course, a little humility is in order. Accounting standards have evolved over hundreds of years. They are spelled out in tomes that run to thousands of pages (and even so, they are still being improved and are not fully immune to gaming and manipulation). We are only now embarking on equally rigorous measurement of customer relationships. So it won't be surprising if we have to experiment a little before we come up with widely accepted standards.

But that shouldn't keep us from getting started. Already, many companies have learned the basics of rigorously measuring customer attitudes and behaviors. We can spell out a set of fundamental principles that can serve any company as a solid starting point. These rules will enable you to calculate your customers' promoter status in a fashion that is accurate, granular, timely, and credible—in other words, to assess what your customers really feel right now. You can also use the principles to focus attention on the customer throughout your organization and to establish accountability for good customer relationships.

Principle 1: Ask the Ultimate Question and Very Little Else

In most businesses, categorizing a customer as promoter, passive, or detractor requires only one question, usually some variant of "How likely is it that you would recommend us to a friend or colleague?" The second question is usually worded something like this: "What is the primary reason for the score you just gave us?" The answer provides an initial diagnosis of the root cause and helps ensure that, if appropriate, the right manager can reach out to the customer for further diagnosis and response. Another good question that can aid diagnosis for any rating below perfection is this: "What is the most important improvement that would make you more likely to recommend us?" Note that the answers to these follow-up questions merely begin the diagnosis; they don't affect the score calculation itself.

To be sure, you may need to gather additional background data on the individual or the account. Once you establish that your feedback system is operating effectively, you can test whether you can add one or two questions without corrupting the measurement process or raising the cost. But be careful! Keep the list short. Adding a battery of generic diagnostic questions is usually counterproductive: the questions yield little actionable insight, waste customers' time, and cut response rates. Moreover, they generate confusion among frontline employees when what these workers need most is simplicity and clarity. We emphasize this point because managers are always tempted to add questions to any survey. But where NPS is concerned, every additional question increases complexity and carries unwanted costs. At Bain, for example, we use the Net Promoter process with our own clients—typically executives of large multinational firms—and we discovered that cutting survey length to just a few questions doubled response rates to over 60 percent.

If you want to find out more about why customers give you the score they do, the best way is to engage managers and frontline supervisors in dialogues with those customers in person, by phone, or if appropriate by e-mail—and to do so shortly after the score is received. Forums that enable group discussions can be effective as well. "We have too many surveys, and they are too long," Intuit cofounder Scott Cook mused. "What we really need is more managers talking directly with their customers, listening carefully, and then responding to their feedback. Sending out more surveys may provide the illusion of customer focus, but this is usually a cop-out for senior managers unwilling to spend face-to-face time with customers." If your current internal (bottom-up) Net Promoter survey exceeds five questions, you will probably be doing both your customers and your company a favor by cutting it back.

Principle 2: Choose a Scale That Works, and Stick to It

Talk to ten research firms, and you will hear ten different arguments for the best scale to use in any kind of customer-feedback system—yes/no, three choices, four, seven, a neutral midpoint or not, whatever, each one advocated with near-religious fervor. But the goal of NPS is not purity of research; it is a reliable operating system. Although we at Bain started out open-minded about the best scale to use, experience with our clients has revealed important practical and empirical advantages to a zero-to-ten scale, where ten means "extremely likely" and zero means "not at all likely." Granted, other scales can work in certain situations. Enterprise has achieved outstanding success with its 5-point scale. Progressive Insurance also made progress while retaining its traditional one-to-five scale, which it did primarily so that its market researchers could coordinate with historic surveys. However, Progressive's executives now wish they had shifted to the zero-to-ten scale since there was little value in creating backward compatibility with the old (ineffective) system. The zero-to-ten scale has many significant advantages:

- Customers find that the scale makes intuitive sense, probably because of their experience with grades in school. They quickly grasp that a ten or nine corresponds to an A or A–, an eight or seven represents the adequate performance of a B or C, and six or below is a failing grade. Even in countries such as Germany, where school grading is different, the zero-to-ten system seems to work effectively. Employees, too, have spent years in the classroom. They can relate easily to these scores, and they don't need a course in statistics to interpret them.

- Most of the world already uses the metric system for commerce and trade, not because the meter is a magical unit but because the decimal system works best for us ten-digited humans. So most cultures and most people already think in units of ten. Everybody knows what it means when an Olympic diver, for example, scores a "perfect 10."

- Customers who believe there is always room for improvement may refuse to give anybody a perfect score, regardless of how delighted they are. The nine response offers an alternative that avoids pushing them into the passive category. Also, it's an early warning whenever a ten drops to a nine on a subsequent survey.

- No matter how carefully the survey is constructed, some customers will transpose the top and bottom on a one-to-ten scale: they will score a one when they really mean a ten since "number one" typically means the best. This confusion rarely occurs with a zero-to-ten scale, since zero always represents the lowest score. Doctors around the world use the universally intuitive zero-to-ten scale when asking patients to rate their pain. Even under duress, patients understand how to answer; no further explanation is necessary. Ditto for the Apgar scale used to rate the health of newborns—doctors, nurses, and technicians all around the world can easily apply this universal zero-to-ten scale.

• Scales with fewer points gloss over important differences in customer loyalty. Customers scoring a ten exhibit markedly stronger loyalty behaviors, such as referrals and repurchase, than those scoring a nine. To be sure, the drop-off for an eight is even steeper, which is why an eight is categorized as a passive. But it still makes sense to maintain the distinction between nines and tens—and to encourage teams to strive for tens.

• Finally, the zero-to-ten standard is being adopted by many of the world's leading companies, including Philips, Apple, General Electric, American Express, Allianz, Intuit, Home Depot, PricewaterhouseCoopers, KPMG, Southwest Airlines, and JetBlue. Companies that adopt this standard will find it easier to compare themselves to the NPS community's growing database of best practices.

It's worth noting that customers in various countries tend to score somewhat differently. In the Netherlands and Japan, few customers give suppliers a ten, whereas tens are quite common in Latin America. Even so, there's no need to adjust scores. Global companies simply need to recognize that it is not meaningful to rank-order units across regions. The relevant benchmark is always local competitors, whose scores will be identically affected by local idiosyncrasies.

At any rate, while we strongly prefer the zero-to-ten scale, the most important message about scales is to pick the one that works best in your business. The best way to tell if your scale works is to test whether it accurately segments your customers into promoters, passives, and detractors, consistent with their behaviors—and whether it inspires employees to take the right actions. Once a scale meets this test, you can establish one consistent standard for every NPS survey in all of your business lines and geographic regions.

Principle 3: Avoid Confusion Between Internal (Bottom-Up) Scores and External (Top-Down or Benchmark) Scores

The best way to determine how you stack up against competitors is the top-down or external benchmark score, which we described in chapter 3. The top-down score is designed primarily to show relative performance rather than to generate diagnostic insights. Companies generally measure these scores through a double-blind research-style survey process; neither the respondent nor the questioner knows who is sponsoring the survey. Every year, for example, Philips hires a research organization to identify comparable samples of Philips customers and customers of each key competitor, for virtually all of the company's major business lines and for nearly every distinct geographic market. The anonymity of the survey eliminates bias in terms of which customers choose to respond, a bias that would otherwise distort the relative scores. Of course, it also closes off the possibility of learning more about the experience of an individual customer and fixing whatever problems may have arisen through a closed-loop process. So companies sometimes include a handful of diagnostic questions in their top-down surveys to provide general information about these customers and broad-brush information about why they scored as promoters, passives, or detractors.

However that may be, the most important rules to follow in a top-down survey are to ensure, first, that the right customers are answering the survey; second, that they are giving candid responses; and, third, that the sample sizes are sufficient to establish reasonable statistical confidence intervals so that variations among competitors are meaningful.

Though the top-down survey process is vital to determine relative scores, think of it as your end-of-the-term report card. It gauges your progress and helps set overall priorities for improvement, but it isn't really useful for driving daily and weekly improvements. For that, you need a separate process: the internal or bottom-up process that facilitates closed loops with customers, generates operational insights, and drives change.

Bottom-up surveys often take place after particular transactions. Enterprise, for instance, surveys a sample of its customers within a few days of the end of their rentals. Apple surveys them shortly after transactions in the store. American Express surveys card members after an important servicing call. In business-to-business relationships with continuous interactions, a bottom-up survey might be triggered by the end of a quarter or an anniversary date. Philips, for instance, surveys hospital decision makers and lab personnel at key accounts about its imaging equipment and services twice a year. Companies vary in which interactions they choose as triggers, and they vary in what they ask. Some feel, for example, that the "would recommend" question is inappropriate in certain circumstances; instead, they ask whether the customer was satisfied with that particular transaction. (And some ask both questions. For a fuller discussion of these issues, visit the Web site www.netpromotersystem.com.) Whatever the specifics, the goal of NPS measurement is to reliably categorize customers so that frontline employees can then diagnose, learn, and take action. The bottom-up process ensures that the person who does the discovery and learning is the same person whose behavior needs to change (or that person's direct supervisor). It is these bottom-up operational surveys and the closed-loop responses they enable that are the sine qua non of the Net Promoter system—so be sure to get this component right.

Principle 4: Aim for High Response Rates from the Right Customers

While it would be ideal to gather feedback from all your customers, it's often wise to begin with the customers you care most about—your core or target customers. This makes good business sense anyway. Your core customers are those who are the most profitable and whom you would most like to become promoters. When you segment customers in this way, you can develop appropriate and economically rational strategies to improve relationships with them. For example, many retail banks are now struggling to retain and better serve their most profitable customers. But can they afford to make the necessary investments? If they focus only on generic feedback—typically dominated by the voices of marginally profitable customers—they may conclude that major investments are unaffordable. But when they segment their customers by profitability, they usually find that there is considerable margin for investment to enhance the experience of high-value patrons.

The goal of NPS surveying, remember, isn't just to research attitudes; it's to sort customers into categories that predict hard, quantifiable behaviors. You want to know precisely how many customers are promoters, detractors, and passives, along with why and how those numbers vary over time. So you can't rely on a small sampling of customers; you need large samples or, better yet, a complete census. You also need high response rates to ensure reliability. At Enterprise, the survey completion rate for customers who answer their phone exceeds 95 percent. At Allianz, response rates for both consumer and business-to-business sectors are up to 80 percent. A good rule of thumb is this: if your survey response rates are lower than 65 percent, your process needs to improve. Similarly, if your response rates are declining, you may need to reexamine your approach.

In business-to-business situations, it can be particularly diffi-cult to get enough responses from the right customers. At Bain, for example, our partners make a point of regularly updating the relevant list of executive decision makers at each client, along with managers at various levels who work directly with our teams. We track responses carefully so we know we are hearing from the right cross section of each client organization. Here, too, a high response rate is evidence of a reliable process. Some com-panies rate every nonrespondent as a detractor, since the choice not to invest the time to answer a brief survey indicates a flawed relationship.

One test that can help you determine the reliability of your sampling method is to examine the behavior of customers who ignored the survey and compare it with those who responded. Progressive Insurance analyzed its policy retention rate for nonre-sponders, for instance, and found that it was substantially worse than the rate for responders. In general, measuring bottom-up NPS with a low-response-rate survey process can lead to confus-ing and misleading results. Consider the example illustrated in exhibits 5-1 and 5-2, which is hypothetical but realistic based on several companies we studied. This company's internal bottom-up survey, which achieved a 20 percent response rate, indicated that its NPS was 50 percent (60 percent promoters minus 10 percent detractors). But when the firm studied the behaviors of the nonre-sponders—behaviors such as repeat purchase, increased purchase over time, and so on—it deduced that the mix of that group was 10 percent promoter, 40 percent passive, and 50 percent detractor. In other words, the 80 percent of customers who ignored the

EXHIBIT 5-1

If nonresponders look like responders, overall NPS is 50%

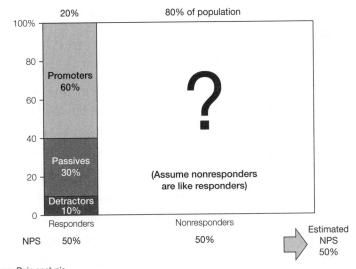

Source: Bain analysis.

EXHIBIT 5-2

But nonresponders tend to be passives or detractors— so true NPS is −22%

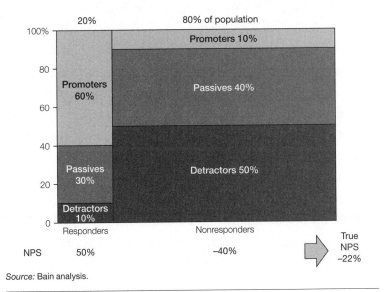

Source: Bain analysis.

survey had an NPS of minus 40 percent. So the true NPS for the company was minus 22 percent.

Principle 5: Report and Discuss NPS Data as Frequently as Financial Data

A well-known high-tech company flaunts its annual customer-satisfaction survey as evidence of its commitment to good customer relationships. The company blasts out an eighty-question e-mail to thousands of customers each spring. By summer, most of the results have been tabulated and reported. Employee bonuses, from the CEO all the way down to service reps, are linked to these results—but the bonuses aren't paid until the end of the year! During this same twelve-month period, of course, the company prepares twelve monthly sales plans and profit budgets, along with four quarterly reports that are carefully calculated by the financial staff and widely speculated upon by Wall Street. Everybody in the company knows that serving customers is an important ingredient for success, but the customer-survey score gets attention for maybe one week a year. The other fifty-one weeks, the company's focus is on the shorter-cycle financial metrics.

So it is with NPS. If you measure and discuss it only once a year or once a quarter, nobody will pay attention except when the results come out; the rest of the time they will focus on profit. Indeed, if you don't develop an NPS measurement process that is just as timely as your financial measurements, employees will dismiss it as one more here-today, gone-tomorrow corporate initiative.

Timely measurement has another big advantage: the more often the reports come out, the more chances there are to try out new approaches and tactics to see if these changes improve outcomes. We saw that Enterprise's more than seventy-six hundred branches and twelve reporting periods add up to more than ninety-one thousand possible experiments. There would be only seventy-six hundred–plus experiments if the analysis of outcomes were generated only once a year. If annual scores were tracked only for the five countries the company operates in, there would be only five.

It may be hard for your business to create a continuous flow of feedback, maybe because customer transactions are infrequent or because groups of customers historically have objected to frequent surveys. But don't stop trying. Few customers refuse to answer just two questions. Survey requests can be sprinkled throughout the year rather than blasted out en masse. The same principle, incidentally, applies to employee surveys. Right now, many companies rely on an annual batch process. But leading NPS practitioners have shifted to systems that create more timely information flows. As we'll see in subsequent chapters, JetBlue, Rackspace, and other NPS trailblazers survey employees ninety days after hiring and then again on each hiring anniversary. This process provides a steady flow of data enabling executives to track trends on a weekly and monthly basis. The data flow informs their priorities and allows them to gauge the success of improvement initiatives.

Principle 6: Learn Faster and Improve Accountability with More Granular Data

Imagine how helpless a physician would feel if he or she could gauge only the average blood pressure of all the patients in the practice, rather than the blood pressure of each individual. Imagine how powerless a police officer would feel if radar tracked the average speed of all cars on the road, but not the speed of an individual car. Businesses learned this lesson a long time ago for financial metrics. Companies don't measure profit only at the corporate level; they break it down by business, product line, geographic region, plant, store, and so on. Granular performance measurements enable individuals and small teams to make better decisions and to be held responsible for the results.

Net Promoter metrics require the same kind of precision and granularity. If NPS is to be viewed as an operating management tool, not as market research, line management has to take ownership of the tool and feel accountable for using it to improve performance. At Enterprise, the crucial breakthrough was pushing the measurement of customer loyalty down to the branch level. The very specificity of the data both allowed and encouraged employees to be much more responsive to customer feedback.

In most companies, of course, granular measurement isn't easy. Many different departments influence a customer's overall experience and therefore his or her loyalty. For example, an insurance client interacts with the agent, with billing, with claims, and maybe even with underwriting. At Intuit, senior leaders realized early on that accurate evaluation of its customers' experience had to include customer service, tech support, software design, sales and marketing, and engineering.

The trick is to distinguish between a customer's satisfaction with a specific interaction, such as a call to customer service, and his or her loyalty to the overall relationship. That's why both bottom-up and top-down surveys are important. On the service front, for example, a company might ask a sample of its customers two questions immediately after a phone interaction: "Did we fully resolve all of the issues you called about?" and "Would you recommend us to a friend or colleague?" Tracking NPS at each interaction would enable managers to spot trends or emerging problems; it would also help them identify which departments and individual reps were doing the best job of turning customers into promoters, and to reward stellar employees accordingly. On the relationships front, the company could continue to sample its broader customer base, asking just the "would recommend" question and why. Ideally, the combination of data would allow managers to summarize results by customer segment, customer profitability, and type of inquiry or service problem. It would also help them understand which dimensions of the customer experience warranted investment.

When managers report that a company already has sufficient granularity in its customer measurements, you should be skeptical. One senior executive at a leading financial services firm explained that the company had organized customer-service reps into small teams and was paying bonuses based on individual performance, thereby pushing accountability to the front lines. But closer inspection revealed a contradiction. The company was measuring productivity (number of calls handled per hour) for each rep, but it captured customer feedback only at an aggregate level, for an entire shift of 150 employees. So the "customer" portion of a rep's bonuses was based on an average score for the entire shift. Trouble was, workers on the same shift didn't know each other and had no incentive to collaborate on problems or to invest in coaching and development. Employees naturally focused on the only thing they could influence individually—their own productivity, which reflected how quickly they got customers off the phone.

Another challenge for many companies is that teams frequently regroup. In a hospital, for example, a single patient may interact with a case manager; professionals in nutrition, oncology, anesthesiology, physical therapy, and radiology; multiple nursing shifts; and administrative services. What's more, each department assigns different staff to each patient. So how can you track the effectiveness of small teams that form around each customer? You can't ask a patient to fill out a survey after each blood test or radiation treatment.

Cancer Treatment Centers of America (CTCA), a chain of specialized oncology hospitals, came up with a clever solution to this problem. It is reworking its patient-care tracking system to register which departments and which employees from each department touch each patient. Scores are gathered from the patient and, when appropriate, from the family caregiver at the end of each hospital stay. This methodology enables CTCA to compute an NPS for every one of its physicians. Ultimately, like a basketball team that compares its points-for and points-against when a given player is on the floor and when he or she is on the bench, a hospital could rank teams and individual members by an NPS that is the average of all the patients they have served. Every department would benefit from this kind of feedback, and best-practice exemplars could be highlighted as role models.

By focusing both frontline and board-member attention on delighting patients, CTCA has achieved eye-popping results, with its internal survey reporting NPS ratings over 80. Steve Bonner, president and CEO of CTCA, explains it this way: "The move toward operationalizing NPS is allowing us to remove the complexity associated with measuring and managing customer loyalty. The results look promising for extending our track record of four consecutive years of double-digit revenue growth in a mature industry."

Principle 7: Audit to Ensure Accuracy and Freedom from Bias

Ironically, the more progress you make toward granular accountability, the more difficult it becomes to gather honest and candid feedback from your customers. If a hospital gets serious about ranking its physicians' Net Promoter scores, doctors will soon be reminding patients to give them high marks. Linking any metric to employee rewards ensures that the rigor of the metric is put to the test, as car dealers demonstrate every day. It could be said that in business—as Heisenberg showed in physics—the mere act of measuring something changes its location and state of being. But you can greatly reduce this uncertainty principle by anticipating potential sources of bias and minimizing them through refined measurement techniques.

Sources of Bias

Net Promoter measurements are vulnerable to four types of bias: fear of retribution, bribery (or mutual back-scratching), sample bias, and grade inflation. The relative importance of these biases will vary according to the nature of your business, but each one requires a practical solution customized to your specific circumstances (see the box "Fighting Bias").

Fear of retribution. If a supplier enjoys market power—say, because the supplier is much larger than a customer or is a technological leader—customers will tend to avoid negative ratings. For instance, an industrial customer might fear that a negative rating for a large supplier would push the customer lower in the queue for the hottest new products, or maybe lead to reduced service levels. One way to coax out candid scores is to offer each customer appropriate levels of confidentiality. In business-to-business settings, you can maintain enough transparency by reporting average scores for an account while keeping individual scores confidential. Even though this complicates the diagnostic process, it helps generate honest feedback.

Bribery and collusion. The flip side of retribution is the risk that suppliers may use bribes and favors to win high ratings. Car dealers offer free floor mats; high-tech salespeople offer free trips or golf junkets. You can counter this by educating customers about the purpose of your system and about the ethical principles that lie behind it. Your customers can learn to resist these ploys and to report them. An even better defense is to educate your employees, emphasizing that such tactics are totally antithetical to the culture of your company. Then, too, you can often rely on community policing, particularly if individuals or teams are rank-ordered. Whenever one person's wheeling and dealing pushes others farther down in the rankings, employees will make sure that their colleagues clean up their act. Finally, unpredictable timing may also deter bribery. When the timing of feedback requests is hard to predict, people find it harder to game the system. A salesperson just won't know when to schedule those golf junkets.

Sample bias. One of the easiest ways to boost Net Promoter scores artificially is to avoid sending surveys to detractors. When a customer who is obviously angry returns his rental car, the agent might find it tempting to botch the phone number or e-mail address on the form, so that the survey never reaches that customer. If you appear enthusiastic when you check out at the local home improvement store, the register clerk may circle the bottom of your receipt in yellow highlighter, point out that the receipt has a survey request printed at the bottom, and note that he or she would really appreciate it if you could call the 800 number and provide a response. Some middle managers find other ways to minimize detractors in the sample. One phone-center manager, for example, determined that, rather than selecting customers for feedback from a pool comprising all calls, the pool would include only customers whose cases were closed. So if an unhappy customer had to call four times to resolve a problem, only that final call would go into the sampling pool for callbacks.

Such shenanigans aside, there is always the built-in sample bias mentioned earlier: it is inherently difficult to get passives and detractors (other than the angriest detractors) to invest the time necessary to respond to the survey and thus join the sample. Promoters nearly always have the highest response rates. The only way companies can minimize this bias is to create a system with very high response rates from the correct sample of customers.

Grade inflation. Some college professors now give A's to more than half of their students. Why? Professors who give fewer bad grades generate fewer complaints, and they don't have to spend long office hours justifying their grading to disgruntled students. Similarly, most customers hesitate to be hard graders, particularly when they have to provide the negative feedback directly. In a restaurant, for example, when a server asks whether you enjoyed your meal, you're likely to say everything was fine. But if a stranger on the sidewalk outside asks the same question, you will probably be far more candid about the inferior quality of the food or the noisy guests at the center table.

Customers will also hesitate to give negative comments if they don't believe their feedback will lead to actual improvements or if they fear that saying something negative will get them entangled in a time-consuming and potentially awkward follow-up discussion. So, typically, the only negative scores come from those who are profoundly disappointed in their purchases or service.

One way to deal with these problems is to have a third party ask for feedback at the right moment. For example, Enterprise's phone vendors call customers shortly after the rental ends. Customer names remain confidential unless the customer gives permission to pass along the feedback to branch personnel. A second solution is to demonstrate that it's worthwhile to grade accurately. If customers see that lower scores lead to improved service, they will be more likely to be honest. Also, instead of asking for an absolute score, it's wiser to ask for a ranking of experiences. "Grading on a curve" forces the truth because someone has to be number one, someone else number two, and so on. If this is impractical, simply asking the "would recommend" question helps reduce grade inflation because it, too, forces customers to think in relative terms. Unless you truly outshine the competition, your customers will not become enthusiastic promoters.

Fighting Bias

There is no simple recipe for neutralizing biases that thwart honest and candid customer feedback. You must assess the four sources of potential bias in your specific situation and craft an appropriate solution from the following strategies:

- Use e-mail, with its lower costs and its built-in audit trail for forensic analysis, whenever feasible, but only if you can achieve high response rates. Otherwise, rely on third-party phone calls as Enterprise does—they're very difficult to game.

- If the only way to achieve high response rates is through Enterprise-style phone surveys, be sure to adjust for the shift to cell phones, where call screening is more prevalent.

- Time feedback requests unpredictably if employees have an incentive to manipulate responses.

- Make team or individual employee scores transparent in order to enable community policing.

- Use a third party to collect feedback so that customers can be completely candid—and so that the promise of confidentiality is more credible. This also reduces the potential risk of gaming.

- Educate employees and customers about the goals and ethical principles of your feedback process; incorporate this training into customer on-boarding and employee orientation programs.

- Develop appropriate audit procedures that will uncover gaming and manipulation.

- Craft a simple and consistent process that makes it easy for customers to participate.

- In bottom-up surveys, consider scoring all nonrespondents as detractors (probably not too far off in business-to-business settings), or as a fifty-fifty mix of passives and detractors (a reasonable estimate for consumer businesses).

Consistency for Accuracy

Another key to accurate metrics is simple consistency. A restaurant chain, for example, was considering acquiring another, and its management wanted to collect feedback on the target company in order to measure customer loyalty. The chain first had a market researcher ask customers leaving the restaurant how likely they were to recommend the restaurant to a friend or colleague. Measured this way, the target company's NPS was almost 40 percent—quite respectable compared to other chains'. Later, however, a due-diligence team polled a broader sample of the restaurant's customers via brief e-mail surveys and calculated an NPS of minus 39 percent. This 79-point swing was alarming, even allowing for the tendency of customers to be more candid via e-mail than they are face-to-face. The team tried segmenting e-mail responses by the number of times customers had visited the restaurant, but the score remained only 13 percent, even for customers who visited more than ten times a month.

Which number was more accurate? Probably the lower numbers, but the acquiring company could be excused for feeling confused. The lesson is that it is vital to use a consistent process for gathering feedback. You can't accurately compare stores, branches, regions, or competitors unless you are using a process that is consistent and reliable. If your initial attempts are flawed, try again.

As more firms link NPS to bonuses and report results to their boards and to investors, they need to ensure that results are accurate and verifiable. Some of the major accounting firms, including PricewaterhouseCoopers and KPMG, have begun making preparations to offer NPS auditing and/or assurance products to their clients. To be meaningful, Net Promoter scores must be reported according to the rules described in this chapter. Hopefully, these principles will be clarified and refined by practitioners and auditors as they are applied in additional settings, both business and nonprofit. Like financial reports, NPS reports must also include footnotes that explain the detailed procedures used to gather these metrics, particularly items such as response rates, sample sizes and selection process, the survey medium, and the degree of confidentiality.

Principle 8: Validate That Scores Link to Behaviors

In the end, there is only one sure way to check whether your system has effectively defused the land mines of feedback bias, gaming, and manipulation: you must regularly validate the link between individual customer scores and those customers' behavior over time. Ongoing analysis of retention, purchasing patterns, feedback, and referrals (as described in chapters 2 and 3) can confirm the integrity of your feedback process. Consider augmenting your routine analysis by randomly spot-checking customer results, monitoring phone surveys, and routing a portion of customer alerts to senior executives.

All this auditing is worth the trouble and expense. Customers react predictably when their loyalty has been fairly earned. One, they make referrals. Two, they buy more. Three, they take the time to give constructive feedback. You need to audit these behaviors periodically for at least a sample of customers, to ensure that they square with the Net Promoter scores. If they don't jibe, keep revising the way you gather feedback—the scale, the question, the customer sample, the candor of replies, safeguards against gaming, and the like—until the scores reliably identify customer segments that behave like promoters, passives, and detractors. Failure to do this kind of auditing virtually guarantees that your system will drift away from reality, especially when scores are linked to employee rewards. Remember that it is the behaviors, not the scores, that define promoters, passives, and detractors. It is the behaviors, not the scores, that drive growth. NPS is a valuable tool only when the scores accurately reflect the strength or weakness of relationships.

If organizations take seriously the goal of turning customers into promoters, then they must take seriously the need to measure their success. As these rules of measurement become more widely practiced, our hope is that they will evolve into a set of generally accepted relationship-measurement principles that can focus organizational energy on relationship quality in the same way that the science of accounting has focused us on profits. Over time, indeed, more and more investors and board members may come to demand an audited set of relationship metrics that accord with the rules of measurement detailed in this chapter.

If your initial impulse is to balk at the investment required to generate solid NPS metrics, consider how much your organization now spends tracking and auditing accounting profits, which can provide only a look in the rearview mirror. Net Promoter scores not only help you see the future, but also help you manage it to improve performance. Until your NPS results are just as solid as your financials, achieving the kind of customer centricity that will enable you to win the quiet revolution will remain an uphill battle.

Conclusion

We have now reached the end of the book's first part. Our goal has been to trace the history of Net Promoter, to provide an updated and refreshed explanation of its core fundamentals, and to review the need for a new approach to measuring customer loyalty. This final chapter in the section has focused entirely on the detailed challenges of measurement, because substantial and reliable metrics are vital for attaining the benefits of the Net Promoter approach. Remember, of course, the most important message of the book: Net Promoter is much more than a score—it is a system of management. Without a robust scoring process as its foundation, however, the system will stall.

In the next part of the book, we will describe the many companies where innovative leaders have applied the principles of the Net Promoter system to generate some extraordinary results. And we'll show you, to the best of our ability, how they did it. Now that you understand the fundamentals, it is time to focus on how you can utilize the system to help drive your success.

Part Two

Getting Results

6

Winning Results with NPS

Why do companies adopt the Net Promoter system? What happens when they do? What are the typical first steps—and the second and the third? What are the keys to success, and the biggest obstacles? What can the adopters hope to accomplish? Where will this journey toward customer centricity take them?

These are important questions to ask before you embark on the Net Promoter journey. The rest of this book will try to provide some answers. Since the first edition appeared, thousands of companies have begun to use NPS to build customer loyalty and to transform their businesses. They have learned a great deal in the process, partly from each other but mostly from their own experience. In chapters 7, 8, 9, and 10, which are wholly new in this edition, we'll tease out the lessons.

In this chapter, however, we want to do something different: simply tell some stories. Sure, the stories have a point, and ultimately they'll help to answer the questions we just posed. But mostly they're just fun, even inspiring, to read and recount. They show businesspeople in a wide variety of situations confronting many different challenges—sometimes enormous ones. They show how companies have learned to tap the power of Net Promoter to resolve those challenges and rack up some truly amazing results. The stories will give you a sense of what the NPS journey is all about, and they'll provide some common reference points later, when we begin to analyze what works and what doesn't.

We'll start with Charles Schwab Corporation, the financial services firm, which in 2004 had taken a serious turn for the worse. So urgent was the company's situation that the board asked founder Charles "Chuck" Schwab, who had retired as CEO the previous year, to take the company's reins once more.

Charles Schwab Corporation

When he returned to work, Chuck Schwab found a company in trouble. Costs were out of control. The company had expanded into businesses where it had no competitive edge. The stock price had dropped over a three-year period from $40 to just $6. Worst of all, in Chuck Schwab's mind, the company seemed to be treating its clients poorly. He had always tried to build a client focus into the company's DNA, and for many years he had succeeded. But now it had lost its way. Nuisance and penalty fees, for example, had swollen to the point where they now accounted for 25 percent of revenues. A bounced check cost the company 82 cents, but the firm charged the client $40. And no wonder administrative costs were high—too many of the company's employees weren't actually dealing with clients. There were seven retail presidents, for instance, each with an entire staff and a separate call center.

Chuck Schwab focused first on cutting costs, which enabled him to reduce nuisance fees and get prices back in line with those of competitors. But by the fall of 2005, he was looking for a way to keep everyone focused on the company's core clients so that it wouldn't again veer off course. Schwab invited one of us, Fred, to address his top six hundred leaders in December; shortly thereafter, the leadership team decided to organize the company's change process around the Net Promoter framework. Soon a team headed by a senior executive was talking to people throughout the organization about NPS. Team members slowly and methodically built support for the idea. Testing survey techniques, they learned how to develop a metric as robust as the company's financial measures. When the time was ripe, Schwab rolled out NPS under the name Client Promoter Score.

That was the beginning of a massive turnaround. By 2008, Schwab had regained its position as a leader in its industry. Its stock had tripled. Its Client Promoter Score, meanwhile, rose from −35 percent to +35 percent, a swing of 70 percentage points in just a few years.

The key to the turnaround was a series of bold moves that began in 2004 and continue to the present day:

• *More value for less money.* Schwab reduced its prices aggressively. But instead of also reducing its services, it improved what customers received. The branches, for example, which in the past had focused mainly on transactions, now began developing relationships with many of their clients. Schwab also overhauled its Web site and online tools, and it introduced compelling new products, such as a high-yield checking account.

• *Eliminating bad profits.* The nuisance fees and penalty fees Schwab was charging were damaging relationships with clients. The company couldn't remove all the fees right away, but it mapped out a two-and-a-half-year plan to get rid of them. Today they are gone. Schwab also eliminated account fees and minimum balances.

• *Beefing up the client-facing staff.* To make it all work economically, Schwab took out more than $600 million in costs. But while the company trimmed overhead, it devoted new resources to the parts of the organization that deal directly with clients. Before, for instance, the service offered by call centers was considered an expense, and the incentive system encouraged employees to handle as many calls as possible. Today, Schwab's executives view client service as a competitive advantage, and call centers are given the resources they need to offer the kind of world-class service that creates promoters.

• *Learning to close the loop.* Schwab branch and call-team managers review NPS ratings and client verbatims every day and use them as a guide to action. They target problem areas for reform. They provide additional coaching to representatives and consultants who elicit problematic feedback. Managers call individual detractors, usually within twenty-four hours, to find out the nature of their problem and try to make things right.

"I don't care what kind of business you're in," Chuck Schwab told a newspaper reporter. "Clients referring us to their friends or relatives is so much more powerful than any advertising we could ever do. We talk about that a lot around here."[1] Schwab and Walt Bettinger, who became CEO in 2008, talk about NPS at nearly every employee event and every public forum. They discuss with securities analysts the central role played by NPS, including an economic analysis quantifying the value of promoters and detractors. The company's executive committee has embedded NPS in its Key Business Indicator Reports, and almost every week Bettinger listens to tapes of calls in which his frontline teams are closing the loop with unhappy clients. The practice makes his commute more productive, he says, and it transports him right to the front line, where loyalty is created or destroyed. "NPS is the first screen I look at on my computer when I arrive at the office each morning—it provides a litmus test of how well we are living up to our core values," he says.

Apple Retail

Ron Johnson, the executive who led the creation and rollout of Apple's retail effort, faced a different but equally daunting challenge. In 2001, when Apple opened its first store, the company was a niche computer maker—the iPod was still under development, and the iPhone and iPad were far in the future. Other computer makers, Johnson knew, had failed miserably at selling through company-owned stores.

So Johnson set about designing a wholly different kind of experience. The retail division's mission, he declared, was to "enrich the lives of customers and employees." The stores would be places for people to gather and learn, not just buy. They would be designed to encourage an ongoing relationship with customers, not merely a one-off purchase transaction. The delighted customers, Johnson believed, would tell their friends and colleagues about their wonderful experience at the store. He envisioned the neighborhood surrounding each Apple store becoming populated with customer advocates, who would promote the brand and act as missionaries to help convert PC-using friends and neighbors into Mac enthusiasts.

But how could Johnson and his managers measure whether individual stores were living up to this ideal? Most retailers measure customer satisfaction through register-receipts surveys: messages printed at the bottom of the receipts request customers to call an 800 number or visit a Web site. Typically, only a few customers notice the request and actually follow up on it. That sampling process was too feeble for Johnson's mission, and when he discovered Net Promoter, he quickly embraced it. Since then, Apple has invested substantial resources to turn NPS into a science. Opening an average of three to five stores somewhere in the world every month, Johnson and his team use the metric to gauge how effectively each store is living up to the mission of enriching lives and helping to build the Apple brand.

NPS in Operation

Net Promoter plays a central role in the daily management of Apple's three-hundred-plus stores. New employees get three weeks of training before they fly solo with a customer, and a substantial part of that training focuses on how to create the right customer experience. Net Promoter is emblazoned on the credo card carried by every employee. Apple developed its own NPS branding—a smiley-faced promoter with a speech balloon containing the Apple logo—and puts it on every Net Promoter communication. Comments from customers help store managers prepare for service-recovery calls with detractors to close the feedback loop. The outcomes of these calls, together with the customer comments, provide important coaching and feedback messages that are passed along to employees.

Apple store managers recognize employees who create promoters of their customers; some stores even put photos of these employees next to the promoter's comment text, and then scroll them across a large-screen TV monitor in the employee break room. Meanwhile, Apple's central NPS team analyzes customer feedback from all the stores to understand the systemic reasons for promoters' enthusiasm. Though you might expect that the primary source of enthusiasm was Apple's amazing products or its cool store design, by far the most common reason promoters give for their happiness is the way store employees treated them.

Employees of an Apple store know where they stand among their peers in terms of NPS and where their store stands relative to the rest of the stores in the region. They know that the score is telling them how they are doing on their mission to enrich lives. Employees discuss Net Promoter feedback at every opening shift huddle (the so-called daily download), thus ensuring that they integrate the feedback into their daily rhythms. Apple ranks its stores every week based on NPS, and each quarter honors its highest-scoring stores and its most improved stores with "Ovation Awards." (A nine or ten from a customer is the equivalent in Apple's view of a performer receiving a standing ovation.)

When Apple stores began measuring NPS in 2007, there were 163 stores, and their NPS was 58 percent. Today, there are more than 320 stores, and the NPS is a lofty 70 percent. The best stores in the system achieve NPS above 90 percent, a score as remarkable as it is unusual. But as Johnson is quick to point out, the mission of enriching lives focuses on employees and investors as well as customers. The reason Apple is so committed to Net Promoter is that it helps everyone do the right thing—to enrich the lives they touch. And that opens up opportunities for profitable growth. Where a typical electronics store might record $1,200 per square foot in sales, mature Apple stores exceed an estimated $6,000 per square foot. This is by far the highest productivity in retailing of any kind—and the number is undoubtedly understated since it ignores online sales inspired by the stores.

Apple Retail was also a pioneer in adopting the Net Promoter framework to employees. Johnson's team knew that only employees who were promoters themselves could turn customers into promoters. So team members developed what's called Net Promoter for People, or NPP, under which stores survey their employees every four months to determine how likely the employees would be to recommend the store as a good place to work. We'll discuss this initiative further in chapter 10. It's just one of the many innovations that Apple Retail has developed around NPS to gauge how closely it is living up to its mission—so that enriching lives can become every bit as important as profits.

Ascension Health

Not every Net Promoter adopter is a for-profit business. Ascension Health, for example, is the largest Catholic health-care system in the United States. In 2010 it included more than 500 locations in 20 states and the District of Columbia. Its health ministries—as the organization calls its regional units—operated 78 hospitals, employed 112,500 associates, worked with 30,000 physicians, and recorded operating revenues of $14.8 billion. Ascension Health was also working on an ambitious 15-year "Strategic Direction" that began in 2005. One key part of this effort was absolute patient satisfaction. "We strive to deliver the kind of healthcare experience each of us would want for those we cherish most," says John Doyle, Ascension Health's chief strategy officer.

Many of the health ministries that had become part of Ascension Health were already measuring patient satisfaction in their hospitals, but in a variety of different ways. Among them, they engaged seven different vendors who asked nearly six hundred questions in all. So leaders were drowning in data, yet they didn't really know how to compare patient satisfaction across the system. In response, the working group focusing on patient satisfaction conducted research on nearly two thousand patients to define the desired experience and to determine how to measure whether Ascension Health was delivering it. In June 2006, the group recommended that the entire system adopt NPS.

Launching NPS

Once the organization's board gave the green light, a team charged with implementing NPS began communicating with the CEOs of Ascension's health ministries. "It was a multi-pronged approach," says Peggy Kurusz, senior director of operational excellence and leader of the NPS effort. "First the CEO meetings that summer. Then at the systemwide Leadership Convocation, where trustees, sponsors, and leaders from across the system come together. We shared the research and the definitions of patient experience we had come up with." Kurusz and her team began to send out regular information on NPS, including a report highlighting where each local system and each individual hospital stood relative to others. Meanwhile, the board decided that NPS would be incorporated into system executives' long-term at-risk compensation, a three-year measure, and that it would be included on the organization's Integrated Scorecard. Both these measures gave the new approach a high degree of visibility.

Not all the communication was top-down, however. Kurusz's operational specialists regularly visited hospitals to do *patient experience snapshots*, as they are known—a systematic method of studying patients' experiences. That gave them an opportunity to talk with middle managers and frontline employees about NPS and how to foster loyalty.

Creating a Plan of Action

Ascension Health's research identified the factors that mattered most to patients by gauging each factor's impact on Net Promoter scores. "Care responsiveness," "communication and empowerment," and "compassionate and respectful care" were at the top of the list. Kurusz's team visited many of the system's hospitals to identify best practices and trouble spots. Team members listened closely to what clinicians and administrators had to say. "I think the fact that we went out and took the time to understand who they were and what they were doing, what was working well and what wasn't working well, was probably the most critical component of our ultimate success," says Kurusz.

The research and information gathering, in turn, allowed the organization to map out a plan of action resting on four cornerstones:

- *Staff empowered and equipped to solve problems.* Ascension Health encouraged its hospitals to empower staff to put patients' needs first, to raise productivity, and to eliminate waste. Tools and techniques included Lean Six Sigma and the Transforming Care at the Bedside (TCAB) toolkit, a program developed by the Institute for Healthcare Improvement and the Robert Wood Johnson Foundation, which involved the participation of one of the Ascension Health ministries.

- *Emotional, social, and spiritual support.* Internal research had shown that personal support along these three dimensions was a key part of the ideal patient experience. The organization sponsored workshops and follow-up programs designed to make providing personal support an intentional part of the "Ascension Health Exceptional Experience."

- *Real-time, closed-loop feedback.* Several practices enabled associates to receive and respond to patient input as quickly as possible. One practice is called *hourly rounding*: staff members visit patients every hour or two, query them about their specific needs, and then respond to those needs. A second technique: postdischarge calls from nurses to patients, asking them about their experience in the hospital. In both cases, documentation systems ensure that problems were resolved and systemic issues addressed through process improvement.

- *Aligned people practices.* Recognizing that only through an engaged and caring staff could they hope to turn patients into promoters, Ascension Health began to modify its human resources policies. It enhanced its selection and performance management processes, and it increased training to provide the skills required to deliver the desired patient experience. It also established rewards and recognition programs to highlight both the top scorers and the most improved teams on both customer and employee feedback. Accountability was also ramped up through "crucial conversations" with associates who did not model behaviors consistent with the organization's values.

Based on these four cornerstones, Ascension Health teams defined a variety of specific practices that would improve patients' experience. Admission and discharge, for instance, were critically important parts of a patient's stay in the hospital and had a significant impact on patient loyalty. Some hospitals created discharge checklists, complete with time commitments, to ensure that the process ran smoothly. Some created welcome videos for each unit. Some made a point of coordinating therapy schedules so that patients could be handed off from one department to another without a glitch.

There are plenty of remaining challenges, to be sure. For example, Ascension Health's efforts have so far focused primarily on its inpatient population. Kurusz hopes to extend that to outpatients as well. In addition, top performers and weak performers were quick to latch onto NPS, while those in the middle weren't so enthusiastic. Kurusz's team had to devote more time to this group, helping them understand the benefits. And some of the top performers were so excited about NPS that they sometimes bit off more than they could easily chew. "We've had to say, 'Wait a minute, why don't you try just this one tool and not all four of these tools, and let's see if we can get one wired into the organization before we take on the others,'" says Kurusz.

Meanwhile, Ascension Health's accomplishments have been remarkable. The organization's initial measurement in 2007 established baseline levels for NPS: its seventy-six units (at the time) ranged from a high of 83 to a low of 21. Today that range has been significantly tightened, with the highest health ministry at 93 and the lowest at 40. Many individual hospitals recorded increases of more than 30 points. Systemwide performance improved from 58 to 68, clear evidence of progress toward the overarching goal of absolute patient satisfaction. "The Net Promoter Score gave us a quantifiable way to gauge how well we are living up to the values and expectations we had for ourselves," says chief strategy officer Doyle.

Carolina Biological Supply

Many of the companies that have adopted Net Promoter are large organizations with marquee names, like Apple or Schwab. But you don't have to be a big company to benefit from NPS. Just ask Jim Parrish, CEO of Carolina Biological Supply, a 450-employee, family-owned business in Burlington, North Carolina.

Carolina Biological provides products and services for math and science education. Its primary customers are high school and college teachers. When Parrish arrived there in 2004, sales were falling and the company had just experienced its first unprofitable year in a decade. Many of its customers were grievously unhappy, and employee motivation was low. Five years later, Carolina Biological was earning record profits and was gaining market share, growing at a double-digit rate in the stagnant education-supply market. "We did a lot to turn things around," says Parrish, "but I believe the most important change we made was implementing Net Promoter."

Parrish, who had worked at Bain in the 1980s, discovered NPS when he read Fred's original *Harvard Business Review* article introducing Net Promoter. He liked the idea of a metric that would provide continuous feedback and track the company's performance in the eyes of customers. He also felt that NPS could inspire people—that it could help the company grow and be more successful.

Carolina conducted its first NPS survey in February 2006, scoring 33 percent overall. It also surveyed customers on specific trouble spots, such as on-time delivery and responsiveness. Many of those results came out negative. Parrish went on "roadshows" around the company, with the various numbers displayed on poster boards. He talked to everyone about the scores and why they were important. Soon the company began doing NPS surveys every couple of months. It also created internal metrics tracking performance on issues such as on-time shipments and product availability. By the summer of 2010, the firm's NPS had improved from 33 percent to 70 percent, so the series of moves that Parrish and his team undertook deserves scrutiny.

Making NPS Work

Parrish and his team attacked on several fronts. Inventory levels were one issue; customers had told the company that product availability was a major concern. The fill rate per line item stood at only 92 percent—and with an average of 2.5 lines per order, Parrish says, "that means 20% of the time we didn't have everything the customer wanted." A significant investment in inventory management brought the fill rate up to 98 percent on the top items and 95 percent on the rest.

The company also mounted an in-house program designed specifically to reduce errors. Customer-service representatives (CSRs) learned how much incorrect address entry or incorrect item entries cost. Each one could see a tally of his or her own errors, along with a dollar figure showing the total cost for a six-month period. That encouraged everybody to take personal responsibility to reduce the mistakes and led to a significant decline in the error rate. Fewer errors led to more promoters and fewer detractors.

A third move: eliminating bad profits. "We had a freight model that calculated a surcharge for this and an additional cost for that," says Parrish, "and sometimes it added up to more than the order, particularly if you ordered something small and wanted overnight delivery and all of that." At first, Carolina gave its CSRs the authority to alter the charges if the customer complained. Then it reprogrammed its system. Now, CSRs talk to customers up front about freight charges and how to ship things more economically.

Tom Graves, Carolina's director of customer service, played a key role in supporting the NPS effort. He wowed customers by sending personal thank-you notes to detractors, writing, "Thank you for letting us know about this problem. Your help in letting us know about it not only helped you, but it helped your peers as well." This communication was so well received that Graves developed a program for his CSRs to send personal thank-you notes to the company's top one thousand accounts. "The teachers would get the note at the end of the school year," he says, "or if it got mailed out late they'd get it first thing next school year. We got more calls than ever over August and September. People were so enthused. No one had ever done that for them before!"

Carolina's NPS rating began climbing steadily, and in 2010 hit 70 percent. Remaining challenges? Parrish thinks of customer feedback as "fuel for the company's engine" and believes that Carolina still doesn't get enough of it. The survey includes ten questions, and response rates are between 14 percent and 16 percent. The number of questions may reduce response rates, but "everybody is attached to 'their' question," says Parrish. Despite the challenges, Parrish is happy. "To me, NPS is the most powerful communication tool that I've ever run across. Last year our core business grew in an economy where we thought we were going to shrink. And this year we're coming out of the gate growing at double-digit rates, which is extraordinary given the market environment in education right now.

"I can't think of anything else I've done that could possibly contribute more to doing the right thing for customers—which of course is the right thing for the business."

The Progressive Group of Insurance Companies

One thing we noticed as we watched NPS spread was that companies were learning from each other. Progressive, for instance, is one of Enterprise Rent-A-Car's largest customers. Progressive CEO Glenn Renwick had long admired Enterprise's commitment to earning customer loyalty, and he knew Enterprise well enough to understand the important role of customer feedback. That helped convince him he should adopt Net Promoter at Progressive.

Renwick had an urgent economic reason as well. Progressive had carefully quantified the financial impact of customer retention, or "persistency," as it is known in the industry. Increasing average policy length by just one month would increase premiums over the life of all policies by more than $1 billion—an impressive amount even to a company such as Progressive, a large U.S. property and casualty insurer with more than $14 billion in premiums.

But how to encourage loyalty? In the past, says Renwick, efforts aimed at being "nice and supportive" to customers never really took a deep enough view of customer retention. "We had a strong analytical side, but we had trouble embracing things that were soft." NPS, with its rigorous numbers-oriented methodology, helped bridge that gap. "NPS could be an analytical measure that to us could be equivalent to the power of 'loss ratio,'" Renwick says. "It creates a measure of customer relationship health that is as analytically powerful and actionable as our other hard metrics.

"The beauty of NPS," he adds, "is that it's a common language— you don't have to reinterpret it to the different people you're talking to. We can go to the most analytical people in the organization and ask them the NPS of everyone who had a claim serviced in Florida. They could understand this and act on it."

Renwick began to talk about Net Promoter to employees, his board, and investors. He included progress reports on NPS in the company's annual report. Asked about the most effective tactic for winning acceptance, he explained that he, as CEO, could insist on including NPS as one of the company's key metrics, and he could demonstrate a direct link between NPS and retention and therefore profits. But what really drove acceptance was when the most independent and hard-nosed department in his operation put NPS to the test—and liked what they saw. "Our claims operation was among the first on board. Once they adopted it, it validated NPS for the rest of the organization, because they are a no-nonsense, pragmatic, and results-driven group."

It also didn't hurt that Renwick assigned a direct report, Richard Watts, to become the executive sponsor of the NPS initiative. Watts was group president of sales and service. With six call centers and about nine thousand full-time-equivalent employees under him, he was responsible for more than 60 million customer interactions and the overall customer experience. Watts, though he had grown up in the firm's numbers-driven culture, believed that NPS could help get the company more customer-focused. But he also saw that it would take work.

An early initiative, for example, was to search out policies and procedures that were creating detractors. When one executive discovered that his own mother's policy at Progressive had been canceled because of bureaucratic rules, he commented, "Is that any way to treat your mum?" The phrase became a rallying cry across the organization: people began to challenge more and more policies and procedures with the same mantra. Joining the NPS Loyalty Forum, Watts witnessed the power of closed-loop feedback and adopted the process at Progressive, first in claims and eventually in all the company's customer-service operations. Today, Progressive monitors NPS by team and by individual, and it ensures that star performers receive widespread recognition. The company holds local lunches and award ceremonies, and each year CEO Renwick invites the top 1 percent (about two hundred claims reps) to fly to headquarters for a dinner with him. There, the reps receive a hardbound book including verbatim comments that their own customers gave them through the Net Promoter survey process.

Progressive has not yet linked compensation to NPS. But its gain sharing is heavily driven by customer-retention figures, and NPS has become the primary tool for prioritizing improvements that lead to greater retention. At any rate, the company is doing well: revenues and the number of customers continue to climb.

Incidentally, just as Progressive adopted Net Promoter because of Enterprise's positive results, Progressive's vendors now are adopting NPS. An example is Belron, the world's leading supplier of replacement auto glass. Progressive is also an advertising sponsor for KOA, the camping franchise system. KOA, too, has become an enthusiastic adopter of NPS.

Rackspace

Take a young, entrepreneurial business in a fiercely competitive high-tech marketplace. Add in the financial crisis and stock market collapse of 2008. You'd think the results would be disastrous. But Net Promoter has helped a San Antonio–based company called Rackspace weather the storms and shoot to the top of its industry.

Graham Weston and his partners founded the company in 1998 to compete in the managed hosting and, later, the cloud computing space. Weston was a real estate entrepreneur, and early on, like most landlords, he wanted only the kind of tenants who paid their rent on time and never bothered him. Rackspace started with what Weston now calls a "denial-of-service" model: it warned prospective customers not to do business there unless they were IT experts and could handle their own computing problems. But Weston and Lanham Napier (then CFO and soon to become CEO) quickly noticed that even tech-savvy customers were clamoring for more help in dealing with complex and fast-changing IT issues. The two men also noticed that none of their competitors was meeting this need. So they decided to differentiate their company around world-class customer service.

Napier is an unusual manager, as attuned to the leadership and motivational side of business as to the financial and analytical side. He recognized the power of Net Promoter to help drive both sides of the business by boosting what the company terms its "Fanatical Support" for customers—and Fanatical Support, Napier says, "is the reason we have grown to be the world's leader in hosting over the past ten years." The company's first annual report after its initial public offering described the connection this way:

> *[Fanatical Support] is our unique way of caring for customers and our point-of-difference in a competitive hosting market. Fanatical Support underpins our operating philosophy and permeates our entire business . . . The goal of Fanatical Support is to create customers who are Promoters. Promoters recommend us to their friends, becoming an extension of our sales force. Customers who are promoters are also more profitable, staying with us longer and buying more of our services . . . The creation of loyal promoters not only reduces customer acquisition costs, it improves retention rates and inspires our Rackers [employees]. We have witnessed these results firsthand.*

When the downturn hit shortly after the IPO, Rackspace shares plummeted from their initial trading range of $10–12 a share to just over $5. No matter: the company redoubled its commitment to customer loyalty and NPS. The management team agreed to a broad set of initiatives, including a change in pricing strategy, a reorganization of frontline phone reps into cross-functional teams that could serve customers better, and a commitment to build a state-of-the-art closed-loop feedback process. At first, frontline reps and team leaders were reticent to call detractors. Thanks to extensive training and the launch of a recognition program for top teams, however, Rackers are now contacting more than 90 percent of detractors and passives.

The results of this doubling down have been impressive. As competitors in the core managed hosting business stalled, Rackspace NPS increased by 20 points to 63 percent, making it the industry leader. Customer churn rates declined by more than a third, from 3.0 percent to 1.9 percent; they are now the lowest sustained levels in the company's history and by far the best in the industry. Both factors helped the company continue its double-digit growth: revenue at this writing is closing in on $1 billion, and the stock price increased by 50 percent in 2010 to more than $30 a share. CEO Napier announced to the board, to stock market analysts, and to employees that NPS would provide the gauge by which the company tracked its progress toward its goal of becoming one of the world's greatest service companies. Nobody thinks small in Texas— but Napier is dead serious about the lofty goal. As he told Rackspace employees in a blog post, "Greatness is achieved when customers say we're great. We obsess about NPS for a reason. When ALL of our customers are Promoters, when all of our customers are giving us a 9 or 10 out of 10, THAT's when you know you've become One of the World's Greatest Service Companies."

Virgin Media

Like the executives at Progressive and Rackspace, Neil Berkett understood the economic links between churn rates, customer longevity, and the lifetime value of customers. When Berkett became CEO of Virgin Media in March 2008, he took on an organization with substantial potential for improvement on these dimensions. Virgin Media's customer-service ratings were at the bottom of its industry. So were its retention rates. Berkett put the problem simply: "Our number one problem was that customers didn't stay with us long enough!"

Virgin Media is the largest of the Virgin Group of companies. The product of a series of mergers and acquisitions of phone and cable properties in the United Kingdom, the company has $6 billion in revenues, around thirteen thousand employees, and millions of customers. One of Berkett's first steps in turning the company around was to adopt the Net Promoter system. He launched the initiative with an NPS workshop (run by Rob and several colleagues) for his top twenty executives. The workshop covered the economic rationale for the initiative as well as the cultural realignment that would need to take place. The group began to lay out scenarios describing how the change would play out over a number of years. They also paid close attention to the need to achieve quick wins. They decided to make NPS an important element of the company's balanced scorecard and to link it to executive bonuses.

"NPS is a simple concept to understand and rally around," Berkett points out. But, he adds, it means different things to different layers of the organization. Virgin Media's senior leaders were most impressed by the economics of NPS. The front line was most excited about the cultural impact. "With effective communication, the front line was positively euphoric about the process of putting customers at the heart of everything we do. The lives of front line employees get much better when their company is helping them find ways to delight customers."

Berkett reorganized the company to clarify accountability for creating more promoters and fewer detractors. He continually communicates to people at the company that the goal is not to record a better score; the goal is to *use* the score for learning, improvement, and motivation. A recent presentation on the company's NPS journey ended with a slogan that captures the essence of Virgin Media's approach: *Net Promoter—It's the way we do things around here.* In just two years, the company improved relationship NPS 15 points, from 3 to 18, resulting in a decrease in customer churn from 1.8 percent to 1.1 percent per month. This brought the company from the back of the pack up to the middle, but Berkett is clear that it's not yet enough. "We are very pleased with progress to date," he says, "but we are certainly not satisfied. Our goal is to become the industry leader in NPS." If he can accomplish that goal, Virgin Media will have the lowest churn rates, lowest cost of acquisition, and highest sales per customer. That will produce the highest lifetime value per customer—an enormous strategic advantage.

More Success Stories

There are more NPS success stories than we can possibly cover in this book, let alone in this chapter. But a few quick summaries highlighting other noteworthy accomplishments may provide a sense of the scope of progress companies are achieving through NPS in a wide array of industries and business situations.

British Gas Services

British Gas Services (BGS), the largest supplier of gas in the United Kingdom, utilized Net Promoter to help turn around its home heating installation business, which was losing money and hemorrhaging cash. The installation business trained all of its personnel in the NPS framework. It developed a rigorous scoring process, reporting daily NPS for all of its seventy-five districts and for each individual installer and sales adviser. Ironically, BGS's marketing team had been sending out detailed surveys for years with little impact, and there was some push-back from that team when its surveys were to be replaced by NPS. But the executive in charge of the turnaround initiative, Eddy Collier, explained, "Large sums of money were being invested in anonymous survey approaches. We cut back all that wasted effort because we knew the best way we could change the culture was to hear directly from our customers and put their issues right one by one. We had to win our customers' loyalty because we knew the only way we could afford to grow was through recommendations and referrals."

The company established closed-loop follow-up to resolve customers' problems. It also established a standard process whereby engineers who installed a boiler called their customers the next day to see if they had any questions or concerns. Net Promoter scores in this business increased from 45 percent to 75 percent over two years. Customer complaints declined 75 percent, which enabled BGS to reduce the number of people handling complaint resolution, also freeing up the time of managers to lead their teams. Bad debts declined more than 90 percent, since happier customers are more likely to pay their bills; cash flow turned positive; and profit margins increased to double digits. At the start of the period, the unit's revenues were shrinking; by the end of the period, growth rates had surged to 30 percent a year. "This was a serious turnaround situation with negative cash flow," says Collier. "NPS helped us stop the bleeding and turn the ship around—it was an incredibly efficient way to put each and every customer at the heart of everything we do and get the business back to health."

Collier and his team were then promoted to run a major new business in North America for Centrica, British Gas's parent company. One of the first things they have done once they hit the ground? Install the Net Promoter system.

American Express

Over the last five years, American Express has reinvented its approach to customer service. The new approach focuses on the "voice of the customer" and is measured by NPS (which the company refers to internally as "Recommend to a Friend" or RTF). It has produced benefits for both customers and the business, including an increase in customer-satisfaction scores, improved efficiency and service margins, and 50 percent lower employee attrition in the United States between 2006 and 2009.

When CEO Ken Chenault appointed Jim Bush to lead American Express's U.S. service organization in 2005, he asked Bush to help the company realize its vision of becoming "the world's most respected service brand." Over the years, service had become "a back office cost center, focused on reducing expenses and executing transactions," Bush recalls. "We were effective and efficient when it came to handling our customers' needs and requests, but we were missing out on an opportunity to establish bonds with them and build more meaningful relationships. To achieve this we clearly needed to shift the mentality and culture of the service organization, not only for the sake of our customers but to invigorate our employees and limit turnover as well."

Bush engaged his leadership team in rethinking the organization's role. "One of the first things we did was to survey our employees to find out what they needed to deliver extraordinary care for our customers, and we then made changes based on that feedback. For example, we stopped calling our people 'customer service representatives' and started calling them 'Customer Care Professionals,' or CCPs. We stopped hiring only from other call centers and started hiring people from industries like hospitality and retail that fundamentally 'get' service. We also changed the metrics we used to gauge success. We stopped measuring our performance through traditional call center metrics like internal quality monitoring and just 'satisfaction,' and we began focusing on the importance of *what the customer thinks* after every interaction, measuring the likelihood they would recommend American Express to a friend."

Using RTF to gather and act on customer feedback, Bush was able to help his team see the vital role they played in overall customer-relationship development. In effect, he elevated their mission. He instilled the belief that every interaction provides a chance to deepen relationships with customers. Setting a dauntingly aspirational goal of doubling RTF in just three years, Bush was also able to engage colleagues from other groups, including product development, risk management, and marketing, in the job of improving policies, product features, and other elements of the business system that could contribute to creating promoters. In addition to changing hiring criteria and performance metrics, Bush and his team achieved that aspirational goal. They took CCPs off the clock and off the script. They removed average handling time goals for calls, instead allowing the customer to decide how long he or she wanted to spend on the phone. They increased emphasis on first contact resolution by getting to the heart of the matter more quickly, and they addressed policies that stood in the way of creating promoters. Where previously 70 percent of training time had been focused on technical skills and 30 percent on relationship and personal skills, Bush and his team reversed that ratio. "We are always looking for ways to continue to improve, but I'm incredibly proud of the progress our team has made and the external recognition we have received along the way," says Bush, "Our goal remains not only to be the best at service in our industry, but to be considered among the elite service brands in the world."

Vanguard

Vanguard Group used the Net Promoter approach to uncover opportunities to improve an already-great business. Several years ago, the big financial services firm focused on its Flagship Services program, designed to provide exceptional service to people with more than $1 million invested in Vanguard funds. While the program created significant client loyalty, Bill McNabb, Vanguard's CEO, and Tim Buckley, managing director of the firm's Retail Investor Group, were not satisfied. McNabb observed, "We had an 80% NPS in Flagship. But we were convinced we could do even better, and we knew we had a few 'pain points' that we wanted to address."

John Marcante, a principal with Vanguard's high net worth services unit, was given the task of rethinking the Flagship service model. "We had such high Net Promoter scores to begin with, it was hard to imagine how we could improve," Marcante says. "So we focused on activating Promoters. We had to give them such an extraordinary experience that it was truly worthy of telling friends." Though Vanguard already was doing this occasionally, Marcante and his team set out to learn how the Flagship Services unit could provide such experiences more systematically.

One improvement involved Vanguard's unit for providing investment advice. The Flagship representative assigned to deal with the majority of a client's issues would refer requests for advice to a licensed investment adviser in another unit. But these advisers were often unfamiliar with the client's account, and usually didn't even know the Flagship representative making the referral. Under Marcante's leadership, Vanguard changed this model, embedding investment professionals in Flagship teams and even training Flagship reps to handle many routine requests. Before the change, about 33 percent of customers scored the advice model a ten. Just a few months after the change, the figure had doubled to 66 percent.

The Three Keys to NPS Success

These stories indicate that companies can achieve impressive results with the Net Promoter system. That holds true across a broad array of industry situations: large global firms and small private ones, high-tech and low-tech, rapid-growth companies and mature businesses. Of course, each situation is unique. But virtually every successful application of the system seems to have three specific characteristics. Whenever NPS helps produce extraordinary improvements:

1. The senior leadership team and especially the CEO personally embrace the improvement of customer loyalty through the Net Promoter system as a mission-critical priority. They understand both the economic imperative (it creates opportunities for profitable growth) and the inspirational and moral imperative (it measures how well a company is living its core values).

2. They hardwire NPS customer feedback into key decision processes up and down the organization, creating closed learning and improvement loops. They don't treat it as a separate department or program; they fully integrate it into the fabric of daily and monthly priorities.

3. Companies organize the Net Promoter initiative as a long journey of cultural change and growth, not just as a short-term program or initiative. They understand that NPS must touch every part of the organization if it is to succeed in generating profitable, sustainable growth.

These are three keys to success, and the next three chapters will address them in more depth.

7

Economics and Inspiration: The Dual Imperatives

L
ike a well-built arch, the Net Promoter system rests firmly on two distinct pillars. If either one of the pillars isn't attended to, the whole thing collapses.

One pillar is economic. Net Promoter makes it possible to invest in customer loyalty, and to calculate the return on that investment. It creates the possibility of a virtuous cycle—greater customer loyalty leading to higher profits, higher profits enabling more loyalty-building investment, and so on. Companies with that kind of accelerating economic advantage can leave competitors in the dust.

The other pillar is inspirational. Most people want to do the right thing by customers—to affect customers' lives in a positive way. Net Promoter helps them know when they're succeeding, when they're falling short, and why. It helps them improve. Apple believes that earning a nine or a ten is like getting a standing ovation. It's the mark of a job well done, a source of deep satisfaction.

Either one of these pillars can be overdone—built too high for the arch, so to speak. Team members may be so enamored of the feel-good dimension of Net Promoter, for example, they imagine that creating promoters is all that matters. With enough promoters, the thinking might run, profits will take care of themselves. That makes no sense, of course, because there are plenty of ways to create promoters in the short term that would bankrupt the company. Slash prices! Give stuff away for free! Net Promoter scores might soar, but profits would plummet. "Be sure," cautions Apple's Ron Johnson, "that your people understand that the goal of creating promoters has to be balanced with the need to ensure your store is profitable."

Many executives, for their part, want the economic advantages of customer loyalty but ignore the inspirational side of NPS. They forget that it's impossible to create loyal customers without first inspiring a team of employees so they become promoters themselves. Who would go out of their way for a customer unless he or she is proud and inspired to be part of the team? And while there are many ingredients of employee engagement—the right training and development, rewards, opportunity for growth, the feeling of being valued, and so forth—the real foundation is this: employees must be able to treat customers and colleagues in a manner that makes them proud. When leaders and their teams consistently treat people right, when they can be relied upon to do the right thing, then an organization can truly be worthy of loyalty.

The Net Promoter system provides the link—the arch—between these two pillars. It combines economics with Golden Rule thinking and behavior—doing well and doing good. When Chuck Schwab chose NPS as the framework to help turn his company around, he was acutely aware of the fact that his name was on the door, and that the firm's reputation was deeply connected to his own. Schwab was committed to earning customer loyalty because it was a symbol of doing the right thing by people. Eliminating bad profits and investing to create promoters offered a way to build a reputation he could be proud of. But he also recognized that client recommendations are a critical ingredient of profitable growth. Roughly half of all new accounts at Schwab come through recommendation or referral.

These customers are superior, in both quality and profitability, to customers attracted for other reasons. So the two functions of NPS—measuring how well you treat your customers and measuring the power of your company's economic engine—are inseparable. They are simply two parts of the same reality.

This chapter will show how companies have learned to focus on both pillars, and to avoid neglecting either one.

The Inspiration Pillar: Measure Your Mission

Great companies typically have great values, and they take those values seriously. They want to do the right thing for the customer. They want to create a great place to work. They want to do well for their communities as well as for their shareholders. The values become part of their mission, their vision, their reason for being. Some organizations, such as Four Seasons and Southwest Airlines, use the language of the Golden Rule. These organizations ask employees to treat customers and other stakeholders as they themselves would want to be treated if they were in those people's shoes. Progressive Insurance's value-laden question—*Is that any way to treat your mum?*—is in the same vein. Whatever the language, the central idea of treating people right provides the foundation for any truly inspiring mission. Only an organization that lives up to that standard can attract great employees and can motivate them to accomplish great things.

But how can an organization know whether it is really living its values every day? That's where the inspiration pillar of Net Promoter comes in, and that's why it's so powerful. NPS enables a company to measure its success in realizing its values and achieving its mission. It's a metric of greatness.

Take Charles Schwab Corporation. Walt Bettinger, who was tapped to lead Schwab's retail division through its turnaround and who later became CEO, worked with his team to clarify Schwab's core beliefs. He then published them and distributed them around the company. The list includes statements like these: "Every client interaction changes our company's future . . . ," "We will view all clients as a whole person . . . ," and "Investing in our people is core to our success today and in the future." Bettinger regularly challenges team members to justify policies, decisions, and recommendations based on their consistency with these principles.

He also views the firm's Client Promoter Score primarily as an indicator of how well Schwab is living up to its principles. Schwab developed a process for tracking NPS every day for each branch, at every phone center, by team, by employee, and so forth. "There are lots of decisions that get made up and down the organization every day, both big and small," Bettinger explains. "The beauty of Net Promoter is that it helps to simplify complex issues and helps people to make the right decisions. NPS makes people ask themselves: Is this the right thing to do for our customer, and is it economically appropriate for the firm?" Bettinger also reminds his team that the intent of measuring NPS is to make sure the company is living up to its client service values.

The mission of Apple Retail, similarly, is to enrich lives. And a vital role for NPS is rigorously measuring how consistently the division achieves this mission. When customers score their experience at a store as a nine or ten, Apple can assume that the store's employees have enriched those customers' lives, and in so doing have enriched their own. When customers score their experience from zero to six, it is a fair bet that something or someone diminished their lives. By tracking and managing NPS results daily—by store, by product, by team, by employee—Ron Johnson has established a discipline around living the mission that extends to every Apple store from Paris to Dallas to Beijing. The real-time feedback scores indicating mission accomplished (promoter) or mission failed (detractor) lead to daily discussions between store managers and team members. The scores make the mission of enriching lives both more immediate and more real.

The Economics Pillar: Ensure Your CFO Embraces NPS

Bettinger, Johnson, and nearly every other successful NPS practitioner are realists as well as visionaries. When asked what he would tell CEOs about to embark on a Net Promoter journey, for instance, Bettinger replied, "You must have the board with you. There will be an investment required, and they must understand the economics that support this investment." Since the chief financial officer in most firms is the ultimate arbiter of whether an investment makes good economic sense, the CFO has to be a friend of NPS. Otherwise, he or she is likely to become its enemy.

Don't misunderstand: we don't mean that a CFO who isn't on board with NPS will necessarily be hostile. There is much in the Net Promoter system that appeals to CFOs, such as the well-documented linkages between scores, individual customer behaviors, and economic results. But CFOs left out of the loop will become de facto enemies over time. An earnings shortfall, for example, might motivate the finance staff to search out opportunities to reduce costs. The first cuts almost always attack line items with longer-term or less-certain payback. Unless the staff has a rigorous understanding of the economic consequences, investments to create more promoters will very likely fall into this category. Similarly, in a hunt for quick sources of incremental revenue, the temptation to increase the sorts of fees that create detractors—bad profits—often becomes overwhelming. Again, unless people have quantified and understood the impact of creating more detractors, the company is almost certain to resort to bad profits. If the economics *are* spelled out clearly, the CFO will know to defend the most profitable investments in loyalty and avoid bad profits.

Some examples will clarify the point. At Apple, store managers call every detractor within twenty-four hours, but there are some whom they never reach. Apple tracked the purchase patterns of detractors who spoke with a store manager compared to those of detractors who didn't. Over the subsequent two years, the detractors who were contacted purchased substantially more Apple products and services than the others. Apple calculated the time required to make these closed-loop calls and quickly discovered that every hour spent calling detractors was generating more than $1,000 in revenue, or additional sales of $25 million in the first year—a very good return on investment. This figure, moreover, ignored the benefits of avoiding negative word of mouth, not to mention whatever managers learned from the conversations that helped them run a better store.

Given this result, any CFO concerned about growing revenues would make sure the allocation of managerial time to calling detractors was one of the last things cut. But what if Apple had never bothered tracking the difference in purchase patterns among detractors? Or what if this analysis had been done for marketing purposes, and had never been shared with or vetted by the finance staff? Chances are, somebody in finance would commission a time-and-motion study aimed at freeing up managers' time for "more important" things—reducing shrinkage, say, where the link to profits is clear to all.

Another example comes from one of the world's leading credit card companies. The marketing team at this company realized that careful customer selection—targeting the individuals most likely to become loyal customers—played a vital role in generating sustainable growth. But the marketers performed their calculations inside their own department and never involved the finance staff. The CFO, meanwhile, encouraged Wall Street analysts to focus on statistics that he could rigorously quantify, such as cost per new customer.

That put pressure on marketing to bring in lots of new customers on the cheap, even if those low-cost customers rarely turned into promoters. The company continued to allocate too many resources to acquiring new accounts and too few to building loyalty.

When Schwab adopted NPS as a key element of its turnaround efforts, CEO Chuck Schwab assigned Chris Dodds, who was then chief financial officer, to lead the project. A substantial part of the turnaround involved cost reduction and elimination of activities not crucial to building the core business. Because the CFO was responsible for both cost reduction and increasing NPS, he developed the economic linkages within his staff group, using data that both he and the staff trusted. Consequently, Schwab has a highly sophisticated understanding of NPS economics. For example, it has quantified the economic value of moving a customer along each point of the scale from a zero to a ten.

One good test of CFOs' confidence in Net Promoter is whether they make the score part of their reports to investors and analysts. Many of the companies that have generated impressive results with NPS, including Schwab, Intuit, Progressive, Philips, and Allianz, regularly report their scores externally. Another test is whether NPS is integrated into the company's standard financial controls and reporting systems. These numbers drive budgeting and resource allocation. They constantly influence trade-offs and priorities. The CFO must bless them; they underlie the reports he or she shows to investors. If NPS and its key linkages to customer and company economics are not part of these standard reports, the system will never achieve its full impact. In too many firms, the economic benefits of loyalty never receive this kind of rigorous scrutiny from the finance staff—they simply never graduate from the informal spreadsheets back in the marketing department.

It is worth examining the process by which the companies most serious about NPS develop a solid economic foundation for reporting and analytics. They may begin with the theoretical framework described in this book, but they then test out the real economics in each of their business lines. In chapter 3, for example, we saw that Philips quantified the relationship between relative Net Promoter scores and growth compared to key competitors in each of the company's product and geographic markets. But the team didn't stop at this macro level; it also developed a detailed understanding of Net Promoter economics at the level of individual accounts. For instance, the lighting team tracked NPS for a sample of accounts over time. Team members then examined the annual revenue growth for accounts where NPS increased (revenues grew 69 percent) and compared it to accounts where NPS remained steady (revenues grew 6 percent) or declined (revenues decreased 24 percent). These striking results are summarized in exhibit 7-1. Combined with account profitability, they provided

EXHIBIT 7-1

Lighting accounts with improving NPS show increasing purchases

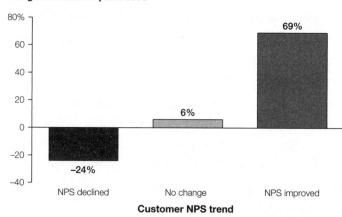

Change in customer purchases

Source: Q2 2009 Royal Philips Electronic Earnings presentation.

the detailed economic knowledge enabling managers to develop the right investment strategy for each customer account. The finance staffs at Charles Schwab, Allianz, and other members of the NPS Loyalty Forum implemented a similar approach. It should serve as a model for all Net Promoter practitioners.

Reinforcing the Two Pillars: Confront Bad Profits

When NPS is properly implemented, the twin pillars of economics and inspiration reinforce each other. Employees' engagement and commitment help build customer loyalty. Ever-growing customer loyalty generates an upward spiral of profitability. But any company that tolerates bad profits will undermine both pillars at once. Bad profits make a mockery of commitments to customer centricity.

Bad profits—profits derived from nuisance fees, onerous contracts, exploitative pricing, and the like, discussed in chapter 1—usually creep into a company's operations as a response to short-term earnings pressure. They can and do boost a company's bottom line for a while. But bad profits alienate customers, creating more and more detractors. Over the longer term, they undermine the virtuous cycle of loyalty economics. They also demoralize employees. When people have to enforce shameful policies and practices in the name of profits, their energy and engagement flags. That diminished inspiration, in turn, spirals downward into poorer levels of service, less innovation, less enthusiasm, and so on, all of which further diminish customer loyalty. Before long, the whole NPS edifice collapses.

That's why companies adopting Net Promoter must be ready to fix the problems unearthed by root-cause conversations with customer detractors. Detractors represent failures. The more detractors there are, the more likely it is that bad profits are helping to create them. If the leadership team is to maintain credibility about its commitment to core values, then it must confront and eliminate contradictions of those core values, which is what bad profits represent.

Verizon Wireless provides a good illustration. Verizon's senior executives understood that the economics of loyalty were particularly powerful in their industry because of the high cost of acquiring customers. In an effort to increase loyalty and reduce customer churn, the company introduced Net Promoter in its stores and call centers. Today the results are quite impressive: Verizon's NPS ranks the highest among national mobile-phone carriers in the United States. (MetroPCS, which competes only in the prepaid segment and only in selected cities, won the top rating in the most recent surveys, which is why it appears on the list in chapter 1.)

Curious as to how Verizon overcame the challenges inherent in an NPS launch, we interviewed frontline team members during one of the NPS Loyalty Forum gatherings. We asked them what helped move the program past the usual skepticism—the belief among employees that this was just one more customer-satisfaction initiative that could safely be ignored. The answers were remarkably consistent: the key factor was senior management's decision to confront bad profits. Before, for example, Verizon required any customer changing his or her plan to sign a new contract for two years, with early defection incurring substantial termination fees. The policy applied even if the change in contract was an upgrade to a more expensive plan. This seemed unfair to customers. When the NPS feedback confirmed that this policy was creating detractors—and when the project leader forcefully pointed out the problem to top management—senior executives acknowledged the contradiction and decided to change the policy. Employees cheered the move, and began to believe that the executives really were serious about doing the right thing for customers. Energy and commitment levels in phone centers and stores increased, and Net Promoter earned its place as the core system used to drive improvements in customer experience and loyalty.

Schwab, too, confronted its bad profits, eliminating the "gotcha" fees and charges that angered customers and humiliated employees. What led CEO Bettinger to this decision were his conversations with customer defectors. Schwab's initial success reflected the fact that it offered Main Street customers good value relative to traditional brokers. Later, however, the company had added fees on balance transfers, inactive accounts, low-balance accounts, and so on, in hopes of propping up profits. One particularly memorable conversation, Bettinger says, was with a customer who had moved more than $5 million away from Schwab. When Bettinger noted that the customer had never been charged any of these nuisance fees because of his large balance, the customer explained that the fees on lower-balance accounts were embarrassing to him. He had done business with Schwab partly because he liked the way it treated customers— not just himself, but his friends and relatives. Now he saw these people getting hit with unfair fees and charges, and it embarrassed him. So he left.

Bettinger heard similar stories from employees about their own embarrassment at enforcing these fees. His conclusion: the company had to eliminate bad profits if the firm was ever to regain the moral high ground. A couple of years later, he could finally report that all the objectionable fees were gone. It was a large part of Schwab's successful turnaround.

Bad profits tend to pop up and multiply whenever an industry enters times of economic duress. But these customer-unfriendly practices often just make things worse. The airlines, for example, have been through a rough patch during the last several years, and have instituted any number of additional fees, such as for changing flights and checking bags. The fees have infuriated passengers, which makes them a little more surly in their treatment of airline employees, which spirals into resentment and bad service, which further alienates passengers. A similar dilemma faces the banking industry. Bain's recent analysis of Net Promoter scores for retail banks in North America (see chapter 3) found that the average U.S. bank with a national network of branches scored a minus 6 percent. Is it any wonder? Consider what the *New York Times* reported in August 2010: a federal judge "ordered Wells Fargo to pay California customers $203 million in restitution for claims that it had manipulated transactions to maximize the overdraft fees it charged. Instead of processing transactions in the order in which they were received, Wells Fargo put through the largest to smallest." The judge also accused Wells Fargo of going "to lengths to hide these practices while promulgating a façade of phony disclosure."[1] While the judge's criticism was aimed at Wells Fargo, the truth is that most of the industry follows this practice. And while consumers may not know what their bank is doing, employees surely do. Practices like these convince branch and phone personnel that whatever executives may claim about their commitment to ethical behavior and putting customer interests first, they have no intention of walking that talk.

Several major airlines have announced that they will be implementing NPS programs. Some of the big banks have done so as well. But until they confront their bad profits, it is unlikely they can make much progress. Meanwhile, JetBlue has managed to minimize bad profits, and Southwest Airlines avoids them altogether. As a result, the two airlines are stretching their competitive advantage versus the rest of the pack.

At times, an industry's customary business practices lead to bad profits. In property and casualty insurance, for instance, insurance companies often take a long time to issue a check against a claim. Their argument is that they need the time to guard against fraud. Meanwhile, the customer whose car may be a total loss gets no cash to buy a replacement vehicle. Companies that really care about doing the right thing for their customers could find ways to accelerate payments in those situations where fraud is minimal, but instead they choose to stall payments to all customers.

Until leaders get serious about eliminating bad profits, they will not be able to earn the loyalty of their employees, which means that customer loyalty, too, will remain a pipe dream. One good signal of serious intent: at some companies, leaders ask their employees to rank-order the items that they consider the most egregious examples of bad profits. Sharing this data in an open and direct discussion can lay a foundation for inspiring and economically sustainable growth.

Balancing the Two Pillars: Measure Employee Loyalty

Over the past few years, Apple's retail stores have developed a process for measuring employee Net Promoter scores (eNPS) as well as customer scores. Apple's data supports the argument of this chapter: you can't create loyal customers without first creating loyal employees. Stores that regularly rank in the top group of customer NPS, such as Boston's Boylston Street superstore, also rank high in employee NPS. And stores with the lowest employee engagement also tend to have the lowest customer Net Promoter scores.

Many companies now recognize that employee engagement plays a vital role in building customer loyalty. Engaged, loyal employees reduce costs, improve productivity, and come up with more creative ideas. But the measurement and management of the engagement process has remained largely independent of the process for strengthening customer loyalty. Most large firms have looked to their human resources executives to measure and manage employee engagement, which puts HR in a difficult position. The primary factor in making a company a great place to work is how often it puts employees in situations where they can be proud of the way they treat customers and colleagues—situations where they can serve customers so well that they deserve and receive a standing ovation as evidenced by a promoter score. That requires a lot more firepower than an annual employee survey, which remains the primary tool of HR departments around the world. Like Apple, some companies are rethinking their approach and integrating customer NPS with employee NPS. That typically makes the HR team far more influential because its work now connects directly to revenue generation—that is, creating more customer promoters.

One of the recent converts to eNPS is Rackspace. "We want Rackers to feel that this is a great place to work," says CEO Lanham Napier, using the company's in-house name for its employees. "It is one of our highest priorities. Fanatical Support is our fundamental strategic differentiator, and we can't consistently deliver that to customers without engaged employees. In this age of low-cost computing, instant information, and sophisticated IT analytics, it just seemed absurd to be reliant on an annual batch processing system to track and manage employee loyalty." Partly because of the technology bust of 2009–2010, Rackspace lost its coveted slot on *Fortune*'s list of 100 Best Companies To Work For. With the implementation of eNPS and an increased focus on creating engaged employees, the firm was able to earn a return to the list by the following year.

Most adopters of eNPS, such as Rackspace and Apple, have settled on one central question to determine employee engagement. It is usually something like this: "On a scale of zero to ten, how likely is it you would recommend this company as a place to work?" Companies try to keep the survey short: a brief survey is respectful of employee time, and it doesn't generate reams of data that lead to analysis paralysis. But because employee names must be kept confidential to encourage honest feedback, the survey can't be as short as the typical transaction-based NPS customer survey. With customers, the closed-loop response process provides the lion's share of root-cause diagnosis and problem solving. With anonymous employee surveys, it makes sense to gather a little more information about possible root causes on the survey itself. But eNPS surveys are still much shorter than the typical annual employee survey because they are designed to help frontline teams recognize and prioritize issues, not for headquarters to figure out the solutions to everyone's problems.

Because eNPS serves the needs of operational teams rather than headquarters staff, companies often adjust the frequency of the surveys to support improvement cycles that make sense to those teams. For example:

- Apple Retail began its Net Promoter for People process using quarterly surveys. But it found that store teams didn't have sufficient time to diagnose root causes, implement solutions, and achieve measurable improvements before the subsequent survey. So Apple shifted to a four-month cycle, which at this writing seems to be working well.

- JetBlue began its eNPS journey by sending a survey to every employee ninety days after hiring, and again on every anniversary of the hiring date. This gave managers a steady flow of information to keep them abreast of developing concerns and help them track whether employees were reacting to improvement efforts. The initial survey, ninety days after hiring, catches on-boarding issues and selection mistakes early enough to allow corrective action.

- Rackspace adopted a process similar to JetBlue's and found that it helped to identify and prioritize leadership and organizational issues. For example, low eNPS scores helped the company come

up with improvements in the recruiting process that made
employees more likely to recommend that friends apply for a job.

Employee NPS data makes the people side of the business far
more transparent and subject to learning and experimentation.
Rackspace, for example, has learned which departments represent
liabilities and which represent best practices. The company can
track which team leaders are doing the best job, even in departments that might be earning low scores overall. It can also see at
what tenure stages the various career paths seem to demotivate
Rackers. That information enables Rackspace's HR people to work
on new training, organizational solutions, and career paths. When
JetBlue first began its eNPS surveys, it discovered pockets of detractors. Upon deeper investigation, management learned that some of
these unhappy employees were preparing a union-organizing
campaign. Rapid intervention helped resolve the key issues before
things reached that point.

At Apple, the eNPS process helps each store manager determine
the right priorities for team development. Stores with similar
issues—like the need for better coaching and career-path planning—
get together to develop effective solutions. Sometimes the themes
have been consistent across the store system, and headquarters has
helped develop systemwide solutions. An example is the Apple Store
Leader Program, which rotated 150 college graduates through a variety of store jobs in preparation for becoming store managers. This
program was a direct response to concerns about career paths highlighted on the surveys. But most of the employee issues are store specific. After each survey wave, store managers review the data for their
store with all employees. Employee focus groups then identify key
themes and issues, and employee teams help develop solutions,
which they present to store management. By the time the next survey
comes around, managers can see whether the solutions have had the

desired effect. This process enables the entire store team to get involved in identifying, prioritizing, and fixing issues that keep employees from feeling like promoters.

A note of caution: eNPS scores tend to be substantially lower than customer scores. Employees seem to hold their company to even higher standards than customers do. So before leadership teams initiate the survey process, they had better be ready to process some tough feedback and respond with appropriate action. In addition, it is usually a mistake to set absolute improvement targets for eNPS as if it were a goal independent of customer NPS. One of the early adopters of eNPS was so enamored with the logic of the metric that the board designated eNPS a key performance indicator for the corporation and linked it to executive bonuses. It set a bold target for improving absolute levels of eNPS before the company had developed much experience tracking how eNPS responded to changes in industry growth or capacity utilization, to say nothing of general economic conditions. When the economy deteriorated (leading to more unhappy employees and customers), the company missed its eNPS target and execs failed to earn their bonuses. Confidence in the metric was undermined, the eNPS initiative stalled, and the organization launched a reevaluation of the entire process.

Someday, it may be possible to obtain relative eNPS—eNPS compared to competitors'— which will provide a more useful lens for improvement targets. In the meantime, it is very productive to rank-order internal teams based on eNPS, and to learn more about the linkage between eNPS and resulting customer NPS for those internal teams. These relative scores can drive learning and progress. We expect that as practitioners gain more experience with eNPS, they will use it to hold team leaders accountable at various levels of the organization for their performance versus peers'. But it is hard to imagine that absolute improvement targets for companywide eNPS will lead to anything other than unhappy results.

Getting Started: Inspirational and Economical Tips

Chapter 9 explains the importance of organizing your adoption of the Net Promoter system with the long journey in mind. Even for loyalty superstars, the quest to improve NPS requires constant effort and continuous rethinking of strategies and tactics. Moreover, plenty of roadblocks crop up along the way, especially as companies begin to improve their performance. Success tends to foster both arrogance and complacency—two mortal enemies of great relationships.

But for most companies, the more relevant and pressing question is this: how do we get started? This question has received regular attention at the NPS Loyalty Forum, and members have come up with a range of useful tactics for launching NPS initiatives. A company that traditionally gave the biggest recognition and rewards to top-grossing salespeople turned heads by creating an even bigger and more prestigious award for the sales rep with the highest NPS. A company famous for its stinginess with IT resources funded the full request for the NPS initiative. Another linked NPS to the bonus plan of its CEO.

As these examples suggest, the most common theme among the success stories is that a company needs some kind of big bang to get everyone's attention. Given daily pressures to meet financial targets, many time-starved managers and employees have become jaded about "customer focus" initiatives. They have seen those initiatives come and go over the years, and they have noticed that quarterly pressures to meet the budget remain ever constant. So leaders need to do something highly visible, with the kind of emotional impact that employees will notice. Moreover, the actions must be credible: employees not only must see that leaders are committed, they must understand how the change in direction will yield economically sustainable results.

When Walt Bettinger was assigned to take over Schwab's retail business, he interviewed one hundred recent customer and employee defectors. By the time he finished, he felt that he had a pretty good idea of the key issues—and one of the biggest, he realized, was the lack of customer focus among the leadership. He came to believe that several members of his executive team were only superficially committed to Schwab's refocus on customer loyalty. When he fired these disbelievers, the organization took notice. Then he began asking the executives who remained what they were hearing from customers. In addition to regularly listening to tapes of calls with detractors, Bettinger began hosting half of his monthly senior leadership team meetings in the field and invited clients to attend and speak to the executives in person. That level of interest in learning about customer issues through the NPS feedback process got plenty of visibility, and the rest of the execs saw that they had better take a similar interest. In other words, Bettinger made sure he had the right people on the bus—executives who really did care about treating customers right—and then he drove the bus out to visit with customers on a regular basis.

Allianz, a global insurance company with €107 ($142) billion revenues in businesses spread across roughly seventy countries, was one of the earliest adopters of the Net Promoter system. The firm announced at its most recent investor day that it has successfully implemented the system in businesses representing more than 80 percent of global revenues. The process has moved remarkably well for such a large and complex organization. During the first eighteen months of its journey, Allianz clearly established the link between top-down, competitive (or relative) NPS and relative growth rates in its top fourteen markets. It developed a rigorous analysis of the economics of creating more promoters and fewer detractors at both the individual and the business-unit level. And it created closed-loop feedback systems enabling customer-facing employees to learn from customers and solve problems for detractors. In 2006, CEO Michael Diekmann reported to investment analysts the results of this economic analysis and the company's goal for improving NPS. This public statement of commitment galvanized the organization as Allianz rolled out its implementation around the world.

At Virgin Media, CEO Neil Berkett knew people in his organization would embrace NPS only if they believed that it would make their lives better—that it represented a path they wanted to follow. Given that the firm was starting from a low Net Promoter score, Berkett was careful to ensure that the organization didn't get overwhelmed by the negative energy of detractors. So he focused first on tens. Teams posted verbatim comments from promoters on what they called a "10-wall." Every company, even one with low overall scores, earns tens from at least some of its customers; recognizing these successes not only feels great to employees, it helps to demonstrate that creating promoters is realistic. Only after that process was well established did Virgin Media's frontline teams begin closing the loop with detractors. To keep the volume of closed-loop feedback calls under control, the company started by calling only those customers who scored it a zero. Later it expanded the calls stepwise, including first ones, then twos, and eventually all detractors.

Like Virgin Media, Progressive began its Net Promoter journey aware that the company needed a more customer-friendly culture. The hole that CEO Glenn Renwick found himself in was not as deep as the one at Virgin Media, but Progressive was an NPS laggard in the U.S. property and casualty insurance business. The celebration of successes played a big role in Renwick's strategy to create energy around NPS. Recall from the previous chapter that he invited the top two hundred claims reps—those with the highest Net Promoter scores from customers—to fly to headquarters for a gala celebration dinner with him. The company created a memento for the honorees—a leather-bound book full of laudatory customer verbatims that would remind them of the energy created by earning a ten and their recognition by the company's top leadership.

Even companies with a strong tradition of customer focus point to highly visible and emotionally memorable actions that helped them intensify this focus. In the early days at Rackspace, chairman Graham Weston worried that it was getting too easy for tech reps cocooned in San Antonio cubicles to forget the importance of providing Fanatical Support. The phones, for instance, might ring many times before customers could get help with their problems. One of the culprits was the automated phone queue—which, like most others around the world, started off every call with the famous recorded words: "Your business is important to us. Your call will be answered in the order it was received. Please press 1 if . . ." Weston recognized the absurd irony in this message: no matter what the words say, making a customer talk to a computer shouts out, *We don't care enough about you to hire a human being to answer your call—because your time is not as valuable as our time.* Weston also noticed that team members became lackadaisical about talking to customers when they were insulated by the automated queue.

So to get the culture back on track, he decided to throw out the phone queue. Now when the phone rings, somebody has to be there to answer it. When people ask Rackers about the beginning of their drive to Fanatical Service, this highly visible action often gets top billing. Rackspace's culture of service continues today: the company's expensive deployment of expert, friendly support techs, available to customers 24/7 by phone or online, continues to distinguish Rackspace from major competitors. Gartner Inc. assesses the strengths and weaknesses of all the key players in this industry. In a report dated December 22, 2010, Gartner says, "Rackspace has long set the bar for customer service in the industry, with proactive, high-touch service and support."[2]

Getting started on the right path usually requires some visible action by senior leadership. The action has to announce that this quest for customer centricity is going to be different—that the organization is really serious about treating customers right. If it is to be credible, people in the organization must understand both the economic and the motivational rationale that support the effort. They must understand that early challenges or disappointments will not sidetrack the journey. And they must begin to see how Net Promoter has an impact on the systems and processes that govern their daily jobs. The following chapter will demonstrate how successful firms have done just this—by starting to hardwire the customer directly into the core processes that drive the business.

8

Close the Loop with Customers

What follows is a story that happened to Fred, so we've written it in the first person. Here's his report:

One April not long ago, I got a mailing from my cable TV provider encouraging me to restart cable service at my summer home. I called the number indicated in the letter, waited two minutes on hold, and finally reached a phone rep. Unfortunately, the rep had no idea how to execute the transaction. After ten minutes researching the procedure, she came back on the line, flustered and apologetic. She told me I would have to call another number. She was very friendly and really wanted to help, but she had never been trained to do this particular task. Since I had volunteered to provide feedback at the end of the call—yes, I was one of those gullible souls who press 1 when the friendly computer voice asks if you would respond to a brief survey after the call—I looked forward to giving some straightforward input. The company was putting this rep in a humiliating situation. And it was wasting my time.

The computerized voice began the survey with these words: "Please provide feedback only on the performance of your representative." I ignored that request because the rep excelled at what she had been trained to do. Question after question droned on; I scored each one a zero, just to be sure the company got the point that something was wrong. Two years later, I have yet to hear anything back from that company, despite what that same nice computer voice said while I was waiting in the phone queue: "We really value your business." Actions speak louder than words, and the clear message I received was that the company couldn't possibly care less about me or my feedback.

Contrast that experience with what happened when a survey from my mobile-phone provider, Verizon Wireless, popped onto my cell phone's message screen. The survey contained only one question: *How likely is it that you would recommend us to a friend?* Of course, I couldn't pass up the opportunity to learn how this company was utilizing such feedback, so I keyed in the score I felt the company deserved—a three (out of ten).

A few days later, I found a message on my home answering machine from a manager at the Verizon store where I had purchased my cell phone. I called her back, and after a couple of rounds of phone tag we finally connected. It turned out she was the area manager, responsible for a handful of local stores. She explained that she had received my feedback, and she wondered if I could take a few minutes to discuss how she might help improve my experience.

I tried my best to be constructive, but a deep reservoir of resentment had accumulated over the previous few years. I launched into the list of complaints: complex pricing schemes; contracts designed to trap me into wasting minutes, incurring outrageous overage fees, or both; inexplicable roaming charges; unintelligible bills; and additional fees for text messages when our plan supposedly included unlimited text messages. You get the picture.

So did the manager I was talking to. First she apologized. Then she explained that most of these things were frustrating to her as well. For a variety of reasons, she said, the wireless industry had adopted these tactics. But her firm was committed to improving them. Some of the changes would take time, but there was one thing she could do for me right now. She had analyzed my recent bills, and she was confident that Verizon had a more suitable plan to offer me. She promised that her store manager would be in touch shortly with a proposed set of changes—and indeed he did get in touch, eventually mailing me new contracts that were much better matched to my needs.

Before the first manager hung up, I asked her what she thought about this system of getting feedback on one question, and then closing the loop with the customer by phone to diagnose the score and determine appropriate responses. Without a moment's hesitation, she exclaimed, "I really love this process." She went on to tell me that for years her company had attempted to put more emphasis on customer satisfaction. But despite all the good intentions, the programs had consistently failed to deliver. "They were add-ons," she explained, "never a core part of the daily workflow."

She continued: "You know, everyone these days is so busy. We're glued to these computer screens that seem to govern our lives. There are not enough hours in the day, so only the urgent items get addressed—and satisfying the customer slips to the bottom of the queue. The advantage of this new approach is that it's simple and practical." She described how the company had hardwired the process into the daily rhythms of team members through their computer screens. Scores are forwarded directly to the store manager, who can then contact customers to understand the situation and resolve problems. Promoter scores receive appropriate celebrations. And all of this feedback informs daily coaching efforts with the team. Managers know that customer responses, corrective actions taken by the company, and promoter celebrations will be part of the weekly staff meeting.

———

Hardwired into the daily rhythms. The companies that achieve outstanding results with the Net Promoter system must do many things right. But if they had to settle on the single most important key to meaningful progress, it might be this: building customer feedback into their regular daily operations and then closing the loop by talking to individual customers and taking appropriate action. "Appropriate action" often involves straightforward service recovery—fixing an individual customer's problem. But it also entails improving products and processes so that every customer gets a better experience and problems don't recur. Ultimately, it may mean reorienting a company's fundamental strategy and priorities to create more promoters and fewer detractors. The key is that the closed-loop feedback, learning, and action must involve everyone, from customer-facing employees through the most senior executives. That way, the entire organization can continually make better decisions—decisions that reflect direct, timely input from customers.

This chapter examines how companies have learned to close the loop with customers at multiple levels of the organization.

Closing the Loop at the Front Line

Every day, managers at each of Charles Schwab's three hundred–plus branch offices and five call centers fire up their computers, log on to Schwab's intranet, and pull up the latest customer-feedback report for their office. Branch manager Cheryl Pasquale, for example, scrolls through the report one day, reviewing how well the six financial consultants she supervises handled the previous day's transactions. She sorts through the aggregate scores from customers, reads the comments from individuals who gave high or low marks, and determines whether any particular kind of interaction elicited praise or complaints.

As she clicks through the screens, Pasquale notices that several customers are frustrated by difficulties in using the in-branch information kiosks. She decides to ask her team for insights about this in their weekly meeting. Some customers are confused by one of Schwab's forms; she reminds herself to raise this issue with other branch managers at the regional meeting later in the month. And she spots an opportunity to counsel a new account rep on how to build better rapport with clients in their next one-on-one training session. Suddenly a *manager alert*—a special notice triggered by a client who has given Schwab a poor rating for a delay in posting a transaction to his account—grabs her attention. The client has indicated that he's willing to discuss the issue in a follow-up call, so Pasquale makes a note to try to reach him that day.

Leading Net Promoter practitioners such as Schwab and Apple work hard to contact every detractor, usually within twenty-four hours. The prompt response not only communicates the important message that the firm really does care about that customer; it also ensures that the disappointing event is still fresh in the customer's (and the employee's) mind. The companies have learned some vital lessons about how to make this process work. Before calling the customer, for example, Schwab managers and supervisors check with employees so that they have the context and background required to help resolve the problem. At Apple, the system automatically forwards details about the customer and the transaction along with the customer's score and verbatim comments so that the call can be as productive as possible. Allianz, noticing that most employees could benefit from training to help them communicate with unhappy customers, developed programs to improve listening skills and teach techniques for discovering root causes. It also scheduled regular forums where employees could share best practices and discuss challenges they could not solve on their own.

Some companies implementing NPS create a separate customer-feedback measurement process and don't integrate it with the standard information flows that drive key decisions and daily priorities on the front line. That's almost always a mistake. At Verizon

Wireless, for instance, only when NPS feedback was automatically integrated into supervisors' daily work systems did the program morph from something nice into something necessary. When people came to understand that root causes, corrective actions, and open detractor alerts would be reviewed at staff meetings, NPS began to get the same level of attention as traditional performance measures such as cost per call and sales quotas.

One of the best ways to ensure that customer feedback packs an emotional wallop is to let employees hear the actual voice of the customer, not just a manager's interpretation or a statistical summary. At Progressive Insurance, supervisors who close the loop with detractors record the call (with customer permission) and then forward the digital voice file to the employee who served that customer. Hearing the customer's voice lets the employee absorb the tone and feel the emotional impact; that alone motivates learning and changes in behavior, with little additional coaching required. Even companies that utilize e-mail surveys and written verbatims have found ways to bring the customer to life. Carolina Biological's customer-service leader selects representative customer comments, and phone reps then read these comments aloud to the entire department at quarterly customer-feedback review sessions. These verbatims are assigned randomly, but the emotional impact is hard to miss. One rep broke down in tears when she realized that the comment she was reading happened to be from a customer she had served.

Finding Patterns

The primary purpose of the frontline closed-loop process is to help individual employees solve problems for individual customers. The process thus helps to shape people's daily priorities and behaviors on the job. But it can also enable companies to spot patterns and thereby determine which processes and policies they need to address at a higher level. In one of Allianz's European health insurance operations, for instance, NPS feedback suggested that unexplained delays were a big source of customer frustrations. When claims representatives followed up with dissatisfied customers, they learned that customers had to call back repeatedly about the status of payments, and that they were expected to describe medical conditions again and again. So a group of reps and supervisors came together to design a process solution. On the initial call, the company would assign a case manager to every policyholder, and the case manager would handle all contact until the claim was resolved. To help manage customer expectations, any delay in the reimbursement process would trigger a call or text message informing the policyholder of the claim's status. Soon after implementing the new protocol, the claims unit saw a double-digit increase in its NPS and a significant rise in policy renewal rates.

Closing the Loop for Mid-Level Managers

Middle managers in operations, product development, marketing, and finance must convert strategies into policies, processes, and products that attract and retain high-value customers. If these managers don't have a steady flow of direct customer feedback, tight budgets and other constraints can lead them to focus on departmental goals and to shunt customer experience to the sideline. If they do receive direct customer feedback, however, they can avoid making poor trade-offs. For instance, instead of spreading improvement efforts equally across every touchpoint, managers can learn to focus on the few that really build or destroy loyalty.

For American Express, one of those vital touchpoints was the replacement of lost or stolen cards. While reviewing the service and operational processes that created the most detractors, company analysts noticed that many initial requests for card replacements went unresolved, requiring a second service call by the customer. Even more alarming, the analysts discovered not only that the highest-value customers experienced a need for card replacement more often than average, but also that their NPS after a card replacement event was almost 25 points lower than the average among other customers. Responding to these findings, the company's operations managers pulled process improvement teams off other, less urgent initiatives and focused them on card replacements. The teams developed new replacement protocols and improved some internal processes, which increased first-call resolution rates by more than 20 percent and raised the NPS of the customers involved to parity with others.

American Express's process offers a good model for any firm. By regularly reviewing each interaction's impact on NPS, companies can identify the biggest culprits—those that occur most frequently and have the greatest impact on scores. They can then devote the necessary resources to developing solutions.

Integrating NPS into Core Processes

Every company has a few core processes that drive its business. NPS must be fully integrated into these processes if it is to produce superior results. Take Logitech, the computer peripherals manufacturer. Logitech releases scores of new or redesigned products each year—a product every four days, on average—and it is the eighteen- to twenty-four-month product design cycle that drives the rhythm of the business. The company makes resource allocation decisions and sets its strategic priorities based on this cycle. It has also designed its management processes and information flows to support the cycle.

Like that of most product-centered companies, Logitech's culture has always emphasized engineering innovation and design.

Since most of Logitech's products are sold through partners or retailers, however, the engineers could find themselves partially insulated from the end user. Of course, the company received feedback through Internet forums, product returns, complaint letters, and its own customer-service phone support. But most of this feedback was anecdotal, and it was often out of date by the time engineers heard it. So it was too easy to ignore. When customer-service reps reported hearing problems about a certain keyboard, for example, engineers might try to re-create the problems on the bench. If they couldn't, they would dismiss the feedback, assuming that the phone rep (who after all was not trained as an engineer) didn't understand the product or had somehow misconstrued the customer's complaint.

Guerrino De Luca, who served as CEO of Logitech from 1998 to 2008 and is now chairman, wanted to make sure that as the firm grew, it would maintain the highest possible level of customer focus. In some ways that meant returning to the past, because Logitech's founders had always believed that delighting customers by providing a superior user experience was a core part of the firm's DNA. "We enjoyed a streak of 40 quarters of double-digit growth," De Luca explains.

> *With that growth came complexity. We were entering new product categories, many with more potentially complex experiences than what we were historically used to, and we were acquiring companies. We quickly found that our culture alone was not enough to ensure great customer experiences. Our independent business units had established their own thresholds for levels of product experience, and increasingly some were overprioritizing cost and schedule at the expense of the user. We decided we needed greater uniformity in our experiences, and generally to raise the bar on what our consumers should expect from us.*

In 2007 he reorganized the executive team, creating a senior vice president of customer experience. Not long thereafter, the company decided to utilize the Net Promoter system.

De Luca assigned one of Logitech's most senior executives to lead the charge. He knew that the only way to really change the culture was to build NPS into the major decision gates along the company's product design cycle. At Logitech, a team of product managers and engineers is responsible for each product. Team members keep a notebook containing the product plan and their progress against the plan, and they regularly present the notebook to senior executives for review. To ensure that NPS would be visible in these reviews, the NPS leader encouraged the redesign of the product notebook's cover sheet. Today, that sheet features three items: the projected release date, the retail price, and the target NPS for the product. If it's a replacement product, the sheet will include the NPS for the prior model as well.

Junien Labrousse, executive vice president of products, reports that every engineer now knows the target NPS for his or her product—and knows how the target compares to the actual NPS the product earns from customers once it's in the marketplace. "The engineers love the rapid feedback they get from customer verbatims," he says. "It creates an emotional link between their work and the customer result."

Success stories reflecting this feedback soon began to spread throughout the company. For example, Logitech found that its much-heralded MX 5000 keyboard—its first to incorporate Bluetooth functionality—was falling short of its target NPS. Analysis of detractor verbatims revealed the three most serious problems: the Bluetooth connectivity wasn't sufficiently reliable, the LCD screen was hard to read, and recharging was difficult. By focusing the engineering redesign on these three issues, the company was able to rack up Net Promoter scores 27 points higher on the next model.

Logitech regularly uses NPS results to rank-order its product lines and was surprised to discover that its webcams weren't doing nearly as well as expected. Detractor analysis again revealed the problem: customers loved the webcam once it was up and running, but they had problems with the setup. Digging deeper, the engineers found that the problem was not the webcam itself but the software applications it was designed to work with. After all other avenues failed, Logitech decided to acquire a software firm that could package software applications together with the webcam so setup would be automatic. The webcam's Net Promoter scores jumped nearly 10 points. Logitech executives believe that the strength of the Logitech brand reflects the NPS of the individual products that carry the brand. So they are particularly pleased that it has become a badge of honor among engineers to have their product ranked near the top of the NPS table.

One of the implementation tactics that most affected Logitech's culture was putting NPS teeth into the final decision gate that each product must pass before it is released to manufacturing. This so-called Gate-X process involves testing of prototypes by twenty-five customers, who then provide feedback. Leaders adopted a minimum hurdle for the NPS from these customers—and if a product fails to meet that hurdle, it is sent back for rework until its NPS passes muster. Any company like Logitech feels pressure to rush products to market in order to meet revenue targets and keep retailers happy. But when the company canceled two products and delayed two others because of low NPS at Gate-X, one executive told us, "people got the message about how serious they were about NPS. The company lost two quarters of revenue from those products, over $4 million. But it was the right decision for their reputation, for the brand, and ultimately for long-term profits."

As with frontline feedback, successful companies ensure that middle management and technical teams hear NPS feedback directly. The same executive adds, "There was a real temptation to build a staff group who could gather the customer feedback and interpret it for the engineers, whose time is precious. But we didn't do that. We made sure the customer scores and verbatims got pushed directly to the product teams so it could affect their thinking. The product teams understood the products better than any central group could. They knew the design trade-offs being considered for upcoming products, and they could make the emotional connection to the end user. Reading a comment from a customer promoter or detractor has far more impact than looking at a statistic on a monthly report from headquarters."

Closing the Loop for Senior Executives

A company's senior executives are ultimately responsible for ensuring that the organization creates more promoters and fewer detractors. And they control many of the most powerful tools for achieving this goal. They determine which customers to target. They decide what strategies to adopt, how to allocate resources, how to structure the organization, and how to measure and reward people's performance. But do these senior executives close the loop with customers to find out what's on their minds? Not often enough. Too many companies delegate the job to sales and marketing departments, to researchers, or to the people who run local branches. Senior leaders peruse market-research surveys and think they are in touch with the customer. But they aren't.

NPS leaders do it differently. Nearly all of them have crafted ways for top executives to stay in touch with customers directly and with the frontline employees who serve customers every day.

Bill McNabb, for example, is CEO of the Vanguard Group, the largest mutual fund company in America with about $1.4 trillion in assets under management. He could easily fill his calendar with administrative duties, managing direct reports, and seeing to his regulatory responsibilities. But he doesn't; he and every other senior executive make time when call volumes are high for what Vanguard calls its Swiss Army. As in Switzerland, where everyone has to serve in the army, every senior Vanguard executive must staff the customer-service phones during peak periods. Working shoulder to shoulder with Vanguard crew members, McNabb and the others find that this time offers an invaluable link to their customers' concerns and priorities. The experience also makes them painfully aware of the challenges presented by the complex systems, policies, and procedures that phone reps must wrestle with every day. In times of crisis, such as a market crash, all execs drop what they are doing and head to the call center.

Scott Cook, cofounder and former CEO of Intuit, a man whose naturally quantitative bent was reinforced by his training as a product manager at Procter & Gamble, puts only limited faith in market-research surveys. The only real way to understand customers, he says, is to observe them in person, and to talk with them face-to-face. Cook established a famous tradition for Intuit executives: participating in customer "follow-me-homes," where two or three Intuit employees get permission to watch over a customer's shoulder as he or she installs and uses the company's software. Afterward they ask questions and probe concerns. Then they share and compare these lessons with the experiences of other follow-me-homes.

When Intuit adopted the NPS framework and generated a list of specific promoters and detractors, the most effective executives did not commission market-research follow-ups. Instead, they and each member of their business leadership teams took the names of ten detractors and called or e-mailed these customers to see what Intuit could learn. When the executives reconvened and shared their conversations, they could begin to implement improvements right away—and they could commission deeper research in the few places where the solutions were still elusive.

So it is at other NPS companies. Each board meeting at Cancer Treatment Centers of America (CTCA) takes place at one of the company's treatment centers rather than at an isolated headquarters facility. The meeting begins with a patient talking about his or her recent experience at that center. After board members chat with the patient—and before they do anything else—they review NPS data and trends. At Rackspace, the company's IT system randomly routes several customer NPS responses each week to CEO Lanham Napier, who then calls those customers. Napier also adopted CTCA's board-meeting practice as soon as he learned of it. Rackspace's board meetings now include a customer visit—sometimes a promoter, sometimes a detractor—and the company has redesigned its board book to focus first on customer NPS, then on employee NPS, and finally on operating statistics and financials. Napier has also made it a tradition to invite a customer to address his troops at each open-book session—regular internal meetings where he explains the company's financial results. Whatever the specific message, flying a customer executive to San Antonio for these events demonstrates a commitment that everyone recognizes. Employees often find that it is easier to hear and accept feedback from a customer than from a boss.

The Top-Level Strategy Processes

At the top of an organization, of course, the job isn't just to listen to customers but to use that information to shape major strategy and resource allocation decisions. Each company has a handful of core processes that drive top-level decision making: the annual budgeting process, strategic planning cycles, capital investment approvals, business reviews, investor days, board meetings, and so forth. At leading NPS companies such as Intuit, leaders have integrated NPS into every one of these core processes.

Every Intuit business, for example, includes NPS targets and key initiatives for boosting its scores in its strategic plan. Top executives discuss NPS at the company's annual Investor Days, and business-line leaders provide more detail about their results and plans. The company's strategic goal, also shared with investors, is to achieve an NPS advantage of at least 10 points more than the nearest competitor. (See exhibit 8-1, which was included in the company's 2010 Investor Day report.) The reason for this goal is that Intuit executives are committed to growth—and they passionately believe that having more promoters than the competition is a prime driver of profitable growth. When the company is considering an acquisition, a major factor in the decision is whether the potential acquiree enjoys sector-leading NPS. One of

EXHIBIT 8-1

Intuit versus competitors

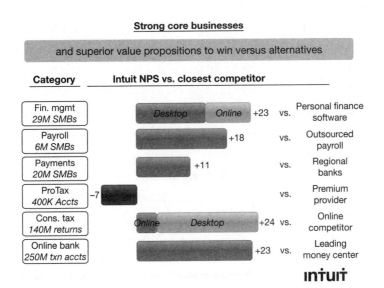

Source: Intuit 2010 Annual Investor Day presentation.

the attractions of PayCycle, the payroll processing firm acquired by Intuit in 2009, was its stellar NPS of over 70 percent.

Rackspace's executive team also uses potential acquirees' NPS in making acquisition decisions. One vital strategic decision, says chairman Graham Weston, was Rackspace's acquisition of Slice-Host. The software developed by SliceHost greatly accelerated Rackspace's entry into the hypergrowth market for cloud computing. "We were trying to decide between two alternative acquisition targets," Weston explains. "They both looked promising from a technology standpoint, but when we examined their customer NPS, SliceHost became the obvious priority. Their outstanding customer loyalty has proven to be an enormous asset to us."

Philips has quantified the strategic value of NPS leadership, setting a goal of earning 50 percent of its revenue from businesses that occupy NPS leadership positions in their industries. To reach that goal, Philips's executives have made a series of bold strategic moves. The company's lighting business, for example, represented one of its strongest sectors in terms of NPS, and in recent years the company made a series of acquisitions to strengthen its position still further. Some major acquisitions bolstered Philips's position in LED technology, which was relevant for the lighting sector over-all, while others extended Philips's leadership position in the pro-fessional lighting business. Reinforcing these acquisitions with additional investments designed to improve quality and service relative to competitors, the lighting division now registers 94 per-cent of its sales in businesses where it holds NPS leadership or coleadership positions. The lighting division is expected to con-tribute 50 percent of the entire company's growth in the current five-year strategic plan.

In addition to feeding its high-NPS businesses, Philips has been starving or divesting businesses where NPS leadership is unrealis-tic. For example, it pulled back from its television manufacturing business for a variety of business reasons, including the fact that it had low potential for NPS leadership, by spinning off its Chinese and Indian operations and licensing the Philips name in the U.S. market. The company also reorganized its health-care business to improve the customer's experience and build customer loyalty, moving from a product-based structure to one based on customers and local markets. This required enormous effort, but it was a necessary shift if the company was to achieve its customer experience and NPS goals in that sector.

Analyzing Customer Verbatims

Like frontline employees, senior executives can establish an emotional connection with customers by reading or hearing verbatim comments directly. Of course, when the volume of responses is in the millions, it's impractical to rely only on scanning a sample of comments. So NPS trailblazers have developed effective tools for harnessing and analyzing this fire hose flow of customer commentary. American Express, Apple Retail, and Intuit, for instance, utilize commercially available software to sort through the comments. These tools track the frequency of various keywords and their relationships to other keywords, and then generate a report summarizing the priority issues. Executives examining the patterns can determine which items require immediate attention from the top and which can inform strategic priorities. Apple, for example, discovered that its popular products and eye-catching store design were not the number one topics promoters cited. Rather, the top reason for promoters' enthusiasm about the stores was the friendly, helpful, and knowledgeable service received from store employees. This message reinforced executives' commitment to investing in hiring, training, and developing outstanding store personnel.

Progressive, the insurance company, decided to create its own internal tool to analyze verbatim comments from customers. But its approach is similar. By tracking the frequency of words and word combinations, Progressive can highlight the most common elements from customer comments. The approach helped the company revamp its online payment process. It had begun to offer customers the option of paying through electronic funds transfer (EFT), believing that this would both improve the customer experience (resulting in higher retention rates) and reduce costs. It promoted the option aggressively, and it found that Net Promoter scores for customers who chose it were well above average for the company at the time. All this data seemed to reinforce the wisdom of the strategy. However, Progressive executives noticed something strange when they examined verbatims. They found that *online payment* was showing up as one of the most frequently mentioned phrases in detractors' comments as well as in promoters'. Upon further analysis, they discovered that when the online payment process went smoothly on the first try, customer NPS was significantly higher. When it failed to go smoothly, NPS was 20 points lower. And the process was failing 18 percent of the time. These failures resulted from bank policies that allowed the first month's payment to be processed with a verbal request while requiring a "wet" signature to continue making repeated payments. If the bank didn't get the signature, the EFT failed, and Progressive then billed the customer via conventional mail. That was confusing, and it was more likely to result in missed payments and cancellations for nonpayment.

Progressive redesigned the payment system by negotiating a new process with its billing partners. The new process enabled customers to utilize an automated phone call ("press 1 if you agree to ongoing monthly payments") to obtain an electronic signature, thus avoiding the wet signature. After implementing the solution, managers were delighted to see that the frequency of detractor verbatims citing *online payment* had dropped out of the top-twenty list, and policyholder retention subsequently improved. That gave executives the confidence to renew promotion of the online payment option—which now generates an average NPS from customers that is 8 points higher than that of non-EFT customers.

Building Customer Communities

Another important tool for integrating NPS and the voice of the customer into vital decision processes up and down the organization is *customer communities*—groups that provide regular feedback on company products and services. For example, Adobe Systems launched a Web-based community for graphic designers and developers in 1999. Marketplace & Exchange, as it is now known, supports millions of regular visitors; the visitors, in turn, provide the company with a regular source of ideas for improvements and new products. At Harley-Davidson, all the senior executives make annual outings to Harley Owners Group (H.O.G) gatherings, relying on those interactions to stay current with their customers as well as with the dealers who sponsor the gatherings. SAS Institute, a loyalty leader in statistical analytical software, involves its phone tech representatives in creating what's known as the SASware Ballot. Each team elects a representative to the customer council, and the representative then polls the team to identify the most important issues arising in their daily telephone interactions. The council discusses these issues, and engineers parse possible improvements into bite-size investments. The company then makes a list of potential improvements—this is the SASware Ballot—and posts it on its Web site. Thousands of users, representing more than ten thousand software licensees, vote on priorities. The last step in this cycle of representative democracy is a set of regional meetings with customers to share the results and discuss plans for addressing the top vote getters.

Many Net Promoter companies take the customer-community approach even further by finding all kinds of ways to involve customers. LEGO User Groups (LUGS), for example, organize exhibitions where members can show off their creative designs, ranging from new urban landscapes to imaginary kingdoms and working robot models. These events serve both as conventions for fans and as public exhibits of the fans' best work. In 2010, more than 2 million visitors, mainly families with children, attended a LEGO fan-organized event. While the LUGS themselves bear most of the expenses, the company in many cases provides in-kind donations of LEGO products and bulk LEGO bricks. Company representatives attend many of the events to learn and get feedback from the community. LEGO fans also participate in events organized directly by the LEGO Group. The peer voting process for best displays at all these events shows the company what kind of products are of greatest interest to the community; some recent LEGO sets have been inspired by winning designs at the exhibitions. Since the LEGO Group distributes most of its products through retailers, the company benefits enormously from the face-to-face interactions at events like these.

The LEGO Group also operates the Web site www.designbyME .lego.com. This site offers customers an opportunity to design and purchase custom LEGO products, including a unique building guide and custom box. It offers a tutorial on how to download and use the LEGO Digital Designer software package, and it provides access to an extensive gallery (with private and public view) where customers can share their designs. The designbyME Web site also offers periodic design and building competitions; it gives awards to the best new product designs and displays them on the site. The design expertise of LEGO community members helps improve existing products as well. When the company halted production on its new Excavator 8043 model because customers were reporting problems with the digging arm, expert consumers came to the defense of the management decision on community boards. (This is an example of what NPS companies often call the "promoter defense shield.") The expert consumers also quickly got involved in suggesting and critiquing alternative solutions. Their engagement and involvement greatly accelerated the firm's response and enabled manufacturing to schedule production in time for the holiday shopping season.

Another leader in the utilization of customer communities has been Intuit's Consumer Tax Group, which developed the Inner Circle program mentioned in chapter 2. More than one hundred thousand customers have volunteered to participate by logging on to the TurboTax Web site and registering by supplying basic demographic information as well as their response to the Ultimate Question: "How likely is it that you would recommend TurboTax to friends or colleagues?" Then, based on whether they are promoters, passives, or detractors, customers are asked a specific open-ended follow-up question. Detractors are asked the reason or reasons for their score. Passives are asked what it would take for them to rate TurboTax a ten—essentially, what it would take to make them a promoter. Promoters are asked what, specifically, they would tell someone to get them to try TurboTax. All three groups can then register their priorities for enhancing service in any area of the customer experience, be it shopping, buying, installing, using, or contacting tech support. In short, what is it that would delight them most?

An additional benefit to the company comes from analyzing verbatim comments—particularly the highest-ranking ones—to understand the language and choice of words that resonate most with customers. For example, Intuit learned from its dialogue with promoters the top items that promoters value and would mention to nonusers. The responses articulated the precise advantages of the products in the language used by its biggest fans. Intuit could then incorporate this learning directly into marketing messages and advertising copy. One final benefit of asking promoters to express what they would tell a friend is that once they articulate the answer, they are more likely to relay it to a friend just because it's on the tip of their tongue and the top of their mind.

This novel approach to gathering customer insight seems to appeal to customers themselves. The completion rate for these sessions is over 85 percent, much higher than that observed for a typical market-research survey. Also, although the sessions are anonymous, users get the option of providing contact information, and more than 75 percent do. This enables Intuit to contact these customers and drill down for additional information or ask them to provide feedback on proposed changes. For example, when customers voiced their displeasure with rebates, the company could go back and ask those customers to provide specific details. Was it the awkward proof of purchase, the slow turnaround time, or the amount of the rebate that needed attention? Similarly a dialogue with detractors could isolate their complaints with tech support and could float alternative solutions for feedback. Barry Saik, vice president of product management for the Consumer Group, notes, "We regularly use Inner Circle to help brainstorm solutions and to understand if our internal solutions are acceptable to customers."

The Consumer Group also recognized that the most valuable feedback might come from some of the company's most unhappy former customers. So staffers monitored message boards and blogs and invited some of the most vociferous detractors to join the Inner Circle. Better to enlist these recruits to help fix the problems, the company figured, than letting them go on venting their anger unconstructively. As it turned out, one of the most powerful drivers of customer delight is a company's commitment to listening and responding to complaints and suggestions. The commitment proves that the company values its customers and takes care of them—basic requirements for any good relationship. When it became clear that Intuit really wanted to listen to their concerns and fix them, many archdetractors of TurboTax became promoters.

Customer communities can help a company improve its business. They can also provide valuable service directly to other customers. Brad Smith, onetime head of the Consumer Group and currently Intuit's CEO, has become a big supporter of customer communities; he likes to tell the story of how one of his consumer tax team members suggested setting up a chat capability inside the TurboTax software so that customers could talk to one another there, rather than searching for external tax forums. Though Smith was initially skeptical, the "live community" feature has proved successful. As Intuit monitored the conversations among customers, it found that the quality and accuracy of suggestions from other customers was impressive. Advice about using the software was just as good as that provided by Intuit's internal customer-service team, and their answers to questions about taxes were superior to the advice obtained directly from the IRS.

————

Most companies want their cultures to become more customer focused. The Net Promoter system offers a broad set of tools and techniques to help accomplish this goal, but none is more powerful than closing the loop to thank customers for their feedback, to probe for root causes, to learn how to serve them better, and to take appropriate action. At its core, however, NPS is much more than a measurement or service-recovery process. It is a way of doing business based on treating people right. When customers signal that you have failed them by providing a detractor score, there is far more than a practical business reason to close the loop;

there is a moral imperative. Failing to close the loop with detractors is failing to treat them with dignity and respect. Whenever a manager neglects to call back a detractor, the message is clear: living up to a customer's expectations and righting failures are simply not top priorities. This message is equally clear to employees. In a world where no one has enough time to finish every task, closing the loop has to be hardwired into the daily workflow so that it becomes an automatic part of the core decision making. Only then can you hope to realize the potential benefits of NPS.

Net Promoter star performers such as Apple, Schwab, Rackspace, and Intuit consistently work to contact every detractor within twenty-four hours. Most achieve this target over 90 percent of the time. How often does this happen in your organization?

9

Organize for the Long Journey

The NPS Loyalty Forum held its founding meeting at the headquarters of American Express in New York City on October 5, 2006. Since then the forum has met dozens of times at member facilities across Europe and North America. Long-term members such as Intuit, American Express, and Apple Retail have been utilizing the Net Promoter system for more than five years. Remarkably, the pace of learning and progress at these quarterly gatherings continues to accelerate, even for the veterans. They continue to discover new approaches and tactics that strengthen basic tools such as closed-loop feedback. They also continue to learn new applications of the NPS framework in areas such as finance, cost management, human resources, and communications. One of the forum's original members often reminds us: "Since NPS touches every part of the organization, it is only reasonable that we prepare for a very long journey."

A long journey, indeed. The amount of work, planning, and follow-up required to achieve the full benefits of NPS came as a surprise to many of the companies. Gerard Kleisterlee, CEO of Philips, expected that the NPS initiative at his company would be at full sail within a year or two, and that he could then turn his attention to other priorities. Three years into the program, he had a different view. "We adopted NPS because it fit so nicely with our 'sense and simplicity' branding," he explains. "The notion is so clear and intuitive, I presumed that the organization would rapidly adopt and integrate Net Promoter into our core processes. But I now realize this level of cultural change management takes time—and lots of leadership attention. It is amazing, given how simple and intuitive the concept is, how much hard work is required. Getting the metrics solid so they can be trusted by the front line and the board, convincing the various business lines that this is the right approach, helping them quantify the economics, training front line and middle managers, creating closed loops for customers and channel partners . . . this was time well spent. But it does take time!"

To accelerate the drive toward a customer focus, Kleisterlee made NPS one of the key performance indicators affecting executive compensation. He also required the organization to report scores regularly to the board of directors. That meant educating the entire organization about both the Net Promoter score and the Net Promoter system. It meant building a reliable measurement process that could be audited. The Philips leadership team had to negotiate performance targets that were both inspirational and strategically rational given the full set of corporate objectives. It also meant building organizational capabilities to act on the feedback from customers. Before long, the leadership team put in place a global network of NPS change agents to work arm in arm with local teams to develop and adapt the system to each business. Team members learned during the first two years that NPS was the right approach, but they also learned that this initiative would take far more support and leadership than expected.

So the payoff and the commitment involved in Net Promoter are both substantial. You can get the most bang for the buck if you understand this going in, and if you organize the NPS initiative with care from the beginning. This chapter will outline what's necessary to prepare for the long haul.

Assign the Right Leaders and Position Them for Success

Leaders who have generated great results through Net Promoter viewed the initiative as a long journey of cultural change and growth from the beginning. It was never a tool or a program, to be used for a while and then discarded. They were looking for a way to create a culture that was centered on the customer. They sought to improve competiveness and accelerate organic growth. Their first step was to assign someone to lead the effort—someone with the right background, skills, and experience. But who should this be?

Sometimes it seems natural to center the NPS initiative in marketing. This was the choice that Kleisterlee made at Philips: he assigned his new chief marketing officer (CMO), Geert van Kuyck, to lead the change effort. Fortunately, van Kuyck realized that his job was really to make sure the operational business heads embraced NPS and became the driving force behind putting the customer at the center of the business. Marketing could play only a supporting role, providing education, communication, tools, and techniques. Giving the responsibility for NPS-driven change management to the CMO worked at Philips, but choosing the head of marketing may carry risks. For example, people may come to see NPS only as a tool for gauging the customer experience, without any other implications. At Enterprise Rent-A-Car, Andy Taylor decided to assign the ESQi process to his rental operations executives rather than the marketing group, specifically because he wanted line operators to own and trust the process.

Chuck Schwab assigned the NPS leadership role to Chris Dodds, who was then chief financial officer. Locating the effort in the CFO's office, Schwab believed, would help ensure rigorous analytics that the entire organization would trust. It would also allow NPS to guide the company's ongoing cost reduction efforts, which were also led by the CFO's office. Moreover, Schwab wanted to report Net Promoter scores to shareholders, and he knew that the CFO would need to have full confidence in the system before he would agree to do so.

At Virgin Media, CEO Neil Berkett appointed Sean Risebrow to lead the effort. Risebrow came out of corporate branding, but Berkett made a point of rotating Risebrow's team through a variety of positions in the organization based on the focus of change. Risebrow describes his journey this way:

> Neil felt it was important to have a single senior leader responsible for ensuring that all parts of the organization were embracing Net Promoter. Interestingly, he regarded success at the start not by how much the leadership team around him was using and talking about NPS but by how much a call center agent or installer knew about NPS when he met them. Originally we were part of the Brand team—great customer service is part of the Virgin brand, and NPS was the operating discipline we adopted at the rebranding of the company. We then moved to Serve—operations and network—when the focus came to be on operational improvements. We are now part of Grow—marketing, sales, and customer acquisition— as the focus is on the end-to-end relationship improvements now required.

Risebrow concludes, "Our goal remains constant: to embed the skills and knowledge in all our operations and not in a central customer experience team."

As these examples suggest, there is no single formula for success when it comes to selecting the person who will lead the adoption of the Net Promoter system. But three guidelines are critical. First, the leader must have the right skills, experience, personal qualities, and energy. At British Gas, for example, Gas Services CEO Chris Weston needed someone who could lead NPS in a turnaround situation. His designee was Eddy Collier, a direct report responsible for residential heating installation services. Collier's background in finance and consulting gave him the necessary skills to lead the turnaround. A second guideline: consider where the greatest changes must be made, and organize the initiative accordingly. A leader who is broadly respected and trusted across the organization can set and reset priorities to focus on finance, human resources, marketing, product development, pricing, or customer service—wherever the need is greatest.

The third guideline may be most important. In every case where NPS has generated great results, the change leader has reported directly to the CEO or an important business unit's general manager. Pushing the leadership role below this level signals to the organization that Net Promoter isn't really a top priority. It also makes it hard to engage senior leaders in situations where they must actively drive change. As we'll see in the following section, NPS often requires major shifts in strategy, structure, or policy that only top executives can initiate.

Pull the Organization Together

Done right, Net Promoter affects virtually every aspect of a company. It always requires buy-in and active support from the finance function. Finance has to develop credible economics and integrate them into the standard analyses and management reports used to make decisions and determine priorities. Process quality and operational excellence executives usually play vital roles too. NPS helps reveal the processes that most need attention, and of course, solutions need to be gauged by customer feedback as well as by internal process statistics. Even the public relations and communications functions may undergo a change. "In the old days," says Allianz's head of group communications, Emilio Galli-Zugaro, "our job was to educate and influence the news media—but today, we realize our reputation is driven by what our customers and employees are saying about us, not by our press releases. By utilizing the Net Promoter framework, we are redefining the role of communications and rethinking the best ways to communicate with our customers and employees."

But the very fact that NPS cuts across functional organizations that may have differing goals and views of what is right opens up new opportunities. Given the right leadership, companies can solve problems that in the past might have run smack into cross-functional barriers. A U.S.-based bank provides a case in point. The firm's CEO—we'll call him James Smith—had stressed the primacy of customer focus for years, and frontline customer-service teams began to make good initial progress within their groups by focusing on transactional NPS. While the company made great improvements in service during the first year or two, progress began to stall because executives from other functions weren't yet on board. The executive responsible for customer service explained, "It was just too easy for execs in other functions to ignore our old satisfaction scores. They didn't identify with the index; it seemed theoretical. That changed only later, when we all shifted to Net Promoter. Now, when customers indicate they wouldn't recommend us to a friend, the whole executive team takes it personally." This personal connection was essential because, as CEO Smith realized, further progress would require help from other functional leaders.

One issue, for example, was that some of the company's most profitable customers were having their identity verified when they attempted to make a purchase at a store with one of the bank's credit cards. Customers found it frustrating and embarrassing to take the phone from the clerk and then recite their mother's maiden name, the amount of their last transaction, or other identifying information. While the process was designed to prevent theft and fraud, it was happening far too frequently for the highest-value customers—and far too frequently for the president of the retail business, who wanted the company's brand to stand for exceptional service and utility. But the fraud control function (which was part of the risk management organization) had a job to do as well. Fraud expense was part of that function's scorecard, which determined bonuses. And while the fraud controllers knew that they sometimes frustrated the company's desire to create promoters from the high-value customers, they dug in their heels. Their analysis showed that, on average, the decision to stop potentially fraudulent transactions at the point of sale was profitable, even when customer dissatisfaction and frustration were taken into account.

The company faced another challenge too. Payment disputes—cases in which a customer challenges a charge appearing on the monthly statement—were costly to resolve, frustrating for the consumer, and often dissatisfying for merchants. While the company had developed a reputation for exceptional service in the case of disputes, its attempt to reduce operating costs by handling these calls overseas had begun to create more detractors. In many cases, a simple explanation of the merchant's full name or a little help remembering a particular purchase was all that a customer required to resolve the question. Without the right level of cultural context, the overseas representatives had difficulty expressing the right level of empathy or jogging the customers' memories.

Smith realized that it would take more than repeating the company's dedication to service leadership to get the various functions to pull together. He had to increase their focus by changing the incentive system for his senior team and others. While the former bonus framework held leaders accountable for a balanced scorecard—the company established goals for improvements in shareholder, customer, and employee metrics, and the board assigned ratings based on performance against those metrics—the customer goals were often shareholder metrics in disguise. For example, new customer acquisition and growth in revenue per customer were part of some groups' customer goals. Smith's new plan increased the weight placed on customer goals and increased the emphasis on true customer metrics, including NPS. Now, even functional execs would not be happy with their incentive compensation unless the company reached its NPS goals. The change led to more energy and cooperation across functional lines to solve root causes of detraction and to discover economical ways of creating promoters.

Neil Berkett of Virgin Media ran into a similar set of challenges when his organization adopted NPS. "The top of the organization quickly embraces NPS," he says. "Once they see the connection to economics and growth, they get on board fast. The front lines come on board even faster. They find it inspirational to focus on making their customers happy—and it makes their jobs easier. The place that takes a lot of effort is in the middle of the organization, which is composed of functional executives." This is understandable. These executives have expertise in running their own function, such as network operations or accounts receivable, and they track progress with function-specific statistics, such as cost per call or percent bad debt. They may find it difficult to relate to the broader customer experience. This, says Berkett, means that any NPS initiative must include a lot of education. It also involves changing the way functional executives measure their success. "They knew how to control the historic metrics to make their bonus," he says. "Adding in some newfangled customer loyalty metric like NPS is more challenging."

The progress at Virgin Media has been impressive—15 points of improvement in Net Promoter scores—but it took even more work than Berkett anticipated. In addition to the shifts in measurement capabilities and bonus programs, Berkett himself had to put a significant amount of energy into communications and regularly reinforce the role of NPS. He also made sure to provide plenty of recognition to the executives responsible for successes. Thanks to these efforts, NPS has received a lot of visibility among the rest of the Virgin companies, many of which have also begun to adopt the Net Promoter system. But they have all heard this warning from Berkett: "This is not as simple as it can first appear. NPS is not just a measure; it is a way of doing business."

Reorganize Around the Customer

Often, the NPS initiative requires reorganizing frontline teams into smaller units that are more accountable, or creating cross-functional teams that can effectively deal with the full customer experience. Either move may require rethinking the responsibilities of the frontline supervisor. In bank branches, for example, managers may need to get out of their office and spend more time on the floor with customers.

Reorganizing the front line was one of the most significant changes Berkett had to make at Virgin Media. Historically, the phone centers that provided customer support were part of the sales and marketing function. That made some sense; as at many companies, it was marketing that cared most about hearing the voice of the customer and building customer loyalty. But locating the call centers in marketing made things difficult for customers, who often needed to make multiple phone calls to resolve a problem. Berkett restructured the organization, grouping the phone centers under the executive responsible for the network and the installation and service crews. The result? Listen again to Sean Risebrow: "Previously a customer could spend days travelling across functional silos, having to make repeated phone calls to manage the process. Today, seventy-five percent of customers now receive resolution the same day or the next day, along with a much better experience. Our cost to serve is actually lower, as we have removed some of the cost of failure." Overall, he adds, the company finds that it costs 25 percent more each year to serve zeros—rock-bottom detractors—than to serve the promoters who give tens.

At Logitech, the NPS journey started with a substantial reorganization. All product business units were grouped under one executive, and all the customer-facing functions under a newly appointed chief marketing officer. The new customer-facing group included marketing, corporate quality, customer care, and a new Customer Experience Team, an independent body designed to represent the customer's voice. Glenn Rogers, the team leader, explains its mission this way: "We just encourage the rest of the company to follow the Golden Rule, which we always found impossible to argue against." At Logitech, most of the customer experience depended on direct interaction with the product, and the hardwiring of NPS into the product design effort, as described in chapter 8, was vital. But the Net Promoter framework also convinced leaders to rethink the way they organized frontline customer interactions. They reengineered the customer care function, shifting from a regional cost center using fourteen outsourced partners to a unified global operation with a single outsourced partner. Where the old contracts were based on handle times, call volumes, and the like, the new vendor agreement depends mainly on NPS metrics.

At Rackspace, the restructuring of the front line was even more extensive. As the firm expanded, it naturally adopted the functional organizational structure of most large companies. The sales group took responsibility for sales, finance for billing and accounts receivable, and so on. As at Virgin Media, however, phone reps often had to transfer customers' calls to one of the functional areas, or else contact that function themselves later in the day and then call the customer back the following day. The communication not only was inefficient; it also caused numerous problems from poor handoffs across departments. For example, salespeople who might not be familiar with a customer's unique technical attributes were writing up new orders that could not be configured correctly by the technical teams. Simple change requests that might take a few seconds ended up being routed to engineering groups, and they sometimes took hours or days to execute.

So Rackspace leaders made a radical move. They asked the account management phone teams to brainstorm with the other departments and come up with the ideal organizational structure for a world-class customer experience. After much debate and discussion, that group recommended creating cross-functional teams staffed with representatives from every major function that touched customers. The leaders liked the fresh thinking but wondered if the proposed solution could work. At the time, the company structured its hiring and career development around the functions. It structured workflow and IT systems around functions as well. Some leaders feared costs might skyrocket in this new "matrix" structure, as it was called, and others wondered whether customers would really be happier. To test it out, they decided to pilot two matrix teams comprising a mix of specialists who would work side by side to serve a defined book of customers.

The results were eye-opening. Net Promoter scores for customers served by these pilot teams were much higher than those for the rest of the company. First-call resolution of customer problems jumped from 55 percent to over 90 percent. Costs and error rates declined substantially. And no wonder. Before the matrix, teams often sat in different buildings, with no easy way to communicate and no personal relationships or team metrics to facilitate accountability and learning. Now, account managers could finish up a phone call with a customer whose order had been entered incorrectly and then ask the sales rep at the next desk to explain the problem. And when a customer called with a technical issue, the account manager could get it resolved promptly by the technician on the other side of the desk (and could learn more about technical issues in the process). The matrix teams showed substantial improvement in the growth of their book of customers as well as in their Net Promoter scores. Interestingly, employee NPS ratings surged as well. For these employees, as for most, it was more rewarding to work in a team setting with easy communication, joint accountability, and all the resources required to get the job done for the customer. This kind of restructuring could never have happened if executives had originally pigeonholed the NPS initiative in the marketing or account service function.

Net Promoter trailblazers such as Rackspace, Virgin Media, Allianz, and others have found that aligning accountability and authority around customers based on the way they interact with the organization provides an enormous boost to Net Promoter progress.

Hire and Fire the Right People

Important as the frontline restructuring may be, Rackspace's leaders believe that yet another factor is even more significant in building and sustaining the company's culture of Fanatical Support. That factor: hiring the right kind of people. "It really comes down to core values, and we don't train our employees in core values," says CEO Lanham Napier. "Their parents did that a long time ago." Though Rackspace seeks technical proficiency in many of its hires, that is not the priority. Tech skills can be taught; attitude cannot. So successful job applicants must demonstrate that they really care about taking care of others. As Napier puts it, "We hire geeks who like to serve." Rackspace holds team members accountable for the NPS of their customers, to make sure that the metric gets as much attention as the financials. But it is not the NPS-related bonus that makes Rackers want to serve. That desire has to be part of their basic makeup.

Barbara Talbott, longtime marketing chief (now retired) for the Four Seasons Hotels group, echoes Rackspace's sentiment. When it comes to delivering a superior customer experience, she is convinced that it is the character of the frontline employees that matters most:

> *Delighting guests means putting kindness and intelligence into action. Often, delight comes from something small that doesn't cost a great deal—offering a pot of tea to someone who arrives with a cold, for example. You can't script or incentivize staff to do this. It would feel mechanical and lack authenticity. And it's not necessary. If you have the right people on board, they come to work with that motivation. They take personal pride and satisfaction in seeing to it that guests are well cared for. Just as important, you must select and develop the right people as front-line leaders so they can create an environment in which people can be their best.*

In other words, if you hire the right employees, you don't need to pay them extra to delight a customer; that should be the most fun and rewarding part of their job. The right people do it with no special encouragement; you simply need to put them in situations where they can delight customers in an economically rational manner—and then get out of their way.

The Four Seasons hotel chain has built a worldwide culture that puts the customer experience at the top of every employee's agenda. And the culture does begin with hiring the right people. Every candidate, from dishwashers on up, will have four or five interviews before being hired. The last interview is with the general manager of the hotel. Since the Four Seasons culture is based on service, managers look for employees who demonstrate the right attitude toward serving others. They don't look for applicants who can be trained to make people feel important; they want people who genuinely *believe* that people are important. The company seems to be unusually successful in achieving this goal. Andrew Harper, the pseudonymous publisher of *Andrew Harper's Hideaway Report* travel newsletter, comments, "Four Seasons seems to have a better instinct for picking the correct employees . . . something they can spot . . . based on enthusiasm or sincerity."[1]

So it is with many leading NPS companies. At Zappos, says CEO Tony Hsieh, applicants who pass the company's thorough screening undergo four weeks of intensive training, so that they understand the Zappos culture and how NPS helps employees wow customers. At the end of that time, Hsieh wants to be sure that he is hiring only people who are truly promoters and who understand what a special opportunity it is to join the Zappos team. So he offers to pay $2,000 to anyone who wants to quit at that point—no questions asked. He keeps raising this offer until some people take it. Bringing those people on board, he believes, will diminish the company's culture and lead to unhappy customers and colleagues, all at a cost that far exceeds the buyout offer. Another leading NPS firm, JetBlue, also focuses on attracting applicants who embody the core values of its service-oriented culture. The airline has developed an online application tool that helps it identify the most promising candidates on this dimension. It also relies heavily on employee referrals as a source of new hires. In fact, it has staffed its Utah customer-service department almost exclusively through Internet postings to existing service agents, who then forward the openings to friends and relatives they think would be a good fit.

Be Careful About Linking NPS to Compensation

Many companies conclude that they must link NPS to the bonus program if anyone is to take the system seriously. That can sometimes be an effective move, especially if it affects only top executives, whose bonus determination typically allows room for judgment. But a premature link between NPS and frontline bonuses can create several problems. First, it focuses the organization on the score as an objective in itself, rather than as a tool to ensure that people learn the right lessons and take the right actions to improve the customer's experience. Second, it puts enormous pressure on the team developing the measurement process to get the metric exactly right; nobody tolerates an error that affects their paychecks. Yet developing a reliable NPS measurement process has far more twists and turns than most executives anticipate.

Finally, the direct link to bonuses will almost certainly encourage gaming and manipulation. Employees may plead with customers for high scores. Or worse: think of the message it sends if checkout clerks circle the register-receipt survey request with a yellow pen every time a customer appears to be particularly happy—and never mention the survey to unhappy customers. Before you know it, your customers' experience will be redolent of the typical car dealership, where the score is everything and honest feedback for making improvements is irrelevant. Most companies that do utilize bottom-up scores begin slowly, by publishing team rankings and eventually using those rankings to determine eligibility for awards, promotions, and bonuses. But even at Enterprise, which took several years to move along this progression, there is still no formulaic link between frontline bonuses and customer feedback scores.

Linking top-down Net Promoter to executive bonuses carries risks as well. The CEO of one global industrial firm, for instance, announced that every manager's compensation would be tied to NPS in the first year of the initiative. A few months later, managers began to see that many of the firm's businesses had no reliable way to create lists of customer contacts. Finance did have accurate contact information for invoicing, but the person responsible for paying the invoice was rarely the right person to give feedback. For that, the company needed the names of senior executives who made purchase decisions, or the key influencers of these decisions, or the employees who used the equipment. This information simply did not exist in any one location—some of it was in the files (or heads) of salespeople, some was in the files of service reps, some was in the files of distributors. Creating the right list for each business around the globe turned out to be an eighteen-month project and revealed some weaknesses in the sales force's account management process.

Still, the CEO had committed to linking NPS to bonuses. So he decided to use a set of market-research firms, which then proceeded to carpet-bomb customer organizations with surveys. The resulting scores proved volatile and unreliable, since response rates were low and no one could tell who was filling out the surveys. Subsequent analysis showed that few senior decision makers or influencers ever responded. Yet the process did yield scores that were used to determine compensation. That led to an uproar from the people affected, who complained that the whole thing was unfair, unreliable, and subject to gaming and manipulation. (For example, lists of customers provided by the sales force to seed the market-research firms' broader lists had a remarkable tendency to exclude unhappy accounts.) When the whole thing was exposed, NPS took a serious body blow. That company has since taken NPS out of the bonus formula and is still struggling to build acceptance for implementation of the broader system.

The experience of Philips Healthcare also provides a cautionary tale, but one with a happier ending. Philips was committed to becoming more customer-centric, and people expected that serious goals would be included in the bonus plan. But few understood how difficult it is to generate reliable top-down Net Promoter scores in a complex, multistakeholder business-to-business setting such as medical systems. Philips sells equipment and services to hospitals and clinics. Relevant customer contacts include hospital CEOs and CFOs, heads of radiology, respected physicians, nurses, and the technicians who operate the machines. Furthermore, Philips competes in several different business lines or modalities that utilize different parts of the wave spectrum. Equipment and supplies to support sonograms, X-rays, CT scans, and magnetic resonance imaging (MRIs) are all sold to a similar set of hospitals and clinics. But the purchase, utilization, and servicing of these different technological solutions are all quite distinct, as was Philips's competitive position in each segment. The first time the organization executed the survey, these groups were not kept sufficiently separate.

There were other problems as well. Philips didn't do enough up-front work to identify the appropriate decision makers, influencers, and users so that it could send surveys to the right people. And because executives wanted a steady flow of scores, they decided to send a stream of surveys and compile results on a monthly basis. As a result, the numbers reported to corporate each month were based on small samples from varying mixes of customers from the several business lines. That resulted in hugely volatile scores. Because this volatility was inexplicable and unrelated to initiatives taken to improve NPS, the credibility of the entire process suffered.

When Philips cut bonuses that first year because it had missed NPS targets, people throughout the organization subjected the system to intense scrutiny. The people responding to the surveys, Philips employees learned, did not reflect a complete picture of the stakeholder ecosystem, just a part of it. Importantly, it underrepresented decision makers and influencers. The sample sizes were inadequate to draw serious conclusions. And, as one would expect with flawed data, the scores did not correlate with subsequent customer behavior and purchases. This linkage to financial results was one of the purported benefits of NPS, and it was failing that vital test.

Rather than pulling back from NPS, however, the leadership team stepped up the effort to design a reliable measurement system. By the second year, Philips Healthcare had built accurate customer lists by business and geographical market. It increased sample sizes for each key competitor. Managers agreed that forty thousand surveys must be completed around the world in order to generate scores for which a 5-point difference among competitors would be statistically meaningful. Gathering this kind of data required an investment of more than $2 million—a substantial cost, but modest in comparison both to the sector's $10 million market-research budget and to the cost of generating reliable financial reports. Like financial information, NPS data at Philips is now audited by KPMG. Auditors thoroughly review the presurvey, the survey, analysis, and score calculation processes as well as the actual numbers. They listen in on a sample of the phone calls, scan verbatim comments, and scrutinize customer contact lists. When they tested the link between the newly rigorous Net Promoter score data and changes in market share relative to key competitors, they found an R-square of almost 90 percent—a very high correlation.

Linking a mature, trustworthy measurement system to compensation can deliver benefits, as the Philips experience shows. CFO Pierre-Jean Sivignon says that making NPS one of the six scorecard elements tied to incentive compensation "raises awareness, not just among employees but also among investors and buy-side analysts." But remember that he is referring to audited top-down relationship scores based on anonymous surveys. The track record of firms successfully linking bottom-up transactional scores to supervisor compensation has only a few success stories and plenty of discredited metrics infected with gaming and manipulation. And many leading practitioners remain cautious. Apple does not publish numbers or link scores to compensation in any formulaic way, fearing that doing so would lead store employees to ask customers for higher scores. However, store managers do use scores to inform coaching, and scores are a factor in determining employee performance ratings and readiness for promotion. Rackspace had linked frontline bonuses to Net Promoter scores, but changed to incentivizing employees only on customer response rates. Even this could create challenges if it motivates reps to direct surveys to friendly customer employees who are most likely to respond rather than to the true decision maker.

So there is still much to be learned about tying NPS to bonuses. Best practices will evolve over time. Meanwhile, it's clear that you shouldn't rush the process. Your organization will need time to learn how to interpret scores and identify seasonal patterns. It will need to get comfortable with the range of random variation in your data collection, with where you stack up compared to competitors, with the range of performance among your own teams, and with how much and how fast you can implement improvements. We recommend that you collect scores for yourself and major competitors, establish closed loops for key parts of your organization, and utilize root-cause insights to drive coaching and improve policies and processes. Publishing rank-order results for your teams will put plenty of attention and pressure on the NPS measures, and that pressure will improve the process. Most people in your organization will already have enough incentive to improve NPS—out of pride, for one, and also because their bonus is already linked to profitable growth, which is driven by NPS. At some point, you may decide to make NPS an official part of your scorecard and link it to compensation. Just proceed with caution.[2]

Don't Skimp on Support from the IT Department

One of the great advantages of the Net Promoter framework is that small businesses find it as useful as large global enterprises do. And small companies can begin making progress right away, using postcards or free survey software. When *Fortune Small Business* interviewed leaders from twenty small companies that had adopted NPS, every single respondent indicated that the system was practical and useful. They didn't need to make major investments in systems or technology.

But this ease of implementation at a small scale doesn't mean much to people in big companies. Large, complex organizations that run on enterprise software require serious IT investments to integrate NPS into their broader operating systems. That level of support is essential even if a company decides to utilize one of the specialized software providers, such as Satmetrix. When we asked NPS Loyalty Forum members to list the mistakes they had made in launching the NPS initiative, a common response was, "I wish we had known to budget more support from our IT department up front."

Consider the challenge faced by a global firm such as Allianz in creating a process to handle just one category of bottom-up transaction surveys. The company must first determine a reasonable amount of time each customer-service representative can devote to calling customers each week. That helps to define the number of customers that can be surveyed. The system must then search the transaction database and come up with an appropriate sample for survey requests to customers who dealt with a particular rep. The sampling algorithm may need to consider rules about how many times a customer can be surveyed in a given period. It may also need to exclude customers who recently filled out a relationship-level survey.

Once the system has sent surveys to the right set of customers, it then must route the responses to the desktop of the appropriate rep, along with the details of the transaction, the NPS survey itself (scores and verbatim), and basic customer information. Once the rep completes the call, performs root-cause analysis, and takes appropriate recovery action, he or she needs to put all that information into the system for future analysis. If, for example, the claims department wants to determine the effect on NPS of the time it takes to handle a claim, it must be able to sort through the responses from the relevant customers. If brand managers want to understand which product lines are helping and hurting customer loyalty, they will need to search through responses by product line. The same goes for geography, customer tenure, share of wallet, and so on. To make this system work, you need some dedicated IT staff.

At Progressive, the NPS leader was Richard Watts, who at the time was responsible for all of the phone reps and customer-service staff at the company. Luckily, Watts already had an IT team to help update the operational scorecard, so the development and integration of NPS tools became the team's top priority. Within the first year, it had created a system dubbed Alchemy, which enabled Progressive to search for any variable included in its customer database and then test for linkages to Net Promoter results. Now product managers around the country could examine NPS by product line, by zip code, by customer tenure, and so forth. Team members could also search for hot spots that seemed to create NPS anomalies. For example, Progressive discovered that new customers who received price increases above a certain threshold at their first anniversary were very likely to become detractors. So even when price increases were fully justified by costs, the company raised its prices less abruptly, smoothing them into the policy over several renewal cycles.

Alchemy flagged another culprit behind low Net Promoter scores, and it turned out to be one of the biggest factors in creating detractors. The customers in question had experienced an accident in which their car could not be repaired—a total loss. Because their car had been totaled, they needed a new one right away. Progressive reviewed its total-loss process to find ways to improve NPS and found that settlement time was one key factor. The team worked to refine the process and get payments to customers faster while maintaining the integrity of its investigations, including fraud. When Progressive implemented its process improvements, NPS and cycle time for this customer segment both improved dramatically.

Apple Retail also learned the power of smart IT investments. Apple might have adopted the register-receipt process that is so common in retail—a survey request printed on the bottom of cash register receipts. But it was unwilling to accept the compromises that most retailers tolerate in these systems, including low response rates, gaming, and no way of closing the loop with the customer. Apple intended to revolutionize the building of relationships in retailing. That required creating a customer contact database that could facilitate real-time communication and feedback. Apple also wanted to revolutionize the retail experience by letting the employee who served the customer also complete the transaction, eliminating the standard checkout process with its potential for long lines.

Apple accomplished both goals by investing in a state-of-the-art customer-relationship database integrated with a revolutionary handheld checkout device. The company issued employees a custom-developed "sled"—a small, flat credit-card reader that converted an iPod Touch into a payment-processing device. The tool thus linked every transaction to an individual employee while also showcasing Apple's use of its own mobile technology. To realize the tool's full potential, Apple needed to incorporate the customer's e-mail address into the system. To that end, the company offered a benefit that many customers would appreciate—if the customer provided an e-mail address, the store would e-mail receipts rather than burdening the customer with paperwork. Of course, many retailers already ask for e-mail addresses. But customers often resist sharing the information for fear of a flood of marketing spam. Apple's intent was not outbound sales efforts but rather a better experience for customers and a reliable feedback process that could build better relationships through the Net Promoter system. Because it built such a system, its store managers can now utilize Net Promoter feedback every day to improve employee coaching, upgrade operations, reinforce the company's cultural values, inform priorities and practices, and track progress toward the mission of enriching lives, all in real time.

So here's how the system actually works. Apple e-mails brief surveys daily to a carefully constructed sample of customers from each store. Store managers receive survey responses in a handy graphical format on their iPhones a few minutes after customers hit the send button. Headquarters staff can access this data and tie it into a rich customer-relationship management (CRM) system for detailed analysis of stores, products, teams, and so on. But the information is most useful at the store. Managers scroll through responses as they arrive to prepare for shift huddles or coaching sessions. Each response shows up on the iPhone screen coded with a Net Promoter emoticon (smiley, passive, or grumpy faces) next to the verbatim comments. To see more information about the customer or the employee involved in the transaction, managers click the screen, and the application displays the full history. To call the customer for closed-loop follow-up, they click the screen again, and the phone automatically dials the customer. When customers receive follow-up calls within a few hours of providing feedback—calls from a manager who read their feedback and researched all the relevant information—they are routinely blown away.

Apple uses the information to rank-order stores each week based on NPS. It constantly tests new approaches to delighting customers. It runs experiments in each store so that best practices can be developed into standard practices across the system. Its IT advantage is helping it achieve its goal of building an army of promoters.

Companies that become more sophisticated in the application of NPS find they continually need to upgrade their IT capabilities. At Rackspace, for example, managers saw that the alert system should identify not just survey respondents who jumped a category, say, from passive to promoter, which might represent no more than a one-point improvement. It should also flag respondents who had *changed* their score by two or more points, whether up or down. The new alerts enabled teams to catch quick signals from customers about improvements and declines in relationship status, to probe for root causes, and to take appropriate action. The score data appears on the account reps' screens whenever they pull up a customer's account, so they can use the feedback to inform their communications with that customer. When customers notice that reps are paying attention to their feedback, they are more likely to take the time to respond thoughtfully to future surveys. Rackspace's IT investments to support NPS and integrate it into daily processes are one reason it has achieved response rates of over 60 percent.

The junk disposal company 1-800-Got-Junk provides another example of how appropriate IT support for NPS can pay handsome returns. During the recession of 2008–2009, the company's competitors were struggling. But 1-800-Got-Junk managed to grow, primarily because its rate of referrals more than doubled. When asked how they did it, CEO Brian Scudamore explained that the company had automated its NPS customer feedback so that any driver paying a repeat visit to a customer would see that it was a repeat on his handheld device. The system displayed the scores from the previous visit along with the explanatory verbatim. Drivers armed with that information could demonstrate that they listen and care. For example, one driver noticed that a customer gave the company a nine, adding that he really liked the team but wished they had swept up a little more thoroughly. Greeting the customer, the driver assured him that they would give everything a clean sweep before they left. When that customer received his NPS survey, he scored the company a ten—and 1-800-Got-Junk's IT department had programmed the e-mail software to provide the customer with a form to list neighbors or friends who might appreciate the company's services. By making customers happy and by making it simple to share contacts by e-mail, the company doubled its referrals—and kept growing through the recession.

Changing the Culture

Becoming truly customer-centric and turning customers into promoters is a very long journey. "It's as much about culture change as it is about organizational design and metrics," says Guerrino De Luca, chairman of Logitech.

> *Ensuring that every employee puts the customer at the heart of what we do is a huge task. Here at Logitech we have customer centricity in our DNA; it just perhaps had become somewhat buried and we needed to force it back to the surface. The recession also reared its head at the start of our journey, which meant we needed to remain steadfast. It was even more important to ensure the loyalty of your customers in difficult economic times. Make sure a culture of the user is ingrained in the organization; make sure the effort is driven at the highest level of the company; integrate NPS into the main processes; report frequently and look for early wins.*

De Luca adds one more piece of advice: "Never give up."

No one has been at this journey longer than Andy Taylor of Enterprise Rent-A-Car, and he certainly has no intention of ever giving up. He introduced ESQi, the forefather of NPS, to his company in 1994. Today, more than sixteen years later, it continues to be one of his top personal priorities. Back then, 66 percent of Enterprise customers were promoters. In 2010 that number stood at 80 percent. When Enterprise acquired National and Alamo in 2007, those brands were number three and number six in the industry customer-satisfaction rankings. The first thing Enterprise did when the deals closed was to introduce NSQi and ASQi with the same rigorous process developed at Enterprise. Within two years, those brands improved so much that Enterprise, National, and Alamo took three of the top four spots in the rankings. Here is a letter that Taylor sent to his colleagues in 2010:

> To: Enterprise Holdings
> From: Andy Taylor
> Subject: Rental brands achieve all-time high scores in customer service
>
> It's no secret that the strength of our brands lies in our focus on providing great service to every customer, every time, all of the time. I am pleased to announce that over the course of the past year, all three of our rental brands have hit all-time high customer service scores.
>
> - *Enterprise* scored an 80 ESQi for its 12-month rolling average for the first time in its history. Maintaining that high level of performance for a full year is a credit to the consistency of the customer experience you have created in our branches.
>
> - *National* hit a six-month NSQi score of 80 as well.
>
> - *Alamo* recorded a 78 ASQi for the month of October, a new high mark for the brand.
>
> The idea of complete customer satisfaction has guided us since our earliest days as a company and will remain at our core. Congratulations on this latest milestone. And thanks for

all of the work you do to give our customers the exceptional service they have come to anticipate each time they visit one of our locations.

Andy

Taylor refers to the recent success as "this latest milestone." He obviously expects there will be many more. Yes, this is a long journey—one that probably has no end. To ensure that your organization achieves the best results possible with NPS, be sure to plan with that in mind.

10

The Road Ahead

We decided to write this revised and updated version of *The Ultimate Question* only five years after the book's initial publication. That's a short time in the publishing world, but we had a good reason for acting sooner rather than later. The reason, of course, is the explosion of learning and progress that has occurred as more and more organizations have put Net Promoter into practice. We have tried to capture some of the lessons and some of the excitement in the preceding chapters.

As people continue to learn about the impressive results of NPS practitioners, the fireworks are likely to continue. More members are likely to join the NPS Loyalty Forum, to the point where it may need to subdivide into geographic and industry-specific chapters. Already, several regional best-practice sharing groups have sprung up around the world—and as we will discuss in a moment, we have already piloted a chapter dedicated to the development of employee Net Promoter. In the future we hope to assemble user groups for health care, education, the arts, and small and medium-size businesses. When people learn what Net Promoter really is, they seem to want to try it. That's why the system has been adopted by California wineries, optometrists, dry cleaners, physical therapy chains, accountants, and so on, all the way to industrial powerhouses like Alcoa and Cummins Inc., the big engine manufacturer. Social media tools are spreading the Net Promoter revolution still further and faster, into new sectors and new geographies. The NPS framework fits so naturally with the social media worldview that leading firms such as Facebook and Zynga have adopted it internally to better manage their own businesses.

But despite all this progress, it is important to remember that the Net Promoter paradigm represents a very young science. New applications and insights will emerge rapidly as more organizations adapt the principles to fit their own situations. Accumulated experience will compound quickly. In contrast to management accounting, which has been developing over several centuries, or even quality management (including Lean and Six Sigma), which has been around for decades, Net Promoter is still in its early stages. We will all learn much more over the next ten or twenty years than we can possibly know today, some of it along dimensions that are hard to anticipate.

Yet we do have a good idea where some of these changes will occur—and where, indeed, they must occur if practitioners are to continue to become more customer focused and more mission driven. In this chapter, we will explore the list of challenges so that you can better anticipate the opportunities and difficulties you will face on the road ahead.

NPS for Employees

Probably the most exciting developments in the Net Promoter community will reflect advances in Net Promoter for employees, which we call eNPS. For many years, companies have known that they can't earn the loyalty of customers without first generating enthusiastic engagement and loyalty from employees, especially frontline employees. But as we noted in chapter 7, many have failed to implement effective processes for building employee engagement. They have placed the responsibility for measuring and managing engagement with headquarters staff groups rather than with frontline operations. Staffers have relied mostly on the annual employee survey, which typically contains lots of questions. They have focused on how their scores stack up against the proprietary benchmarks provided by the survey vendor, rather than on how they rate against competitors and their own historical data. If this sounds eerily similar to the tired old path companies followed in pursuit of customer satisfaction, then you get the picture.

NPS leaders grew dissatisfied with this approach for a variety of reasons. First, the surveys were too long and too infrequent to drive change. They were based on a complex, black-box index designed for statistical research rather than for practical action. Second, survey data remained trapped in HR departments. No one ever developed it into a line tool that could drive daily frontline processes. Third, the framework and language of the surveys didn't readily connect to the more fundamental goal of generating more customer promoters and fewer detractors. The surveys might produce lots of bar charts and correlations; they didn't produce a simple and timely categorization of success, failure, and disaster. Fourth, because of this lack of integration, companies had no way to create economic links to see what employee engagement was really worth. So engagement took a back seat to other priorities whenever finances were tight.

Apple Retail, JetBlue, Bain, Rackspace, and many other firms recognized that they needed the same kind of revolution on the employee engagement front that they had pursued for customer loyalty. And they didn't want a separate but equal revolution; they wanted it to be completely coordinated and integrated with the customer Net Promoter initiative. So these companies developed a process for gathering feedback from employees using consistent language and a consistent framework. On a scale of zero to ten, they asked their employees, how likely is it you would recommend this company (or this store) as a place to work? They followed up that question with the usual open-ended request: what are the primary reasons for your score? When appropriate, they also asked employees how likely they would be to recommend the company's product or service to a friend.

In general, there is much room for improvement. Forrester Research surveyed more than 5,500 information workers across the United States and Europe and found that the Net Promoter score for recommending the employer's product or service was minus 23 percent. Almost 50 percent of employees were detractors. That is more than a little scary in a world of employee blogging and social media.

There has been a great deal of interest and activity in this area—so much, in fact, that we added a day devoted entirely to eNPS to a recent NPS Loyalty Forum. Both the regular customer NPS leaders and their HR counterparts attended the sessions. At the end of the day, the group asked that we continue to meet regularly on this topic. We probably shouldn't have been surprised by the enthusiasm. Joe DiGiovanni, the manager of Apple's Boylston Street store in Boston, says that Apple's Net Promoter for People process "is the most powerful tool I have for improving our store's customer NPS results." FranklinCovey, the well-known consulting, training, and time-management company based in Salt Lake City, was an early adopter of both NPS and eNPS internally; the firm also built a practice to help clients apply these tools. In work focusing initially on multisite retailers and hospitality firms, FranklinCovey discovered that individual store eNPS ratings can range from minus 40 percent for the worst location in a chain up to 100 percent for the star performers. This framework is helping chains recognize the enormous opportunities for learning and improvement. Over time, we expect more and more companies to recognize that they need to take a fresh approach to improving employee loyalty, an approach that fits hand in glove with their customer NPS initiative.

Resistance from Without and Within

As more companies adopt eNPS, you can expect blowback from the employee survey vendors that now serve corporate HR departments. The same thing happened when companies began to adopt NPS for customers. When this book was originally published, it ignited a firestorm of criticism from customer-satisfaction survey traditionalists and their academic supporters (the so-called *Net Pro-moaners*). Many published white papers and journal articles purporting to prove that Net Promoter was a sham. They complained about its lack of statistical sophistication. They said they could find no connection between Net Promoter scores and loyalty, growth, or profits. A few trash-talked NPS on blogs, penned scathing book reviews, and bloated Wikipedia's section on NPS with their critiques. They warned executives that adopting NPS would prove ruinous to business results. One senior executive who implemented NPS was barraged with e-mails protesting that the plan to monitor NPS was simplistic—"based on flawed research, flagrantly illogical, statistically invalid, irresponsible, and fundamentally flawed." At a large European insurance company, the research department commissioned university professors to write a paper arguing that using a zero-to-ten scale in Europe was foolish and that anything based on this approach would be disastrous. Satisfaction-survey vendors and research organizations have much to lose and can be expected to fight fiercely to discredit an open-source metric that can be used without their assistance.

So you can expect more of that. But not all the criticism will come from outsiders. Although adopting NPS to help make your company more customer-centric and to stamp out bad profits may seem like a universally appealing idea, it isn't. An army of adversaries will oppose a system of accountability that really works. In a large company, the biggest internal challenge is likely to come from the company's own market-research department. Like the survey vendors, the market researchers feel a vested interest in maintaining the status quo. Since customer feedback has always been their area of expertise and the basis of their organizational power, they're likely to perceive NPS as a threat. The notion that customer loyalty can be summarized in the response to one question will not be appealing. Shifting the collection and analysis of customer feedback to line managers will be even less so. However, as researchers have become more familiar with NPS, many have found it empowering; it allows them to communicate the value of their insights and drive change more effectively. Market researchers at leading NPS firms are now among its strongest proponents.

But it isn't just the market-research folks who may initially object. Many managers have learned how to play the game in the current system. They know how to milk customers to make their bonus. They know that "their" employees are fully engaged, and they don't want any evidence to the contrary. Any manager, sales rep, or service team who shows up at the bottom of a rank-ordering based on NPS will be inclined to fight the idea or the credibility of the measurement. Even managers who look good on an NPS rank-ordering may be uncertain about their status and the reliability of the process. These concerns are understandable, but they can be resolved by simply measuring NPS and sharing the information for a number of cycles before linking it to pay and promotions. Most well-intentioned participants should be willing at least to test the process to see if it helps them produce better results.

The Real Risk

Critics are supposedly your best allies: they help to identify legitimate shortcomings that you can fix. Ironically, for all their complaints, the critics of NPS have failed to live up to this duty. The most serious risk for would-be NPS practitioners—a risk the most vocal critics have completely overlooked—is adopting the ideas in a superficial and ineffective manner. Because NPS seems so intuitive and straightforward, it is easy to presume you are "doing it" when, in fact, your organization's understanding of the concept is shallow and your implementation ignores most of the lessons from leading practitioners.

Dick Boyce, a partner at the buyout group TPG Capital and the head of its operating group, explains this idea:

> I believe NPS is in a very similar position to where Lean Six Sigma was a few years back. We would go to our portfolio companies when we saw great opportunities to add value with Lean Six Sigma and they would usually say, "Oh, we know all about that—we are already doing it." But they weren't. We would help them come to a deep understanding of the Lean Six Sigma approach, help them really do it right, and that would generate enormous improvements in both quality and cash flow. We are seeing the same thing happen with NPS. Executive teams think they understand it and believe that they are already using it—but then when we provide some deep expertise and help them really do it right, there is enormous value to be realized.

We have seen something similar at the NPS Loyalty Forum. New members often come to their first meeting thinking they already have a pretty good understanding of the Net Promoter system; they come away astonished at how many subtleties and dimensions they had never even considered.

We have developed a few basic questions for companies that believe they are already doing NPS. The questions help us probe the depth of their understanding and whether they have pushed the initiative to a point that will produce real benefits for them. Here are some samples:

- What percentage of customers receive an NPS survey at least once a year, and how many respond? What percentage of your revenues do these customers account for?

- What percentage of detractors do you contact for closed-loop follow-up within forty-eight hours—and of those contacted, how many were happy with the resulting actions taken?

- How many of your employees know their unit's current NPS, its target, and the single most important change they must make to reach this goal?

- What is the difference in customer lifetime value between a promoter and a detractor in your target customer segment?

- What is your most important initiative for creating more promoters—and what will it cost per promoter generated?

Many leaders can't easily answer these questions, which probably means that their journey has not progressed very far. But once firms do have answers, they want to know how their results stack up against NPS leaders. For those companies, we have developed a broader set of questions that provides a self-diagnosis for your NPS initiative. On the Web site www.netpromotersystem.com, we have included a thorough list of these diagnostic questions, as well as the answers or results from best-practice firms from the NPS Loyalty Forum. A good way to ensure that you are doing NPS right is to ask yourself the same questions and compare your answers to those of our NPS leaders. Over the years, we expect that the best-practice thresholds will continue to rise, just as they have over the last few years.

The Issue of Reliable Numbers

NPS, as we have seen, is much more than a score. But if the score itself is unreliable, then the system built around that score cannot be effective. Already, too many companies gather NPS data in haphazard fashion, and the scores don't square with customer behaviors or growth. Companies may not have not developed a timely, rigorous process that asks the right questions of the right customers. They may be oblivious to important seasonality patterns. People on the inside may be gaming or manipulating the scores. Either way, the problem thwarts learning and improvement, since priorities are based on bad data. If NPS is a factor in determining bonuses, then the wrong people will be rewarded.

A lack of reliable scores is a much more serious problem than most practitioners realize. To see the magnitude of the problem, let's examine a sector that has been the subject of rigorous calibration studies. Sandy Rogers, a former Enterprise executive who played a central role in developing that firm's ESQi system, teamed up with FranklinCovey to build a practice that created a comparable measurement process for other industries with many similar sites, such as chain retailers, restaurants, and hotels. One key to Enterprise's success was the development of a reliable score for ranking each branch every month. The system was based on outbound phone calls triggered by a sample of transactions from each branch. Executives established the sample size carefully, so that the rolling average for each three-month period was statistically reliable.

Enterprise could have opted for a cheaper solution, but the company concluded that the extra expense for outbound phone calls from a third-party surveyor was well worth the cost. Executives wanted reliable store rankings for which managers could be held accountable. They viewed the phone process as the gold standard for reliable scores; it was difficult to game and easy to audit. Samples were also easier to control due to much higher response rates. At Enterprise, more than 95 percent of customers who answer the call go ahead and complete the survey. The phone-based approach costs about 50 percent more per store than more conventional approaches, but the results are far more reliable.

Enterprise's system was radically different from the systems most retail and hospitality chains typically employ. Those systems usually use an automated feedback process based on register receipts. Each receipt has a request printed at the bottom or on the back. It asks the customer to call an 800 number or log on to a Web site, enter the transaction number printed on the ticket, and then respond to survey questions. It often offers an incentive, such as a coupon, a free sandwich, or a chance to win a sweepstakes, to induce the customer to complete the survey. These surveys are an efficient way of gathering some valuable customer feedback. But they are not reliable for rank-ordering stores because the sampling methodology is unstable. It fails to identify the truly good and the truly bad stores with any consistency.

FranklinCovey became aware of this problem when its researchers discovered weaknesses inherent in existing survey methodologies for its own retail locations (which the company has since divested). Sandy Rogers and his FranklinCovey practice team then began working with many other retailers and hospitality chains to test out various methods for ranking stores. The most popular solutions were based on register receipts. But it was too easy to game the system; for example, clerks in those stores could circle the survey request for happy customers and never mention it to unhappy ones. Moreover, the type of customer attracted to this method is not necessarily representative of the entire customer base. The low response rates—typically 5 percent or less—also introduced enormous statistical variation, which made store scores volatile.

The FranklinCovey team compared register-receipt scores and rankings to the scores and rankings for the same stores over the same time period generated by the Enterprise-style outbound calling process. In eight different calibration tests, including health care, pet stores, restaurants, electronics, auto parts, quick lube shops, and hair salons, the Enterprise-style system identified different stores as leaders and laggards in more than half the cases. FranklinCovey then tested whether the stores identified as leaders by the phone process were actually experiencing customer behaviors consistent with that categorization. Sure enough, customer-retention rates and average ticket size at those highly ranked stores were superior. In contrast, the stores ranked highly in the register-receipt approach had retention rate and average ticket below average for the chain. One consistent difference between the two methods: the phone approach seems to reach more detractors. Average NPS using the phone was about 15 points lower than the score produced by register receipts.

We suspect that more and more companies will discover, to their chagrin, that the Net Promoter scores they are now using to set priorities, drive bonuses, and allocate resources are not sufficiently rigorous. Many companies, for example, have recently installed e-mail survey systems as the basis of their NPS process. That makes a lot of sense on efficiency grounds, and it allows for easy connection of the survey to customer and transaction data. However, too many of these systems have very low response rates, so it is dangerous to assume that the aggregate scores reflect the entire customer base. We noted in chapter 5 that low response rates almost always result in volatile and unreliable scores, since the distribution of promoters, passives, and detractors among customers who respond to the survey is markedly different from those who choose to ignore the survey request. This is an area where we expect to see major improvements over the next few years as companies develop and implement new and better processes. Phone surveys may not be the right long-term solution for your firm, but beware of defaulting to the cheapest alternative. Best-practice companies are generating response rates between 40 and 70 percent today. Our hope is that these will increase to 90 percent or more as firms recognize the importance of this challenge.

Other Improvements

There are many other improvements that will need to occur as NPS matures—more than we can list. What follows are brief descriptions of some of the more obvious areas where change will be required to move NPS forward.

Combat survey fatigue. Customers already receive too many survey requests, and as NPS spreads, their tolerance will diminish. Response rates will inevitably decline unless companies develop a different approach. It is absurd to smother customers with surveys until the statisticians are happy. So we expect that firms will need to rethink their survey strategy and *earn* ongoing customer participation. For example, they might:

1. *Agree up front with the customer* about the mutual value created by regular feedback, the appropriate frequency of contact, and the best communication channel (phone, e-mail, etc.) given the nature of the product or service and the importance of the relationship. E-mail communications must be approved beforehand anyway so that spam filters don't block the requests. This kind of agreement could be part of the customer on-boarding process, an approach employed successfully by Rackspace. Rackspace uses an online video of CEO Lanham Napier to welcome customers and explain the role of NPS.

2. *Communicate after the survey.* Customers will not continue to give thoughtful feedback unless they know that it is valued and that it is effecting change. So we expect to see more firms getting in touch with customers after the survey

closes. Companies would thank the customers for
their feedback, review the lessons learned from them
and others, and describe the changes they are making as
a result.

3. *Structure surveys like votes.* Many people understand how
   important it is to have the right to vote on issues that affect
   their future. (After all, revolutions have been fought to
   secure this privilege.) If you are willing to share the results
   of a survey, consider positioning it as a voting process, like
   the SASware Ballot. The results may not be binding, but
   the transparency will encourage more people to participate, and sharing the results will encourage employees to
   take them more seriously.

Right now, most companies rely on cultural norms and internal
policing by colleagues and coworkers to prevent employees from
pleading with customers for high scores. In the future, they may
also recruit customers to call out offenders who game the system.

Tap the interest of investors. As more and more investors become familiar with NPS, they are likely to utilize it in their valuation process.
The original edition of this book described how a private equity firm,
Summit Partners, used NPS to evaluate its potential investment in
optionsXpress. When Summit Partners discovered that options-
Xpress enjoyed a Net Promoter score of 52, more than 40 points
higher than the industry leviathans, the decision to invest was an easy
one. In less than three years, the firm grew to hold a leading market
share in retail option trades. OptionsXpress then adopted NPS as
a management tool, which has helped it continue to gain share
profitably.

Today, investment firms such as Bain Capital, TPG, Berkshire
Partners, and Apax are utilizing NPS both as a due diligence tool to
help evaluate acquisitions and as a management framework to

improve results. Tony Ecock, for example, gained experience with NPS when he was an executive at GE Healthcare. When he moved to the investment firm Welsh, Carson, Anderson & Stowe, he helped portfolio companies get better results with Net Promoter. One of these portfolio firms was Concentra, a chain of more than three hundred specialized health-care clinics. Concentra CEO Jim Greenwood credits NPS with helping the company strive for a world-class culture: "It helped the organization take our three core values, Healing Focus, Selfless Heart, and Tireless Resolve, and bring them to life. NPS helped us upgrade our hiring, our recognition and rewards, and our customer service. Our CFO believes that NPS helps us hold and win business. Our salesforce shares our NPS results with prospective customers. I'm convinced the system had a lot to do with our ability to generate same-store sales growth coming through this brutal recession."

Concentra's results were so impressive that, by 2010, the board had decided the company would be an attractive acquisition candidate. When Greenwood explained the firm's focus on customer and employee loyalty to one of the prospective bidders, Humana, he was surprised to see how much Humana's senior executives already knew about NPS. "They were already adopting NPS for their own customers and employees—and seemed very impressed that we were tracking NPS monthly for every clinic and using it to prioritize and drive improvement efforts. I think that our mutual focus on NPS helped both of us come to the conclusion that we were right for each other."

In addition, at least one hedge fund now uses NPS in making investment decisions. The general partner credits the system with helping him anticipate swings in growth and earnings for the retail chains he focuses on. Rather than relying on outside surveys or numbers reported by the retailers themselves, this investor recognizes that it is worth investing serious effort to create reliable data. So he pays a small crew of interviewers to visit stores around the country and gather comparable Net Promoter data through customer intercepts in the parking lots.

As we have seen, executives at companies such as Allianz, Intuit, Progressive, and Philips report NPS to investors and analysts. Philips CFO Pierre-Jean Sivignon notes that the questions he is hearing from these audiences are increasingly sophisticated and relevant. As the investment community becomes more familiar with NPS, we expect its impact will continue to spread.

Bring in the auditors. More and more companies are claiming high Net Promoter results in their advertisements and other public communications. One of Rackspace's European competitors, for example, advertised that its NPS was the highest in the industry. On the other side of the world and in a different industry, the magazine *Computerworld* in Australia recently reported the claim that the Internet service provider iiNet was differentiating itself on outstanding customer service through NPS. "Net Promoter Score (NPS) is our truth barometer," iiNet's Michael Smith said in his chairman's address. "It tracks the net percentage of customers that would refer iiNet to their family and friends, and is closely aligned with customer retention. iiNet's NPS score ranks the Company alongside such great global brands as Apple and BMW. Reflecting our ongoing commitment to first class service delivery, iiNet continues to receive industry awards, with customer retention remaining very high."[1]

All of this may be true. But as more companies make such claims, there needs to be a process to ensure we are comparing apples to apples. (Rackspace's competitor's claim, for instance, didn't seem consistent with studies Rackspace had commissioned.) We need to develop a standards board much like the Financial Accounting Standards Board to determine the general principles and rules for gathering, reporting, and auditing NPS data before it can be published or advertised. The rules laid out in chapter 5 provide a good start. Of course, individual companies can and should develop their own internal NPS systems to serve their management needs. But before advertising their results to investors or the public, companies should meet a common set of standards. Allianz is developing such a set of standards internally. Philips has employed its outside auditor, KPMG, to audit scores so they can be relied on for bonus calculations and reported to investors. Pricewaterhouse-Coopers, which is a founding member of the NPS Loyalty Forum and has used NPS as a core part of its internal management process for years, has already been asked by some clients to explore building an NPS auditing and assurance process. The firm is working with other members of the forum to determine how it might develop the right guidelines and process steps to serve serious practitioners.

Develop better microeconomics. One of our greatest surprises has been the glacial rate at which most NPS practitioners have developed systems and analytics to understand customer economics. As a result, remarkably few firms can confidently quantify the value of improving loyalty (more promoters, fewer detractors) for specific customers or segments. Few have figured out how to track the volume of new business coming primarily from referrals and positive word of mouth. So they typically guess at these benefits, even though referrals and word of mouth are often the single largest component of economic value. While a few firms, such as Schwab, have pushed the analysis to a high level, most are still content to work with rules of thumb and rough estimates. This must change.

It is possible to develop precise and accurate customer lifetime economics that incorporate the value of referrals, repeat purchase, expanded purchase, and so forth. Until they do so, companies will tend to underinvest in the creation of more promoters. They won't have the confidence to make substantial investments until they develop the financial controls and processes to track and account for the benefits of loyal customers. Expect to see books and articles on this topic in the near future.

Engage internal departments. A number of firms, including Allianz, Schwab, and TD Bank, have begun to apply the discipline of NPS to their internal departments. Customer-facing employees are asked to rate how well the various internal teams are supporting their efforts to turn customers into promoters. This kind of accountability is vital. Otherwise, the internal departments will continue to focus on productivity and efficiency metrics rather than on delighting customers. The new approach may require developing ticket systems and survey processes so that each frontline request of an internal department can be tracked and evaluated. We can also imagine an adaptation of the Enterprise vote system, in which branch employees each week rank-order one another based on how well each member helps the team deliver great service to customers. This kind of ranking process could be applied to internal departments.

Improve training and orientation. Many leading NPS companies have integrated Net Promoter into their new-employee training and orientation programs. But we have yet to see the kind of breakthrough creativity in this area that we expect to appear over the next few years. Too many companies that have adopted NPS in operations or marketing have yet to clue in their training departments, which are still using programs developed long before NPS was invented. Verizon Wireless is different: the leader of the NPS initiative personally reviewed all the training programs covering customer experience, customer delight, service recovery, and so on, and helped to rewrite them so that they fully utilized the NPS framework and language. More companies are likely to follow suit. But if you consider the impressive array of materials developed for teaching manufacturing employees the tools of Lean Six Sigma and total quality, and if you then note that every employee (not just manufacturing workers) needs NPS training, you get a sense of how far we have to go. Of course, the Net Promoter Associate Certification program we helped develop for leaders of NPS initiatives, which we mentioned in the introduction to this book, represents one important step. But this level of serious NPS education is required for every level of the organization.

One of the dimensions that ought to be included in NPS training echoes some of the basic quality rules developed for lean manufacturing. Companies should make every effort to reduce the number of surveys and the number of questions asked on each survey. Manufacturing specialists have come to recognize the enormous cost of complexity. Each SKU generates cost. Think of every survey question sent to a customer as an SKU. The company must track answers, create databases, note exceptions—all the way to spelling out the process for responding, thanking the customer, and closing the loop by taking corrective action. Complexity destroys efficiency and effectiveness for NPS just as it does for manufacturing. Another lesson from lean that is relevant to NPS is this: reduce all activities that don't create value for the customer. Every question and every questionnaire should be tested against this standard. Can it be shortened or simplified? Surveys nearly always suffer from question creep. We need a strong countervailing force to overcome this tendency.

Spread NPS to nonprofits. Many nonprofit organizations have already begun to use NPS in their management processes. Some arts organizations, for example, apply NPS both to their customers and to their donors. The NPS discipline is particularly applicable to health care, as we have seen with the success at Ascension Health. We hope that many more companies in that sector will adopt this discipline.

In education, a number of schools have adopted the framework. Several districts in the United Kingdom, for instance, have used the NPS closed-loop feedback process effectively with parents of middle school and high school students. The schools e-mail a two-question survey to parents twice each term asking them how happy they are with their child's progress and with their understanding of the learning objectives for the coming period. Parents rate their satisfaction on a zero-to-ten scale, and any scores of six or below go directly to the headmaster's office. Like the store manager at an Apple store who calls a detractor within twenty-four hours, the headmaster or assistant headmaster calls the parents to diagnose the problem and find a solution. The schools also rank teachers based on the NPS feedback so that top performers can receive recognition and rewards.

Charter schools in the United States have also begun to adopt the Net Promoter discipline with excellent results. Chicago's Rowe Elementary, for example, has adopted NPS for parents (achieving response rates over 70 percent) and has also adopted eNPS to help prioritize efforts to improve the teachers' work experience. Teach For America, the highly successful organization that recruits top college graduates to teach in underprivileged school districts, uses it to gauge progress among its eighty-two hundred corps members and twenty thousand alumni. As more teachers are exposed to NPS, many will take it with them through their careers, just as executives are spreading NPS as they take jobs with new companies. Perhaps this process will even lead to including NPS in school curriculums, so that students learn about the framework at an early age. The notion of holding oneself accountable for enriching the lives you touch is applicable to just about everyone, from elementary school students all the way to candidates for MBAs and other professional degrees.

Why Is This So Hard?

As we did earlier in the book, we want to capture the experience of one of the authors, Fred Reichheld. Here's what he reports.

I remember riding one day with Graham Weston of Rackspace, who was driving me to the San Antonio airport after a board meeting. He was perplexed about the challenges he and Lanham Napier were facing in keeping NPS front and center for their firm. He told me, "Rackspace was built on your loyalty-based principles. It is at the core of our culture. We have always strived to deliver Fanatical Service because it helps our customers succeed, it enriches the lives of our employees, and it makes our business grow. And yet, every time we turn our attention to something else, the company's focus seems to slip away. It makes so much sense—but then why is it so hard?"

That was a great question. After all, NPS is really about helping people measure the success of their careers based on how many of the lives they touch are enriched. What is difficult about that?

Responding to Weston, I believed I knew some of the answers. Today's financial systems work against NPS. Organizations structured into silos have trouble with it. Companies have engineered or reengineered their core processes with no thought of NPS; their process designers had never heard of Net Promoter, let alone received training in the discipline. Conventional budgeting, resource allocation processes, rewards, and bonuses also fight against NPS. Cultures that tolerate bad profits thwart the serious pursuit of NPS. Sloppy measurement systems that generate unreliable scores undermine NPS. So does failing to invest in solid benchmark surveys that track your scores versus competitors'.

The truth is, most corporate systems were not built with customer delight in mind. So leaders need to be realistic about the forces that militate against NPS. Success requires commitment to a long journey, which will constantly require refreshing and resolve.

Companies today operate on legacy systems that overwhelmingly emphasize profit-centric metrics; it is only reasonable that a lot of hard work will be necessary for them to become customer-centric organizations.

Later, however, I received an e-mail from Graham Weston that I think does an even better job of explaining why this is so hard. "Fred," it read,

> I have been thinking about our conversation at the airport.
>
> I believe that there are very few core truths that remain constant through time—but one of these is the notion that we must strive to turn customers into enthusiastic advocates who say great things about us to friends and colleagues. This is the path to greatness.
>
> Greatness often seems out of reach. It is symbolized by people like Mozart, Michael Jordan, and Steve Jobs . . . but at a level that's hard to relate to. In contrast, earning a "10" from your customer seems more realistic. Our teams already do this every day with at least some of their customers. They realize that creating promoters is a practical goal, and desirable. It doesn't take a lot of logical justification to get regular folks to buy into this objective.
>
> The problem is not the regular folks. The problem is leaders and managers. There is a hidden force at play that pulls companies away from the pursuit of greatness. It's like the force of gravity on an airplane. It's always pulling it toward earth. It takes a lot of energy to keep it aloft.
>
> Greed, arrogance, and complacency are part of this force. But I think the biggest enemy is fear. It takes enormous courage to wake up each morning and stare into the Net

Promoter mirror. That scorecard reflects how close you came to greatness, how many lives you enriched.

Maybe it is not NPS that is so hard; it is the underlying *quest for greatness* that NPS is measuring. NPS actually makes the difficult journey a little easier, a little more practical. It helps leaders understand each day where they are succeeding and failing—one customer and one employee at a time. NPS helps them ensure that each day is cumulating into the legacy they want for their team, their business and their life.

Graham

To return to what we said at the beginning of this book: success in business and success in life reflect the impact you have on the people around you, and on the quality of your relationships with them. Too many people measure their success primarily with existing financial metrics. That often leads them down a path away from customer centricity, away from treating people the way you would want to be treated if you were in their shoes. If your goal is to enrich the lives you touch, to build great relationships that are worthy of loyalty, then adopting Net Promoter in a systematic manner can help you measure what really matters. It can put you back on the right path.

Graham Weston described this path as the *"quest for greatness."* We couldn't agree more. Net Promoter illuminates the path to greatness with one constant beacon to guide your journey: enrich more lives, diminish fewer. In other words, create more promoters and fewer detractors. That is the way to ultimate success in your business and in your life.

Appendix

Advice for the Journey

Since 2006, more than fifty senior executives from dozens of companies have shared their experience in open, honest dialog as members of the NPS Loyalty Forum. While the group includes many of the most advanced and experienced users of the Net Promoter system, several members joined relatively early in their process of adopting the approach. Though they come from different industries (the group meets under a nondisclosure agreement, and direct competitors to current members are excluded), they learn from each other. And though they are at very different points along their NPS journey, each has something to teach the others.

We asked members of the forum to share with us their best advice for others who are either just starting out or who may be struggling somewhere along the way. What follows are just a few of the experiences they wanted to share with you. For additional advice and insight, and to share your own, please visit the Web site www.netpromotersystem.com.

Allianz

Top-down push and bottom-up pull

You will never get started and sustain momentum without determined leadership, including a passionate sponsor who truly believes in customer focus and understands it as a multiyear change journey. You will never get anywhere without creating bottom-up pull from the people that deal with customers daily and believe the top-down push is genuine and the new focus and tools can make them better day by day.

Central versus local

Orchestrating a global program across over seventy fairly independent market organizations is very different than just going deep in one country. Winning support of the local country CEOs, choosing a small number of very specific program elements and tools, finding the right balance of central support versus local execution, and getting governance, targets, and incentives right is critical. Fundamentally new approaches like NPS will not spread and stick without the right balance of implementation progress "input" targets versus customer results "output" targets. This requires dedicated central support and operating principles in the early years. Early successes pave a solid path to full ownership and adoption into the local operations and mind-sets.

—*Frederike Hentschel, Group Market Management, Allianz*

American Express

Senior leaders need to take a leap of faith

Any successful journey must begin with leadership. A successful NPS program must have strong, explicit, and public support from the most senior leaders of the company. Don't wait for the root-cause analysis to be completed. Don't wait for proof that promoters drive revenues and enhance your brand. Senior leaders must take a leap of faith and hold organizations accountable for incorporating NPS into their business processes to drive change.

Change the way the business operates

A successful NPS program is not about measuring top 2 box–bottom 6, it's about moving beyond measuring the squiggly line to change the way businesses operate. Implementation of an NPS program should be thought of as a material change initiative requiring constant support, broad-based education, continuous reinforcement, clear accountabilities and goals.

Build NPS into monthly financial reviews and performance assessments

The journey may have been bumpy, but progress is noteworthy. The most senior leaders of the company must talk about NPS publicly and hold their teams accountable for driving change. For American Express, it was important to incorporate NPS data into monthly financial reviews alongside traditional shareholder metrics. In addition, it has been critical that each business unit's customer performance is assessed based on this voice-of-the-customer metric.

—*Adam Rothschild, VP, Global Marketplace Insights, American Express*

Atlas Copco

Don't allow the perfect to become the enemy of the good

Never give up when (not *if*) unexpected situations develop with your NPS program. Continually evaluate and be prepared to adjust your program when required. We found that it is far better to take action based on what we believe may be helpful and then test it to confirm, rather than to wait until we've collected all of the proof we need to ensure our ideas are going to be effective. It is likely to "cost" more to our company if we delay taking a decision than to act now and make adjustments along the way.

Use your own business judgment

The customer is not always 100 percent correct. An example of this is apparent in Henry Ford's quote, "If I had asked my customers what they really wanted in the future, they would have told me, 'A faster horse.'"

This is important for us in our NPS programs; as in Ford's case, his customers were not yet thinking of the possibility of a horseless carriage. Thankfully, Ford did not wait for someone to tell him what they wanted from their supplier/partner. He took initiative to prove the concept, despite the strange reactions from customers who were not yet able to imagine the new concept.

Be patient with those who put up resistance

If there are internal colleagues who are detractors to your NPS program, they typically share similar characteristics. First, they tend to have the lowest NPS results in the organization. Second, they tend to be change resistant. The good news seems to be that success breeds success—the longer and stronger your program becomes, the more internal detractors learn from their peers and begin to "want" to adjust, and then improvements begin to be noticed in their NPS results. Former internal NPS detractors are some of our strongest NPS program promoters today.

—*Ellen Steck, Vice President, Communication and Branding, Atlas Copco*

Cancer Treatment Centers of America

Create transparency, both internally and externally

To be successful, companies must be transparent about their results, and they must share those results across the organization. Further, the organization must respond to comments and provide feedback to customers in order to improve performance and build credibility.

Learn and adapt as your effort evolves

Creating a customer advocacy program/NPS effort within any organization is an evolutionary process. The most important first step is to develop a plan of action, and then be flexible as results begin to come in. Companies need to learn what works best within their own unique environment, and then they must commit to continuous quality improvement over time.

At CTCA, the NPS became a regular part of our management team discussions at both the operating and the corporate levels, which gave the program visibility. We learned through trial and error that the fewer the questions on our survey, the better. So as our program evolved, we continually distilled our questions until only the most relevant and the most necessary remained.

Advice I wish we had before we started

Remember that measuring NPS is only one important part of the equation. At CTCA, the NPS has proven to be a superior indicator of customer loyalty, and its use and its integration into our hospital system have helped drive quality growth. Nonetheless, we've learned that it is equally important to measure vital aspects of our product, service, talent, and delivery that most influence customer loyalty, and to refresh these measures regularly.

—*Christopher G. Lis, Chief Strategy Officer and Vice President, Research and Development, Cancer Treatment Centers of America*

Charles Schwab

Help senior leaders become true, active champions of NPS

Ensure seniormost leadership are deeply passionate about the importance of NPS. Mere "buy in" is insufficient: they need to be vocal and enthusiastic champions, committed to the ongoing success of the program and what it takes to continuously improve.

Our chairman and our CEO, along with the rest of Schwab's senior leaders, made CPS (Client Promoter Score, which is what we call NPS) front and center of virtually every broad-scale employee message that they delivered for the first several years of implementation, usually speaking about NPS results before even mentioning the company's financial metrics. They also hold leaders across the company accountable for developing plans to improve NPS, and track results closely.

Build a science around NPS

Take the time to develop robust survey and feedback processes. We treat NPS as a true scientific endeavor at Schwab, and pursue sampling, surveying, analysis, and interpretation with extreme rigor and discipline. Test and check the methods and the output. Nothing undermines trust and confidence like mathematical errors, suspect methodology, or unexplained variations. Stay curious about both the results and how to improve the process: seek out input from your stakeholders and frontline practitioners.

Make NPS a tool to help people succeed (not just an evaluation metric)

Schwab now enjoys tremendous frontline confidence when it comes to NPS. Our branch manager and call-team leaders use NPS as a tool both to assess and to improve individual client relationships. We build this frontline confidence by demonstrating to our front line that "NPS is a tool that we have built to help you succeed," rather than merely "a tool for us to measure how successful you have been."

Close the loop with customers quickly

Nothing delights a client more than having someone from Schwab quickly follow up with them to address feedback they provided in an NPS survey. It is truly a "surprise and delight" opportunity. It is shocking how few companies make the effort to respond to the feedback that their clients provide, and doing so has been a differentiator for Schwab.

Build controlled experiments to guide improvements

Rigorously test every minor change to survey sampling, design, and execution. Even just changing a font or subject line can impact the score. We put in place rigorous test-and-control experiments before we make any change to our survey processes. CPS is a key operating metric for Schwab, so we need to have complete confidence in the integrity of the numbers.

—*Troy Stevenson, VP, Client Loyalty and Consumer Insight, Charles Schwab*

Cintas

Build allies

Surround yourself with other customer advocates and like-minded coworkers. They can help you weather any "storms" and keep your engine charged. We have created an NPS/Loyalty Spirit-In-Action committee that meets monthly to share best practices across the organization. That monthly meeting also serves to recharge and reenergize the team.

Get started on the right foot

Implement transactional, bottom-up NPS first. This puts the customer feedback directly into the hands of frontline employees. It gives them something to go to work on and instills the importance of closed-loop feedback. We did not do this and I wish we had!

Keep the focus off the score and instead focus on where you need to go to work to improve. We've dropped the word *score* altogether and refer to NPS as Net Promoter System (of improvements).

Celebrate successes along the way

Success is built off of a series of sometimes small improvements. Celebrate and acknowledge progress.

—*Sue Glotfelty, Sr. Director of Marketing Services, Cintas*

E.ON

Bring the finance team into the fold

Get finance involved early. The dead hand of finance can be a real pain where customers are concerned. However, if you can get them to understand the commercial benefit early on, they can be a positive help to get things done. Therefore, plan to collect the data to demonstrate the differential value of promoters, detractors, and so on as soon as possible. Keep it updated and talk to them regularly—don't avoid them.

Create, tell, and retell stories

Human beings are programmed to respond to stories, and if any type of program should be able to create them, it's an NPS program. There should be endless customer stories and tales of how agents responded. Make sure you collect and publicize them, using them to illustrate key issues with the experience you provide. You need to back them up with data and graphs, too, but it's the stories that will be remembered and that gather a life of their own.

Tell people what you've done and what you're doing. The front line are used to being ignored. Telling them how you've responded to the feedback from customers (or them) will give them a genuine boost.

—*Adam Elliott, NPS Centre of Excellence Director, E.ON UK*

Intuit

Link NPS to business economics

Build a rock-solid financial impact case of the value of promoters versus neutrals versus detractors on growth results along with your finance group. Having your finance leader be part of the process will build deep awareness and instant buy-in to the impact that the NPS efforts will have on short-term and long-term financial results. A partner who controls the purse strings is a great ally to have.

Approach NPS as a change management journey

Have patience. This is a marathon, not a sprint. But you can see lots of promising early wins. In most organizations, it's a huge change management journey, and it should follow great principles of effective change management, such as models crafted by Noel Tichy or John Kotter.

With this in mind, building a burning platform, building a strong coalition of champions, and generating early wins are vital. Communication efforts need to be continuous and repetitive. We learned from Apple Retail and LEGO and created some branding for the effort to make it more memorable and inviting. Finally, most companies that are successful understand that it all boils down to the people in the company. Pay close attention to winning their hearts and minds. Build effective ways to select new employees with a "service" orientation. Find ways to on-board them well to capture their hearts from day one. Repeatedly reinforce the company's values through stories and best practices. Partner with your training organization to develop meaningful ways to develop strong awareness and skills.

—*Brian Andrews, VP, Customer Experience and Business Excellence, Intuit*

LEGO

Hold yourself accountable, first

I think the real reason why we're actually making such fast progress is that we have balanced scorecards, and now all employees in the company understand them, because we make this public. Everybody can see every year exactly how I scored on every dimension. So they know exactly how my performance was evaluated by the board of directors. And I think what's important to LEGO employees is, "OK, if he's going to suffer the pain, then OK, I'll take it as well." Who's going to be willing to take a Net Promoter score if top management is still saying, "Well, that's too uncertain. We don't know really how this should be measured. We're not sure we want to be compensated on it."

—*Jørgen Vig Knudstorp, CEO, LEGO*

Experiment your way to success

We have learned that it is more important to get started on the consumer engagement agenda (including NPS) in one area, instead of waiting to have a fully fledged global program covering all touchpoints and products on day one. We consider consumer engagement a journey and a change process that never ends. It is much faster and more effective to learn from your experiences, adjusting the process and activities along the way, so that you constantly get wiser and more professional in your approach. This again helps you bring on board new colleagues, as you can share your learnings and success stories.

Communication is key

It is vital to report on the NPS performance and the actions taken to improve the score broadly and regularly. By doing so, the reporting and process becomes a key storytelling tool in the organization, as it demonstrates the colossal impact taking action on consumer insight has. As such, it motivates the organization to continuously improve the consumer experience.

No matter how much you have shared and communicated about consumer loyalty and engagement, it is never enough.

—*Conny Kalcher, Vice President, Consumer Experiences, LEGO*

Philips

Fight the temptation to let it become just a score

Implementing NPS is not easy to get right, because there is a tendency in the organization to take it as a number, and then the number becomes the object of all things. And of course, it's not about a number. It's about what's behind the number. It's what customers are telling you and how that number stacks up vis-à-vis competition in any particular geography or any particular product area and taking those learnings, that feedback, back into the organization and translating it into effective action.

For me, NPS is successful when I can go anywhere in the organization, not just on the marketing or sales side, but in product development, in supply management, in IT, and I get an answer to the question, "What NPS feedback are you taking into account in your improvement plans?" And if people look at me as if I come from a different planet, then I know we are not there.

—*Gerard Kleisterlee, President and CEO, Philips*

Choose the right leader for the effort—it will run broad and deep

You are going to have to be willing to pick up the fight, so to speak, and address every single process in the company. That also means that the leader will have to be willing to engage in all those different topics and functional areas. So making sure that the right leader for the effort is in place is critical for success.

Make it every bit as rigorous as your financial reports

With NPS, we have the opportunity to make customer experience as hard a metric as currency. People underestimate how important it is to do that, because otherwise you can't touch all the operations in the company. If you choose to make NPS as hard a metric as currency, then you have to define the exchange rates. You have to define the methods of calculating the currency so you can understand the costs versus the benefits. This must be a very rigorously controlled process for any company that does it.

—Geert van Kuyck, Chief Marketing Officer, Philips

Celebrate the first successes, then keep celebrating

You have to celebrate the first successes and make sure that the people who did a nice job become heroes of NPS. It's a journey, and you need to stimulate it all the time. You need to celebrate. You need to ask the questions in every room, in every discussion.

You need to make it very personal for people.

Keep NPS top of mind

When you do business reviews, you know, forecasts, you talk about business targets, balance scorecards, APIs, all these things we do all the time. You need to make NPS very visible, very concrete, very personal. All the time you need to make it as important as the profitability of the company, or the sales growth, or the cash growth.

—Rudy Provoost, EVP and CEO, Philips Lighting

Don't isolate it in marketing

The biggest surprise is how many decisions it actually drives as a result of the evidence you find from your NPS feedback. So my one cent of advice would be not to present it as a marketing project.

—Pierre-Jean Sivignon, EVP and CFO, Philips

Progressive Insurance

Focus on engaging with what your customers are really telling you

NPS is not just a number or a score; it is a means of engaging your company in truly listening to customers and acting on their feedback. It is critical that everyone at all levels of the organization is bought in and accountable to respond to the needs of customers. You can learn so much from the NPS comments customers share with you, and reap gains by acting on them—by closing the loop with individual customers and by sharing the NPS data and comments in relevant, actionable ways so employees, regardless of their role, can effectively act on that feedback.

It is also important to acknowledge that customers may say what they want, but they aren't always able to articulate what they value. This is more art than science and suggests that you find ways to have deeper conversations with customers to uncover those latent needs. NPS has allowed Progressive to open the door to allow more meaningful relationships with our customers and to reap both the cultural and the economic benefits of those relationships.

Set thoughtful goals to focus the culture around customers

It's not the metric that matters. The real value of NPS is the cultural shift to an intense focus on holding ourselves accountable to our customers. That said, to assure focus, setting goals is important. Every employee should share in the goal to improve NPS. It is important to set goals so that any given employee can truly influence the outcome. We have learned that setting goals where the employee does not feel control over the outcome can distract from the positive cultural focus on NPS, so think hard about how you set goals.

Simplicity and consistency will be your friends

Keep the NPS survey process simple and consistent. Changes in the survey process (post transaction or random, branded or blind, relative to competitors or not) or survey delivery methods (e-mail or phone, sampling or timing) can affect response rates, measurement, and score trends. Make good decisions up front, and tamper as little as possible. Focus more on the culture, the customer and improving, and less on the survey or the process.

—*Christine Johnson, Director of Customer Experience, Progressive Insurance*

Qantas

Get the facts and quantify the value

Understand the meaningful segments of customers in your business and understand what matters to them. Understand what drives their behavior and how best to improve NPS. Understand the commercial and strategic value of NPS leadership.

Get the internal communications right

I wish at the outset I had more fully anticipated the importance of and challenges associated with internal communications on the NPS/customer strategy and the transformation program.

Who would have thought this would be as hard to get right as it is in practice? Getting the framework right is hard—and getting the buy-in and engagement in the process is also challenging. Inevitably, parts of the answer are already in action around the business. But they typically are not present across the whole business, nor are they strategically framed or digestible by all levels of the company. This is really hard to get right.

Strong communications can be incredibly powerful if you get them right. The business from the top down needs to speak differently and have the ability to articulate the strategy and how all the various activities of the business fit in—both BAU and program elements. The "what" and the "how" need to be communicated in a simple way, digestible by anyone in the business.

—*Jayne Hrdlicka, Customer Strategy Executive, Qantas*

Schneider Electric

Remember who has the greatest power to make improvement

Since starting our journey, we focused on credibility of the metric and leadership commitment. We have made great progress reducing detractors, but hadn't seen an improvement in promoters. When visiting our customer-facing teams across countries, we realized we didn't have the communications focused on those who matter most—the customer-facing team members!

Direct customer comments are powerful

I wish I had known earlier just how powerful customer comments can be! The metric tells us how we are doing, but the comments tell us what to do in order to improve.

—*Jeff Wood, Sr. VP of Process Excellence and Quality, Buildings Business, Schneider Electric*

Sodexo

Make sure it's integral to the strategy

It is essential that the effort is part of the organization's strategy and has full support and advocacy from the senior executive.

Communicate. Then communicate more

Do not underestimate the value of frequent communication to clarify, direct, and engage your team more deeply in the journey—to fully understand the desired management behaviors which may be different from the current practice.

—*Bret Johnson, Group Senior Vice President, Client Relations, Sodexo*

Swiss Reinsurance Company

Tie NPS to financials early on

Do not wait to tie NPS results directly to financial performance. Client loyalty is only one of many potential economic drivers and it may take years to "prove" the relationship between NPS and financial performance. If you're waiting years to prove your result . . . your program will likely slowly die from lack of engagement.

What's critical to prove as early as possible is how promoters, passives, and detractors behave differently. For example:

- Who stays longer—promoters or detractors? What's the extent of the difference?

- Who gives you a higher proportion of their total spend? How much more?

- Who's willing to pay more for a particular service? How much more?

Expect the unexpected

There will be more moving parts to your program than you think . . . and no matter how smart you think you are, you'll find reasons to adjust processes and tools that you thought were perfect for the job. It's important to remain nimble to be positioned to handle situations as they arise. This ability to quickly adapt will allow quick insight back into the organization at just the right moment . . . providing real value and driving further stakeholder engagement with the program.

> —*Steve Dee, SVP, Innovation and Growth, Swiss Reinsurance Company*

Verizon

It's not (just) about the number

While the whole concept is about a number ("the score"), it's not about the number! Too many executives fall into the trap of overfocusing on moving the score. Of course, that's natural; executives get paid to improve numbers. But in the case of NPS, that same attitude will, almost always, doom the program to failure, or worse, turn it into what most customer satisfaction programs are—something that employees game to get better scores, not happier customers.

The best programs look at the score as a lag indicator—a validation of the improvements the company has put in place because of the voice of the customer received via survey verbatims. And the litmus test for whether the company "gets" this? Listen to the questions that get asked when executives visit the front line. Are they asking about the score, or are they probing the front line for what are the top issues their customers are telling them in their surveys?

Manage for improvement at both the individual and the system level

NPS provides a micro and a macro view into the customer experience:

- *Micro view.* Delivering a positive customer experience takes a dedicated commitment day in and day out. Just because a customer is a promoter today, that does not guarantee they will be one tomorrow. Also, customers that submitted a detractor rating appreciate us reaching out to them to improve the situation.

• *Macro view.* Set up a process to objectively categorize all of the feedback. Change is hard work, but this will position you to turn customer insights into actions.

Focus on what you can control and influence

External influencers, such as the economy, do influence results, but by focusing on internal business improvements, you keep the customer experience moving in the right direction.

—*Kerry Wozniak, Director of Marketing, Verizon Wireless*

Westpac

Keep it simple

Keep things as simple as you can, especially in the goals you set. Customer-based strategies by nature can become complex, but this is where you can lose people or parts of the organization. Alternatively, allowing managers too many goals can give them a way out if they are not performing—that is, they end up doing well in one area, but are below performance on the whole. Many staff in the organization catch on to a customer-based strategy quite quickly because it is so intuitively sensible. By nature people are inquisitive and want to interpret what they think is important, but very easily, collectively these interpretations are not always consistent with your goals. Hence, keep your goals as clear and simple as you can.

Work in stages that build on each other

Don't try and do it all at once. Think of the journey in stages, where your organization builds new layers of capability over time. In any business with high aspirations, at some point you risk managers getting confused and disillusioned when things are tough. Trying to do too much can add to disillusionment in the strategy at these points, but that is exactly the time you want your team to double down on their focus and effort.

—*Anthony Poiner, General Manager, Customer Transformation, Westpac*

Notes

All quotations not otherwise cited are from interviews conducted by the authors or personal communications sent to the authors.

Introduction

1. Ownership of this trademarked term is shared by Satmetrix Systems Inc., Bain & Company, and Fred Reichheld. Our goals are to encourage universal and consistent usage of NPS and to protect against its misappropriation.

Chapter 1

1. Randall Stross, "Why Time Warner Has Fallen in Love with AOL Again," *New York Times*, September 25, 2005.

2. The study analyzed 12,000 companies in 12 developed and emerging economies. It found that only 9 percent of these companies qualified as *sustained value creators*—that is, they grew revenue and profit at a minimum compound annual growth rate of 5.5 percent while earning their cost of capital.

3. *BusinessWeek Online*, "Online Extra: Jeff Bezos on Word-of-Mouth Power," August 2, 2004.

4. Adam Cohen, "Coffee with Pierre," *Time*, December 27, 1999.

5. This data is from the same study described in endnote 2.

Chapter 3

1. Frederick F. Reichheld, with Thomas Teal, *The Loyalty Effect: The Hidden Force Behind Growth, Profits, and Lasting Value* (Boston: Harvard Business School Press, 1996).

Chapter 4

1. This account draws heavily on Andy Taylor, "Top Box: Rediscovering Customer Satisfaction," *Business Horizons*, September–October 2003, 3–14. All quotes are taken from this article unless otherwise noted.

2. Kemp Powers, "How We Got Started—Andy Taylor, Enterprise Rent-A-Car," *Fortune Small Business*, September 1, 2004.

Chapter 6

1. *San Francisco Chronicle*, "Interview with CEO of the Year Charles Schwab," April 9, 2007.

Chapter 7

1. *New York Times*, "Wells Fargo Loses Ruling on Overdraft Fees," August 10, 2010.

2. Gartner RAS Core Research Note G00209074, "Magic Quadrant for Cloud Infrastructure as a Service and Web Hosting," December 22, 2010.

Chapter 9

1. Alexandra Kirkman, "Hotel for All Seasons," *Forbes*, October 28, 2002.

2. Additional information about linking NPS to compensation is available at the Web site www.netpromotersystem.com.

Chapter 10

1. Tim Lohman, "iiNet Seeking to be ISP 'Acquirer of Choice,'" *Computerworld* (Australia), November 23, 2010.

Acknowledgments

We remain grateful to all of the people who made the first edition of this book possible. Here we would like to acknowledge those individuals who helped make this second edition possible. We want to thank each of the following people (organized by company):

Bain & Company: Phil Schefter, Raj Pherwani, Marcia Blenko, Gary Turner, Josh Chernoff, Aaron Cheris, Andreas Dullweber, Julie Coffman, Ron Kermisch, Stu Berman, Sarah Dey Burton, Wendy Miller, Paul Judge, and the entire editorial team

1-800-Got-Junk: Brian Scudamore

Allianz: Emilio Galli-Zugaro

American Express: Jim Bush, Beth Lacey

Apple Retail: Ron Johnson, Catharine Harding, Joe DiGiovanni

Ascension Health: Peggy Kurusz

British Gas: Eddy Collier, Chris Weston

Carolina Biological: Jim Parrish, Tom Graves

Chick-fil-A: Steve Robinson, Jon Bridges

Concentra: Jim Greenwood

CTCA: Steve Bonner, Chris Lis

eBay: John Donahoe

Enterprise Holdings: Andy Taylor, Christy Conrad

Four Seasons: Barbara Talbott

FranklinCovey: Sandy Rogers

Intuit: Scott Cook, Brad Smith, Brian Andrews

JetBlue: Ann Rhoades, Bonny Simi, Julia Gomez

LEGO: Conny Kalcher

Logitech: Guerrino De Luca, David Henry, Junien Labrousse, Glenn Rogers

Philips: Gerard Kleisterlee, Geert van Kuyck, Suhail Khan, Pierre-Jean Sivignon, Rudy Provoost, Laura Murphy, Arne van de Wijdeven

Progressive: Glenn Renwick, Richard Watts, Christine Johnson

Rackspace: Graham Weston, Lanham Napier, Ben Hart, Dan Goodgame, John Lionato

Satmetrix: Richard Owen, John Abraham, Debby Courtney

Schwab: Walt Bettinger, Chris Dodds, Troy Stevenson

Teach For America: Gillian Smith

TPG: Dick Boyce

Vanguard: Bill McNabb, Sean Hagerty, Jack Brod, John Marcante

Verizon Wireless: Kerry Wozniak

Virgin Media: Neil Berkett, Sean Risebrow

Welsh, Carson, Anderson & Stowe: Tony Ecock

Zappos: Tony Hsieh

We especially want to thank all of the members of the NPS Loyalty Forum. Their pioneering efforts have blazed the trail leading from Net Promoter score to Net Promoter system.

On the publishing side, we are thankful to Jeff Kehoe and his entire team at Harvard Business Review Press. Jim Levine has worked most effectively as our agent. John Case, our gifted and unflappable editor, has been a pleasure to work with on both editions of this book.

Finally, we would like to thank our families for their support and their active contribution to clarifying our thinking about loyalty through innumerable dinner table conversations over the past few years.

Index

About the Authors

Fred Reichheld joined Bain & Company in 1977 and was elected to the partnership in 1982. Founder of the firm's loyalty practice, he has served in a variety of leadership roles, including membership on Bain's nominating, compensation, and worldwide management committees. In January 1999 he was elected the firm's first Bain Fellow. His consulting work and research have focused on helping clients achieve superior results through improvements in customer, employee, and partner loyalty. In the June 2003 edition of *Consulting* magazine, Reichheld was included on the list of the world's twenty-five most influential consultants.

Reichheld's work has been widely covered in the *Wall Street Journal*, the *New York Times*, *Fortune*, *BusinessWeek*, and the *Economist*. The *Economist* refers to him as the "high priest" of loyalty; the *New York Times* declares, "[He] put loyalty economics on the map." He is the author of eight *Harvard Business Review* articles on the subject, and his two previous books, *The Loyalty Effect* (1996) and *Loyalty Rules!* (2001), were published by Harvard Business School Press. The first edition of *The Ultimate Question* was published by Harvard Business Press in 2006. He is a frequent speaker to major business forums and groups of CEOs and senior executives worldwide.

A graduate of Harvard College and Harvard Business School, Reichheld lives with his wife, Karen, and their family in the Boston area.

Rob Markey is a partner in Bain & Company's New York office and heads the firm's Customer Strategy and Marketing practice globally. He joined Bain in 1990, where his work has focused on helping clients achieve profitable, sustainable organic growth through customer and employee loyalty. He is also one of the firm's experts in customer experience improvement. While much of his work has been focused in financial services, his clients have also included media, technology, retailing, professional services, and transportation companies.

Markey founded and leads the NPS Loyalty Forum, a group of senior executives from loyalty-leading companies around the world who meet several times a year to share experience and advice about how to create a culture of customer and employee advocacy in their organizations. He has published articles in a variety of business journals, including the *Harvard Business Review*, and was a significant contributor to the first edition of *The Ultimate Question*. He is a frequent speaker on topics of customer experience, customer and employee loyalty, and customer-led growth.

A graduate of Brown University and Harvard Business School, Markey lives in the Boston area with his wife, Lisa, and their children.